FREUD AND AUGUSTINE in DIALOGUE

STUDIES IN RELIGION AND CULTURE

John D. Barbour and Gary L. Ebersole, Editors

FREUD AND AUGUSTINE in DIALOGUE

PSYCHOANALYSIS, MYSTICISM, and the CULTURE of MODERN SPIRITUALITY

WILLIAM B. PARSONS

UNIVERSITY OF VIRGINIA PRESS
CHARLOTTESVILLE & LONDON

University of Virginia Press

Printed in the United States of America on acid-free paper

First published 2013

9 8 7 6 5 4 3 2 1

LIBRARY OF CONGRESS CATALOGING-IN-PUBLICATION DATA

Parsons, William Barclay, 1955–
Freud and Augustine in dialogue : psychoanalysis, mysticism, and the culture of modern spirituality / William B. Parsons.
pages cm.—(Studies in religion and culture)
Includes bibliographical references and index.
ISBN 978-0-8139-3478-5 (cloth : alk. paper)—
ISBN 978-0-8139-3479-2 (pbk. : alk. paper)—
ISBN 978-0-8139-3480-8 (e-book)
1. Augustine, Saint, Bishop of Hippo. 2. Freud, Sigmund, 1856–1939. 3. Mysticism. 4. Spirituality. 5. Psychoanalysis and religion. I. Title.
BR65.A9P375 2013
201'.6150195—dc23

2012050152

CONTENTS

ACKNOWLEDGMENTS

Several people and institutions were instrumental in the production of this book. Foremost among them is the Institute for Advanced Studies at Hebrew University, where I was a resident Fellow during the 2008–9 academic year. To my closest conversation partners—Philip Wexler and Jonathan Garb (who invited me), Yoram Bilu, Elliot Wolfson, Boaz Huss, and David Loy (my housemate)—heartfelt thanks. The assembled scholars at IAS were absolutely instrumental in helping me work through the intricacies of my various arguments. I also wish to thank my chair, Jeffrey Kripal, and my dean, Nicolas Shumway, for their unconditional enthusiasm and financial support.

I am grateful to the anonymous external readers and the series editors, John D. Barbour and Gary L. Ebersole, who substantially enriched the manuscript through their many insightful responses and suggestions. The process of writing and publishing is often a long one, and I am grateful to my editor, Cathie Brettschneider, whose steadfast hand, support, and advice throughout the vetting process sustained me, and Peter C. Reynolds, whose editorial skills vastly improved my grammar and prose. His alternative formulations made the narrative more compelling.

Elliot Berger, my graduate research assistant, went through the entire manuscript with the sharpest of razors. And to the many other students who took my courses on mysticism I can only say this: while it may not be immediately apparent, your feedback can be found infused throughout the text. I work for you, and I can only hope that some of these ideas are of service, if even in the smallest of ways. In all things Augustine I like to keep in mind Bernard McGinn, who introduced me to Augustine the mystic when I was a graduate student and who has continued to offer me support and constructive criticism, and my friend and colleague Diane Jonte-Pace, for her insightful feedback and nurturance.

I also wish to acknowledge the following presses, who have kindly granted permission to develop passages and ideas from some of my previous publications: Oxford University Press for *The Enigma of the Oceanic Feeling: Revisioning the Psychoanalytic Theory of Mysticism* (1999); Rowman Littlefield/Lexington Books for "On Seeing the Light: Assessing Psychoanalytic Interpretations of Vision in Augustine's *Confessions,*" in Sandra Lee Dixon, John Doody, and Kim Paffenroth, eds., *Augustine and Psychology* (2012); Springer Science+Business Media B.V. for "Psychoanalysis Meets Buddhism: The Development of a Dialogue," in Jacob A. Belzen, ed., *Changing the Scientific Study of Religion: Beyond Freud?* (2009); Rodopi Press for "Psychoanalysis and Mysticism: The Case of St. Augustine," in Jacob A. Belzen and Antoon Geels, eds., *Mysticism: A Variety of Psychological Perspectives,* (2003); and Peter Lang for "Freud's Last Theory of Mysticism: The Return of the (Phylogenetic) Repressed," in Philip Wexler and Jonathan Garb, eds., *After Spirituality: Studies in Mystical Traditions* (2012).

FREUD AND AUGUSTINE in DIALOGUE

INTRODUCTION

It is arguably the case that no two figures have had more influence on the course of Western introspective thought than Freud and Augustine. As they wrote centuries apart, we might assume that it would be Freud, the more contemporary of the two, who would have the last say. But the primordial wisdom contained in Augustine's substantial written corpus and the unpredictable nature of cultural eddies have ensured the continuation of numerous long and protracted debates revolving around the very different perspectives on human nature each bequeathed to culture.

Traditionally, Freud is considered to have had little, if any, sympathy for religion, much less for what today passes under the rubrics of "mysticism" and "spirituality." But things are rarely simple with Freud, and there is some evidence to think otherwise.[1] Augustine, on the other hand, is often characterized as an apologist and ecclesiastic, but Abbot Butler, writing many decades ago in his classic book, *Western Mysticism,* read Augustine not merely as a mystic but, as he put it, as the "Prince of Mystics." This designation has been furthered more recently by Bernard McGinn and John Peter Kenney, both of whom have unveiled Augustine's sustained teachings on mystical contemplation.[2] Even so, it seems unlikely that Freud and Augustine would have anything to say to each other with regard to mysticism and spirituality.

This book argues the contrary position. It does so by calling attention to a contemporary cultural movement that has commanded the allegiance of many and is succinctly summed up by the phrase, "I'm spiritual but not religious." The proponents of this movement have a deep distrust of orthodoxy and its institutional enforcement, yet also claim there are genuine pearls of wisdom to be found in any and all traditional religions. They are decidedly psychological, seek wholeness and individuation, and are willing to cobble together practices and ideas from multiple traditions in an effort to satisfy their desire for personal insight and growth. It is precisely this cultural milieu that welcomes Augustine's personal reflections on the mystical as part of a wider and enduring religious quest for wholeness and meaning.

Along similar lines, if Freud and indeed multiple theorists in the psychoanalytic tradition are seen within this emerging cultural perspective, then a new relationship of psychoanalysis to religion begins to emerge. This book aims to show that the methodological perspectives on and insights into the human personality Freud bequeathed us have, even against his wishes, played an instrumental role in the cultural ascendancy and personal orientation of those professing to be spiritual but not religious. Both the suspicion of religious orthodoxy, on the one hand, and the construal of religion in psychological and therapeutic terms on the other owe no small debt to the psychoanalytic tradition. The question before us, then, is how to bring into true dialogue insights into the depths of the mind as enduring as those of Augustine and the mystics yet also as imaginative and potentially destabilizing as those of Freud and his heirs. In pursuit of such a dialogue, we may find there is something distinctly Freudian about Augustine and something distinctly Augustinian about Freud. Certainly it is this kind of progressive exchange of ideas that characterizes modern spirituality at its best.

But this is to telescope things to come, to provide a bird's-eye view, so to speak. To properly engage with the argument to come, we need to take each element in turn. Turning first to Augustine, the initial move must be to articulate more precisely what we mean when we speak of his mysticism. And that entails beginning with one central text, the *Confessions.*

The Prince of Mystics

Augustine's *Confessions* has been designated a classic for many reasons, not least its continued ability to speak to generations of seekers over the centuries. From his early socialization into Christianity (described in books 1 and 2) and adolescent attraction to the dualism of Manichaeism (books 3–6) to his encounter with Neoplatonism (book 7), conversion to

Christianity, and reflections on scripture (books 8–13), Augustine depicts the journey of a religious pilgrim guided by "faith seeking understanding." Ostensibly the reflections of a single man seeking wholeness, the narrative of this classic text, punctuated by numerous episodes laced with literary motifs and trenchant philosophical insights, transcends Augustine's own biography. It offers a prognosis of the universal existential themes and conflicts that constitute being human, and prescriptions for our communal redemption.

In books 1 and 2 Augustine describes his socialization into the Catholic Christianity of his mother. Reflecting years later as a bishop of the faith on this early phase, Augustine was at times sharply critical, stating that he did not understand the profundities of scripture in an existential sense. His apprehension of God, he tells us, was limited by his still developing intellectual capacities, and his soul, mired in sin, was ruled by a perverse and disordered will. Augustine the boy was not directed "inward and upward" toward the "unchangeable Light" but enchanted by the vanities of the world and caught in the web of earthly attachments. In books 3–6 Augustine relates that, during his stint as a young teacher of the rhetorical arts, he had become enamored of Manichaeism. But again, he retrospectively criticizes his youthful folly, claiming that the conception of God he entertained under their influence was still "an empty fantasy, a creation of my own error" (4.7), and that he "preferred to think that you [God] also were subject to change rather than I was not what you are" (4.15). Moreover, the dualistic worldview of Manichaeism catered anew to his still "disordered" desires. He used it to defend against the need for introspection and responsibility for inner change: "I was still of the opinion that it is not we ourselves who sin, but some other nature which is in us; it gratified my pride to think I was blameless" (5.10). While other flirtations with philosophy of his youth, notably with Cicero and his *Hortensius,* were not without their beneficial effects, it becomes clear that at this stage in his journey Augustine did not feel he had experienced direct communion with the true God or had arrived at the true rest for which his restless heart yearned.

In book 7, however, something quite dramatic occurs. In a pivotal episode Augustine relates his introduction to "some books written by the Platonists" (7.9). Earlier in the *Confessions* Augustine had prefigured the impact Platonism had on his understanding of God by describing a movement to a place "deeper than the deepest recesses of my heart" and above the summit of his soul, "higher than the highest I could reach"

(3.6). In book 7 he becomes more specific by describing how, once having arrived at this inward place, he glimpses an ineffable light:

> I was admonished by all this to return to my own self, and, with you to guide me, I entered into the innermost part of myself, and I was able to do this because you were my helper. I entered and I saw with my soul's eye (such as it was) an unchangeable light shining above this eye of my soul and above my mind. It was not the ordinary light which is visible to all flesh, nor something of the same sort, only bigger, as though it might be our ordinary light shining much more brightly and filling everything with its greatness. No, it was not like that; it was different, entirely different, from anything of the kind. Nor was it above my mind as oil floats on water or as the heaven is above the earth. It was higher than I, because it made me, and I was lower because I was made by it. He who knows truth knows that light, and he who knows that light knows eternity. Love knows it. O eternal truth and true love and beloved eternity! You are my God; to you I sigh by day and by night. (7.10)[3]

This vision at Milan, which the modern mind is apt to think of as a mystical experience, signals a crucial juncture in Augustine's spiritual journey. For the first time, Augustine claims that he understands the changeless, incorporeal nature of God, that he loves God "and not a phantom instead of you" (7.17), and that he knows that evil is not a "substance," as he had been taught by the doctrines of Manichaeism, but located in his own will: "a perversity of the will turning away from you, God, the supreme substance, toward lower things" (7.16). Indeed, the importance of vision for Augustine cannot be overstated. As Robert J. O'Connell observes, Augustine's mysticism is the central thread coursing through his works: "If there is one constant running through all of Augustine's thinking, it is his preoccupation with the question of happiness. . . . But the answer is equally uniform: what makes man happy is the possession of God, a possession achieved by way of vision."[4]

This was not, however, the end of Augustine's mystical journey. The problem was that he could not "stay in the enjoyment of my God" (7.17). It was the weight of his "carnal habit" that tore him away from God, thrusting him down toward lower, earthly things. Augustine goes on to say, in words now constructed almost entirely of the ocular experience:

> And when I first knew you, you raised me up so that I could see that there was something to see and that I still lacked the ability to see it. And you beat back the weakness of my sight, blazing upon me with your rays, and I

> trembled in love and in dread, and I found that I was far distant from you, in a region of total unlikeness. (7.10)

Augustine was now faced with a problem: how could one live the "happy life," one in which the true One bathed the soul in its continuous light? The Platonists had afforded Augustine a glimpse of the truth. But while a pivotal breakthrough had occurred, much inner work awaited. He needed a soteriological regimen, something that to the modern psychological mind might look like a form of therapy, to train and reform the *imago Dei*. This is the case for if, as stated in Genesis, we are made in the image of God but, through Adam, have fallen into a state of sin that has tarnished that image, then the task of a Christian therapy implies restoring or reforming that image. As we shall see, for Augustine this was a lifelong process that required allegiance to a Christian worldview and its practices. Again, as I have indicated and will elaborate later, this specifically Christian understanding of the person became the basis for his criticisms of Platonism. So it is, for example, that Augustine states that the difference between the Platonists and those who confess Christ is that "between presumption and confession, between those who see their goal without seeing how to get there and those who see the way which leads to that happy country which is there for us not only to perceive but to live in" (7.20). And so it is that in book 8, Augustine goes on to speak of further introspective insights, including those concerning his "divided will," the link between such a will and sin, the influence of Saint Paul and the book of Romans on his newfound subjective awareness of two wills in conflict, and his need for Christ as mediator.

It is here that Augustine's famous *tolle et lege* ("take and read") of book 8 belongs. It is also here, in *Confessions* 9.10, that Augustine speaks of another mystical event, more pivotal than the first and involving Monica:

> She and I were standing alone, leaning in a window which looked onto the garden inside the house where we were staying, at Ostia on the Tiber. There we were out of the crowds and after our long and weary journey by land were resting ourselves for the sea voyage. So we were alone and talking together and very sweet our talk was, and *forgetting those things which are behind, and reaching forth unto those things which are before,* we were discussing between ourselves and in the presence of Truth, which you are, what the eternal life of the saints could be like, *which eye hath not seen, nor ear heard, nor hath it entered into the heart of man.* Yet with the

> mouth of our heart we panted for the heavenly streams of your fountain, the fountain of life, which is with you, so that, if some drops from that fountain—all that we could take—were to be scattered over us, we might in some way or other be able to think of such high matters.

As they talked, they began to consider how much greater the pleasures and joys of eternal life were than anything that could be granted by the senses and by transient, earthly, corporeal delights—of how it was that they went beyond their own souls, inward and upward, "to reach that region of neverfailing plenty where *Thou feedest Israel* forever with the food of truth and where life is that Wisdom by whom all these things are made, both what is past and what is to come." It was here, states Augustine, that "we did, with the whole strength of our hearts' impulse, just lightly come into touch with her" (i.e., with Wisdom). The two then said:

> If to any man the tumult of the flesh were to grow silent, silent the images of earth and water and air, and the poles of heaven silent also; if the soul herself were to be silent and, by not thinking of self, were to transcend self; if all dreams and imagined revelations were silent, and every tongue, every sign; if there was utter silence from everything which exists only to pass away (for, if one can hear them, these all say: We did not make ourselves. He made us that abideth forever) but suppose that, having said this and directed our attention to Him that made them, they too were to become hushed and He Himself alone were to speak, not by their voice but in His own, and we were to hear His word, not through any tongue of the flesh or voice of an angel or sound of thunder or difficult allegory, but that we might hear Him in Himself without them, just as a moment ago we two had, as it were, gone beyond ourselves and in a flash of thought had made contact with that eternal wisdom which abides above all things—supposing that this state were to continue, that all other visions, visions of so different a kind, were to be withdrawn, leaving only this one to ravish and absorb and wrap the beholder in inward joys, so that his life might forever be like that moment of understanding which we had had and for which we now sighed—would this not be: *Enter into thy Master's joy*? And when shall that be? Shall it be when *we shall all rise again,* though we *shall not all be changed*?

This vision at Ostia, as the scene has come to be known, has both notable similarities to and notable differences from the vision at Milan, as will be examined in a later chapter. What is significant now is that Augustine understands the Ostia vision as a foretaste of the life to come. This new theme is echoed again in one last pivotal text (*Confessions*

10.40), in which Augustine returns to a consideration of his search for God in the fields of memory (*memoria*):

> And sometimes working within me you open for me a door into a state of feeling which is quite unlike anything to which I am used—a kind of sweet delight which, if I could only remain permanently in that state, would be something not of this world, not of this life. But my sad weight makes me fall back again; I am swallowed up by normality.

The ascent at Ostia marks for many of Augustine's readers the denouement of the pilgrim's religious journey. It is a veritable ascent to the presence of God and offers a foretaste of the heavenly life to come. There is, then, a discernible movement in the *Confessions.* As Henri Marrou, Karl Weintraub, Robert O'Connell, and other scholars of Augustine have noted, the *Confessions* is in some fundamental sense an *exercitation animi,* an exercise of the soul or mind.[5] That is, if we are made in the image of God, and if that image needs restoring, then one could say that the apex of that restoration, and thus the central theme of the *Confessions,* is the achievement of the mystical vision of God (the *visio Dei*). As Augustine describes this yearning in the first paragraph of the first book of the *Confessions:* "Our hearts are restless until they can find peace in you." But carnal habit—the entrapments of and attachments to the things of the world, fueled by the disorder and sin of the soul—keeps us from turning our minds and hearts in the proper direction and from cultivating, strengthening, and reforming the *imago Dei* within, the eye of our soul that sees God.

It is this movement that animates Augustine's retrospective critique of the religious pursuits of his youth, his boyhood understanding of Christianity, and his youthful infatuation with Manichaeism. And while the Platonists glimpsed the One, only the mystical ascent at Ostia is portrayed in singularly Christian terms as a foretaste of the life to come. From this perspective, the various reflections and episodes animating the narrative of the *Confessions* can be seen as so many edifying instances of how the mind and the affections are caught in the web of earthly attachment; of how, by reflecting on the past, laying bare our soul before God the "inner physician," and reforming the image of him who created us, we can hope to effect the ascent to the incorporeal God. As Weintraub has put it, "all the early books [of the *Confessions*] are an exercise which the things of this world prepare for the soul," and "the account of the vision at Ostia becomes a compressed presentation of all the steps whereby the soul is freed from such entrapment in order to reach the infinite."[6] If this is so, then the mystical ascent at Ostia is rhetorically linked to the sweep of the narrative of the *Confessions:* it is the paradigmatic instance of that reordering of the will, refinement of the *imago Dei,* and exercising of the mind that leads to touching God.

The notion that Augustine's episodic mystical experiences at Milan and Ostia cannot be wholly separated from his emerging theological reflections has important consequences for a proper understanding of what is meant when we refer to the term *mysticism.* Most important, it is crucial to distinguish between the mystical *experience* and what may be called the mystical *process.* While the two admittedly are inexorably related, a mystical process expands the episodic, finding the latter's meaning in the context of the course of a religious life and in the cultivation of various dispositions, capacities, virtues, and levels of consciousness. This general point finds specificity in the ways in which many mystical authors have integrated episodic mystical experiences under the broader umbrella of a spiritual path. For example, in Christianity, perhaps the best-known examples of what is here termed process occur in the Spanish mystics Saint John of the Cross and Saint Teresa and their use of "mansions" and "stages"—purgation, illumination, union—to describe the development of the mystical path. For Augustine, raising episode to process necessitates broadening the view of his mysticism to include not only experience but also his ruminations on the nature of confession and memory, as well as his reflections on contemplation, all set in the broader context of his thought on ecclesiology and Christology, and his mystical readings of scripture. In theological terms, it is the totality of Augustine's reflections on mystical ascents and process in a churched context—which is to say his mystical theology—that needs to be fully taken into account when speaking of Augustine's mysticism.[7]

This conclusion also has consequences for those who wish to use psychoanalysis as a methodological tool to investigate Augustine's mysticism. Most foundationally, the psychoanalytic tradition has generally assumed that "mysticism" is a relatively self-evident, unambiguous term. However, in the academic study of comparative mysticism, this is far from being the case. A definitional problem attends terms like mysticism, mystical theology, spirituality, and modern spirituality, a problem manifested in a host of academic controversies and debates. How these terms are defined and unpacked, and how that unpacking plays out with regard to psychoanalytic inquiry and to the argument presented here, is a central concern of this book.[8]

Reception: On Reading the *Confessions* Psychologically

In light of the importance to and influence of Augustine's thought on the course of Western history, it should be no surprise that the passages from the *Confessions* cited thus far have been the object of intense interdisciplinary scrutiny. At various points theologians, historians, literary critics, classicists, and philosophers have all entered the fray. Most important, at least from the methodological perspective adopted in this study, is what amounts to a psychoanalytic reception history of the *Confessions*, a reception whose history now spans more than a century. Such interest in part owes to what many scholars see as the work's seemingly modern character. For example, the historian Karl Weintraub notes that in the *Confessions*, we see the historicizing of the self and a new, modern notion of selfhood. Although the genre of autobiography—indeed, the word *autobiography* itself—is not older than the eighteenth century, the *Confessions* has elements that define what autobiographies have always been, namely, in Weintraub's words, "self-questioning by asking the context of one's life to surrender the secrets about the self; self-discovery, by perceiving the order in the disparate elements of life; self-evaluation, by tracing the meaning as a continuous pattern. . . . No self-written life before Augustine had this scope, fullness, intensity, and lifelike quality."[9] Peter Brown, Georges Gusdorf, and Krister Stendahl have further observed that Augustine extended the ascetic and monastic fascination with the interior life in a historically new direction.[10] In the hands of Augustine, personal experience, past events, and introspective probes into internal conflict and the mysteries of the elusive and opaque nature of consciousness become integral aspects of ever-deepening religious subjectivity. It is the latter fact that led A. C. Outler to suggest that Augustine "was far and away the very best—if not the first—psychologist in the ancient world. His observations and descriptions of human motives and emotions, his depth analyses of will and thought in their interaction, and his exploration of the inner nature of the human self—these have established one of the main traditions in European conceptions of human nature, even down to our own time. Augustine is an essential source for both contemporary depth psychology and existentialist philosophy."[11] Extending these observations, Donald Capps adds that the *Confessions* is a text in which catharsis, the recall of past events, and an attempt at self-transformation are apparent.[12] Even the noted Augustine scholar Eugene TeSelle has been moved to echo these sentiments, adding that "Augustine is the one who taught the West about selfhood, its freedom, its affections and their disordered orientations, its object-relations, especially in the model of love. Perhaps these insights are the result of Oedipal or narcissistic conflicts, resolved or unresolved. But even if they are unresolved, he did conceptualize the dynamics of the self."[13] Indeed, recalling the importance to psychoanalysis of the power of sexuality and aggression, the universality of repression, and the depths of the unconscious, what are we to make of Augustine's insistence that his personal experience led him to conclude that there is a "stomach to the mind," that "what is inside the mind is mostly hidden"? Or that there exists a "sad kind of darkness" that circumvents the mind's ability to enlighten itself? Or his admission that, despite his avowed celibacy, the war of the Pauline "two wills" continues to haunt him; that in his slumber sexual dreams continue to occur—a fact that leads him to wonder, "Does reason go to sleep when the bodily senses sleep?"[14]

It is understandable, from the above, that Augustine's autobiographical, case-history style of narration, complete with revealing portraits of his relationships with his parents and significant others and accounts of pivotal life events, has occasioned multiple and varied psychological analyses of the nature and determinants of his religious journey. Several notable twentieth-century studies can be traced back to sources that are not specifically Freudian: to William James, who saw in Augustine an instance of the "divided self"; to the classicist E. R. Dodds, who used both Jamesian and Freudian categories to render his opinion of Augustine as a sick soul besieged by self-reproach; and to Bernhard Legewie, who used Ernst Kretschmer's correlations between physique and character to develop the position he published in *Augustinus: Eine Psychographie*.[15] But the most determinative post–World War II studies have been psychoanalytic in orientation. Dozens upon dozens of psychoanalytic essays as well as multiple books have appeared on the topic, ranging from early oedipal perspectives to those championing the preoedipal to those using narrative theory.[16] One wonders what truly new psychoanalytic perspective can be brought to bear on a text that has been the subject of a scrutiny bordering on tiresome overanalysis.

Yet this book proposes just such a new perspective, one originating in a specific sociocultural context. As the sociologist Philip Rieff noted, parts of Western culture have become wholly intertwined with the therapeutic, and psychology has become a dominant if not determinative mode of introspection. Western culture has, in a very real sense, seen the "triumph of the therapeutic."[17] This undeniable social reality has forced earlier seminal theologians and religious studies scholars, among them Paul Tillich, Paul Ricoeur, and Reinhold Niebuhr, to engage with psychological models of various stripes. Freud, of course, was an avowed atheist and arch reductionism, suggesting that religion be replaced by his "secular cure of souls" (as he once remarked to the pastor Oskar Pfister).[18] However, other psychological models have been more sympathetic to religious claims, a posture that at times earns them such treatment as "psychology *as* religion" or, more typically, the label of psychospirituality.[19] In turn, psychospirituality is but one important strand in the complex cultural weave termed "modern spirituality."[20]

The defining characteristic of what has become known as modern spirituality is that it intentionally offers itself as a nontraditional or, if one were to emphasize its Christian roots, an "unchurched" way of organizing and expressing the existential search for wholeness, numinous experiences, and individuation. With respect to its psychological component, studies of modern spirituality trace its roots to the originative figures and movements of the initial decades of the twentieth century, such as James, Carl Jung, Frederic Myers, R. M. Bucke, Roberto Assagioli, and Mesmerism, as well as to mid-century efforts like those promulgated by Abraham Maslow with humanistic/transpersonal psychology. Today this religious style, being unchurched, is often portrayed as commensurate with the rise of Max Weber's "inner-worldly mystic" and responsible for the now popular cultural phrase, "I'm spiritual but not religious."[21]

As intimated above, psychoanalysis, traditionally regarded as hostile to religion and historically at pains to divorce itself from anything that hints at psychospirituality, is generally thought to have withstood such cultural trends. However, this is clearly not the case. Spirituality has crept into the practice of psychoanalysts, into the therapeutic expectations of analysands, and even into psychoanalytic theory itself.[22] Yet despite its underground and repressed character, one can point to practitioners, sometimes referred to as "psychoanalytic mystics," whose theoretical formulations exhibit a marked sympathy with the mystical.[23] This situation indicates that psychoanalytic therapy is engaging a new social base with spiritual concerns. And it is this social base that makes possible a new perspective on the role of Augustine's visions in his journey of faith and initiates a psychoanalytic dialogue that can be truly transformational. It asks, with an eye to both the perils and benefits of modernizing an ancient text, how a mystical work like the *Confessions* might speak anew to a more receptive psychoanalytic culture and to the proponents of modern spirituality.

Psychoanalytic Studies of the *Confessions:* A Brief History

In placing the totality of Augustine's teaching on mysticism, or what might be called his mystical theology, at the heart and core of the *Confessions,* this book departs radically from previous psychoanalytic readings of Augustine. Such a move offers not only a new base from which to critique past studies but also a theoretical space in which to integrate and reorder them. To see how this is so, we must backtrack a bit and ask what previous psychoanalytic studies have made of Augustine's mysticism. The answer, at least to those convinced of the core significance of Augustine's mystical ascents, is "not much." Even a cursory review of the history of psychoanalytic studies of Augustine reveals that they have found other, more important episodes and events: the bath episode, the pear-stealing episode, the gravitation toward Manichaeism, the garden conversion experience of book 8, and so on. Generally speaking, and with respect to method (and with the caveat that many studies use more than one psychoanalytic model), the psychoanalytic studies of Augustine can be divided into two groups: the (earlier) classic oedipal studies and, later, those that championed theories relating to the preoedipal or narcissistic aspect of the personality. With respect to diagnostic categories, the studies can be further characterized as falling on a spectrum, from those that emphasize Augustine as hopelessly conflicted, fixated, and regressed to those that see some adaptive, healing value to his religious journey—and including a number of nuanced studies that do not hew strictly to either pole. In all cases, however, Augustine's journey is presented as explicable within the terms of the models of self and development found in these theories.

For all intents and purposes, the modern psychoanalytic study of Augustine started with Charles Kligerman's 1957 article, "A Psychoanalytic Study of *The Confessions* of St. Augustine," and the famous symposium on Augustine, "St. Augustine's Confessions: Perspectives and Inquiries," whose proceedings were published shortly thereafter (1965–66) in the *Journal for the Scientific Study of Religion.* Many of the participants in the symposium, whose number included James Dittes, Joseph Havens, David Bakan, Philip Woollcott, and Paul Pruyser, followed Kligerman in his claim that the *Confessions* could be read as "a psychiatric personal history without the contaminating presence of an interviewer . . . the text has the spontaneous quality of free association."[24] In other words, these studies assumed (as do many extant psychoanalytic studies of Augustine) that the reader could access the real, historical Augustine behind the text and make pronouncements on that person. Further, as one might expect, their attempts at a "hermeneutics of suspicion" centered on Augustine's relationship with his mother, Monica, and his father, Patricius. A developmental portrait of Augustine thus emerged that highlighted the role of Oedipus and various derived themes relating to guilt, conflict, repression, castration, and self-reproach.

As concerns Monica, the general thrust of these early studies was to depict her as fostering an erotic attachment to Augustine, as hypermoral, frigid, and hostile toward sex, as well as domineering, controlling, and ultimately winning the battle with her submissive son. Much evidence was amassed to buttress these claims. Monica did, after all, play a role in foiling Augustine's attempts at marriage not once but twice, and she did relay to him prophetic dreams and visions about his future conversion to Christianity and follow him all over the Mediterranean seaboard, only to play housemother (and wife?) to him and his friends in Italy. Moreover, did she not undermine the role of Patricius as Augustine's father ("She earnestly endeavored, My God, that you rather than he should be my father" [1.11])? And was she not, in Augustine's own words, possessed of an "overly carnal" (9.13) attachment to him?

Similarly, these early studies made a point of noting how Augustine's comments about Patricius fuel the oedipal fire. There is, in fact, a dearth of information concerning Patricius. But this in itself could be pounced on as revealing, since Patricius was a catechumen, who converted shortly before his death (9.9), and thus could be seen as an instance of the prodigal son. Moreover, even though Patricius tried to facilitate Augustine's education, the bishop of Hippo claimed that he "only thought in the most trivial way about me" (2.3). Indeed, in what little Augustine does say about his father it becomes clear, at least according to these early studies, that he saw him as an unempathic, hot-tempered, lusty, willful pagan. Whereas Augustine spends pages eulogizing his son and his mother, he passes coldly over his father's death (3.4), devoting to his passing a single dismissive parenthetical sentence. Surely more could be expected from a son, even if the father was a latecomer to Christianity!

This triangle of relationships then became, in the earlier, oedipal psychoanalytic studies of Augustine, the basis for interpreting the various episodes that punctuate Augustine's spiritual narrative, such as the famous observation of the nursing infant jealously guarding his rights to his mother's milk (1.7). Does this scene not reflect Augustine's strong and unresolved feelings of sibling rivalry? As for Augustine's moving portrayal in book 1, chapter 13, of his childhood infatuation with Virgil's *Aeneid* and its description of Dido's suicide, is this not a "screen memory" revealing neurosis and a sadistic sexuality? In the same way, the bath episode of book 2, chapter 3, became a window into his relation with Monica and the conflicts of his sexual life, and a key to explaining his later conversion to celibacy. By similar logic, Augustine's attraction to the dualism of the Manichaeans, as detailed in books 3–6, was construed as an effort to stonewall the conscious acknowledgment of adolescent feelings of lust, rage, and guilt through splitting and projection. Even his conversion to Christianity, detailed in book 8, was held up as evidence of his final capitulation to Monica and the ascendancy of a harsh maternal superego.

It is hardy surprising that these studies went even further, to suggest continuities between Augustine's life and thought. Donald Capps and James Dittes referred to this as a "basement theology"—one in which the various elements of Augustine's theology are traceable to the relationships and events that marked his developmental past.[25] For example, Dittes noted that Augustine's meditations on God as impersonal force, the elevation of primary authority to the church, the framing of evil as "privation," and the denial of human initiative and freedom (to take but a few instances) were traceable to his relationship with Monica and the conflict between autonomy and dependency, prompting speculation about a veritable "theology of dependency."[26] There were a few exceptions, notably Woollcott's ego-adaptive approach to Augustine: "The Confessions represent beyond doubt a great therapeutic effort. . . . [He] *used* his conflicts."[27] But by and large, these early essays can be accurately described as reductionistic. David Bakan exemplified the most reductive and pejorative stance of the oedipalists when he concluded that Augustine's *Confessions* played a role in the "spiritual retardation of mankind" and that his historical influence reflected the "immaturity of mankind."[28]

Starting in the 1980s a number of studies appeared that reflected advances in psychoanalytic metapsychology, particularly with respect to the narcissistic personality trait. This line of thought found fruit in a second symposium on Augustine, whose proceedings were published in 1986 in the *Journal for the Scientific Study of Religion*, as well as in some books and articles, such as the edited book by Donald Capps and James Dittes, *The Hunger of the Heart: Reflections on the Confessions of Augustine* (which, as an edited volume, also included reprints of many of the earlier oedipal studies), and Sandra Dixon's *Augustine: The Scattered and Gathered Self.* These studies tended to focus on the dyadic relation between child and mother, the analysis of archaic narcissistic structures, and the vicissitudes of separation and individuation. In contrast to oedipal readings, such studies highlighted the preoedipal themes of merger, individuation, fluctuations in self-esteem, self-fragmentation, idealization, and the search for self-objects. The very language of narcissism—shame, vanity, and humility, along with guiding metaphors such as "the hunger of the heart"—is seen to be at the center of the *Confessions.*

Like the oedipally based studies, studies in the preoedipal category found deficiencies in the relation between Augustine and his parents—deficiencies that were interpreted as having had an impact on the bishop's narcissistic development. For example, Augustine's continued deprecation of Patricius and the virtual omission of his father from the text were no longer read as indicative of oedipal hostility but as evidence of Patricius's failure to provide an idealized parental figure for Augustine's budding sense of his male self. In the same way, Monica's "overly carnal" attachment to her son, as revealed by her weeping fits, the dream of the ruler, and the need for control, was no longer simply incestuous gratification but evidence of her depressive narcissistic personality and her need to use Augustine as a self-object to regulate her fluctuating self-esteem. Indeed, in parallel with their foregrounding in the oedipally based studies, the episodes that punctuate Augustine's narrative now became grist for the preoedipal mill. The parade of male figures whom Augustine idealizes—Faustus, Ambrose, Simplicianus—reinforced the interpretation that Augustine failed to idealize Patricius. The "disorder" of his youth, exemplified by the pear episode, became seen as a consequence of narcissistic injury and rage, traceable to the emotional and physical abuses suffered at the hands of his parents.[29]

The more pejorative of these studies agreed, in the apt phrase of William Beers, that "key narcissistic elements were never fully integrated into Augustine's developing self, and remained split-off parts of his adult self."[30] Others, however, following the more "adaptive" reading advocated in the earlier studies by Woollcott, saw in the *Confessions* an act of therapy. Some spied in Augustine's journey elements of the adaptive transformation of archaic narcissistic structures into the mature attainments of humor, empathy, wisdom, and creativity. Yet others, utilizing the formulations of Winnicott, Erikson, and Rizzuto, saw the epigenetic evolution of Augustine's "God representation," arguing that Augustine's spiritual journey exhibited personality shifts resembling those found by Erikson in Luther. Still others, most notably Dixon, found evidence in the text indicative of Augustine's move to a Kohutian-framed cohesive and "gathered" self.[31]

Vision and the Developmental Cycle

Within this general set of psychoanalytic studies one can glean, here and there, both oedipal and preoedipal perspectives that specifically tackle Augustine's mysticism. As with readings of many other episodes in the *Confessions,* these perspectives follow essentially two lines of interpretation, one castigating mysticism as regressive and defensive, the other extolling it as healing and adaptive. Both lines view the presence of Monica in the ascent scene at Ostia as symptomatic, stressing the presence of the mother and the array of instinctual and relational oedipal and preoedipal developmental vicissitudes associated with her.

A paradigmatic example of the early studies is that penned by Kligerman, who sees at the core of the *Confessions* an unresolved oedipal complex. It is not surprising, then, to find him interpreting the Ostia vision as essentially incestuous and erotic:

> Augustine relates in equally masterly fashion quite a different sort of experience. He tells how they leaned together in a window overlooking the garden "discoursing together, alone, very sweetly" what the eternal life would be like. He goes on to describe a mystical ecstatic experience he shares with his mother which in rhythm, flow and imagery strike the reader as passionately orgastic.[32]

But Kligerman goes further, intimating there was a homoerotic component to the ascent. He observes that the "end result" of Augustine's conversion was

> an identification with the mother and a passive feminine attitude to the father displaced to God. . . . The feminine imagery is unmistakable: Augustine constantly addresses God with the intense love he could never allow himself to feel toward his own father, and this love is expressed in openly sexual terms. Even in the ecstatic experience with his mother, he gives the impression that he is one with her in panting for God.[33]

Kligerman's initial psychoanalytic foray has been followed by a long line of studies focusing on the presence of Monica at Ostia. For example, Dittes links Monica with Augustine's turn to the mystical worldview of Neoplatonism. For Dittes, Augustine's development left him with a central conflict: whether to be dependent or autonomous. This is Augustine's "identity theme," which can be traced to his relation to Monica and is expressed through the vision at Ostia, in which Monica and Augustine are emotionally and symbolically one. To use Dittes's terminology, "Momism" rules Augustine's vision at Ostia.[34] Variations on this line of argument can be found in later studies of Augustine. Both Capps and Beers, for example, utilize Heinz Kohut's self psychology in elaborating on the preoedipal basis of Augustine's vision of ascent at Ostia. For Capps, Augustine never had approval from Monica for acts of independence. In other words, an affirming self-object response of the mother to the child's thrusts toward independence, crucial to resolving the dependency of the preoedipal stage of development, never occurred in Augustine's case. The fusion detected in the Ostia vision is interlocked with the developmental fact that Augustine was never given that empathic response from Monica that would have allowed him to feel good about acts of independence.[35] For Beers, Augustine's archaic narcissistic structures (the "grandiose self" and "idealized parent imago") were never integrated in a phase-appropriate developmental manner. The Ostia vision, according to Beers, reflects this developmental theme:

> Augustine soared to his longed for idealized Mother imago. . . . The fact that the mystical area is beyond language (i.e., silent) suggest the pre-structural, pre-symbolic, and pre-linguistic realm of dedifferentiated narcissism. And, the reference to carnal pleasure suggests a degree of "telescoping" of narcissistic forms and energies onto later oedipal themes.[36]

On the other hand, some contemporary studies valorize Augustine's visions as adaptive and healing. Dittes's second and much later study of Augustine, for example, begins to move in this direction by seeing in Augustine's mystical visions the encounter with a God who will not fail him. The central issue here is Erikson's epigenetic understanding of the preoedipal stage as constituting the basic dilemma of trust versus mistrust. It is in his visions of God that Augustine "discovers God to be trustworthy."[37] Volney Gay has a Kohutian take on the vision at Ostia: "Mother and son engaged in a kind of spiritual ecstasy that unifies them in a common bond of selfobject merger with God," and the presence of God "corresponds directly to the universal human need to find, somewhere, another who knows us to our depths, recognizes our faults, yet loves us completely."[38] Again, Dixon acknowledges the preoedipal basis for Augustine's mysticism when she states that the ascent with Monica to the "region of unfailing richness" is to a "*regionem ubertatis indeficientis,* the region of inexhaustible fertility, or, at its root, of the inexhaustible breast"[39]—a statement that reveals longing for the idealized parent. However, she also notes that the noetic element one also finds in the vision (where Augustine and Monica "extended their reach and in a flash of mental energy attained the eternal wisdom that abides beyond all things") "sounds like an evocation of what Kohut called 'cosmic narcissism.'"[40] While this comes close to acknowledging that a truly transcendent dimension to Augustine's visions exists, and whereas Dixon leaves open the possibility that Augustine glimpsed something "More," she qualifies this line of argument by stating that Augustine's own grandiosity and inability to accept his death render the achievement of cosmic narcissism open to doubt.[41]

Responses—Historical, Literary, Theological

In the analyses just reviewed, Augustine's mystical ascents do not fare too well. Indeed, if the above were left to stand, Augustine's journey of faith and mystical ascents could be fully explained by interpretations that range from a developmentally regressive "conditioned mode of response" to an adaptive attempt at self-healing. No room can be found here for what James would call a "More" to Augustine's mystical visions.

However, in the last few decades psychoanalytic studies of Augustine have met with responses from numerous quarters, the most effective of which can be grouped into three methodological perspectives: historical, literary, and theological. These diverse approaches have collectively yielded a wide-ranging critique of the reductionist literature: psychoanalytic interpretations often misread the text; they do not take into account Augustine's rhetorical strategy; they do not adequately situate the author in his sociocultural context; they do not restore the full scope of his teaching about mystical ascents with respect to the larger context of his teaching; and they are necessarily limited by the narrowness of their theories concerning the nature of psyche and soul. Overall, the message is that unless such psychological forays engage the *Confessions* in true dialogue they are bound to be misleading and reductive.

Taking each of the above responses in turn, historians have put forward the view that in many ways Augustine is a "modern" man and that his writings are in part responsible for the ways in which contemporary Western persons think of self, world, and other. But they are also apprehensive about psychoanalytic projection (and here the historian and anthropologist have much in common), cautioning researchers of the requisite to engage in cultural contextualization while refraining from imposing normative psychoanalytic notions on an ancient text.[42] For instance, where Augustine's references to "carnal desire" and "fornication" are seen in psychoanalytic studies as revealing important and unconscious sexual meanings, historians such as Paula Fredriksen rightly point out that a phrase such as *Et illius carnale desiderium* is to be construed more widely as "earthly (or worldly) affection" and attachment.[43] Similarly, Augustine's use of the term "fornication" occurs in nonsexual contexts and is to be understood as pertaining to his important religious construction of the "disordering" effect of desire. In both cases the meaning Augustine intends to convey is existentially deeper than that captured by a theory focused on conflicted sexuality.

Again, to give more substance to the important matter of history and cultural differences and the role these can play in misinterpretation, some psychologically oriented readers have interpreted Augustine's relationship with his concubine as evidence of pathology. Some psychoanalytic studies are guilty of figuring Augustine as callously abandoning his first concubine (the mother of Adeotatus) and, in conjunction with his celibacy and seeming dependence on Monica, as evincing the kind of inner conflict that rendered him incapable of engaging in intimate, loving relations with women. David Bakan, for example, concludes that Augustine was a narcissist who, unable to reconcile elements of lust and love, alienated himself from any chance at real love.[44] But historians insist that while a case could be made that Augustine's sexuality was problematic, at the very least the cultural context would have to be admitted into evidence. Bakan's conclusion, for example, is based on the conjunction of a misreading of the cultural context of concubinage in the ancient world and the projection of twentieth-century values concerning wished-for ideal relations between men and women. Eugene TeSelle and Paula Fredriksen, drawing on Peter Brown's work, note that it was an accepted and encouraged cultural practice for a man to dismiss his concubines and "marry up," as was the unnamed concubine's subsequent vow to live the life of a Christian widow.[45] Thus, while contemporary readers may cast a skeptical eye on Augustine's having as a sexual partner a concubine, whom he never names or marries, and then leaves, it is clear, as Jonte-Pace argues, that neither Augustine, nor his family, nor his peers, nor his wider religious culture would have shared this opinion.[46] What was shameful for a socially mobile man like Augustine would have been to have married below his rank. Thus Jonte-Pace concludes, "culture, in these analyses is ignored, resulting in an erroneous diagnosis of pathology. Our denial of Augustine's cultural differences leads us to find him psychologically different: it is our very insistence upon his (cultural) sameness that leads to our evaluation of him as (psychologically) different and pathological."[47]

At the same time, such critiques do not preclude the possibility or the validity of psychobiographical adventures into the *Confessions,* or even the notion that Augustine had problems with intimacy. Frederiksen, who also sees Peter Brown's monumental biography of Augustine as a "closet psychobiography," heralds the "important" and "sensitive" observations of psychologists, which could, if properly contextualized, lead to finding real "continuities," as Dittes would have it, between Augustine's life and thought. The point historians wish to drive home is that psychologically interesting lines of questioning can be easily marred and easily dismissed if their proponents are found guilty of mishandling of texts and willfully ignoring the cultural context. The latter can only lead to misinterpretation and overinterpretation.[48] Perhaps the psychoanalytic treatment of Augustine's mysticism reflects a similar insensitivity to the cultural and literary context?

Literary critical methods have noted that Augustine's narrative is composed not only out of actual existential life experiences but also out of elements taken from scripture, philosophy, and literature. In contrast to Kligerman's claim that the *Confessions* can be read as revealing fantasies and free-associative material, literary perspectives stress that Augustine was educated, as he himself says, to realize the cultural idea of the orator. What this means, as has been traditionally argued by Pierre Courcelle, Leo Ferrari, and Robert McMahon, and more recently with respect to the psychoanalytic literature on Augustine by Jonte-Pace and others, is that Augustine's narrative in the *Confessions* must be taken for what it is: an intentional, constructed work of art that borrows heavily from literary sources.[49] In portraying his own self, Augustine undoubtedly utilized some of his own personal experiences. But in the last analysis, as Jonte-Pace writes, the *Confessions* portrays a "fictionalized self, an allegorically and rhetorically constructed self, rather than a literal self."[50] Augustine used his own life experiences in conjunction with literary sources to construct an archetypal self that transcends his own biography, speaks to the universal human condition, and functions as an instructive discourse concerning the nature, limits, and possibilities of human transformation. Augustine's teaching—his theology, so to speak—is found transmitted through a rhetorically crafted historical narrative. In rhetorically weaving his narrative, Augustine "makes the truth," and hence sublates the distinctions among autobiography, theology, and history.[51] Failure to take the rhetorical nature of the *Confessions* into account can, as in the case of ignoring historical and cultural considerations, lead to misinterpretation. For example, as Jonte-Pace notes, the interpretation by some of Augustine's account of the death of his son, Adeotatus, as evidence of feelings of shame and coldness neglects to take into account the rhetorical structure of the text, a structure designed to convey the Christian parameters for acknowledging and expressing grief. Properly internalized, Christian doctrine, as it concerns the linkage among baptism, death, and salvation, lends optimism to a seemingly tragic event. As Jonte-Pace comments, "the psychohistorian misinterprets here. The anxiety that Augustine *does not feel* is anxiety over salvation, not shame over the conditions of his son's birth or character. It is the *baptism* of Adeotatus which releases Augustine from anxiety."[52]

Taken to the extreme, this perspective casts doubt on any approach that construes the *Confessions* as a simple case history filled with revealing symptomatic and free-associative content. As a result, it mitigates if perhaps does not entirely undercut the attempt to isolate the real, historical Augustine behind the text. It argues that psychology is better off engaging Augustine's narrative on its archetypical level—his teaching, as it were. Again, as is true of the cultural-historical perspective, this literary critical perspective does not entirely undercut the psychohistorical enterprise. The issue is how to engage the problems of the constructed subject and what is clearly the use of borrowed literary elements in narrating a life history. For our purposes, and with respect to the famous vision at Ostia, literary perspectives allow us to inquire in a new way about the meaning of Monica's role in the ascent to the divine—a meaning that, as I shall argue, indicates a "trans" beyond the "pre" of Oedipus.

Finally, theological perspectives ask us to consider whether there are limits to the models employed by psychoanalytic probes: whether extant psychological models possess enough explanatory power to illuminate the deepest recesses of Augustine's religious nature. On the one hand, those theologians who have endeavored to work with psychoanalytic interpretations of Augustine have been respectful of such probes. Eugene TeSelle, for example, agrees that "there is much in the *Confessions* that is psychologically revealing" and that "Augustine seems almost to invite psychoanalysis."[53] Paul Rigby agrees in noting that "Augustine's intimate, developmental self-portrayal of his *Confessions* must be read by Freud, modernity's master of the psyche, if it is to win space for his theology and worldview in the human sciences."[54] Rigby goes on to say that "Freudian pessimism with respect to Augustine's sublimation of his Oedipus Complex cannot be finally rejected, has much textual support, and demands that we search for its traces not only in his doctrines of predestination, the damnation of unbaptized infants, and the use of religious coercion but also in his understanding of grace, original sin, creation, church, sacraments, and the image of God as father that underpins them."[55] David Burrell insists that psychology can show us how Augustine's conflicts continued to handicap him.[56]

But theologians also raise the familiar cry of reductionism and insist that psychoanalytic analyses are all too ignorant of the depths of Augustine's religious journey. Thus, Rigby employs Paul Ricoeur's dialectical interplay between *arche* and *telos* to argue (over against Bakan, Dittes, and Augustine's oedipal interpreters) that some of the archaic determinants of Augustine's unconscious were superseded and transcended, and Burrell notes not only that Augustine had the ego strength to put his psychological conflicts to use but also that the element of dependency psychologists spy in Augustine can be answered theologically: genuine autonomy accrues as a result of a realization of one's limits and reliance on a therapist beyond our control.[57] Additionally, Ricoeur and TeSelle point out that psychologists could avoid hasty conclusions if they took care to contextualize their attempts by "making the detour of an exegesis of the texts in which his faith is documented."[58] Contextualizing the events and ideas found in the *Confessions* with elaborations of the same found in Augustine's other works could help mitigate psychoanalytic overinterpretations and misinterpretations while suggesting alternative intellectual perspectives.[59]

Although theologians are willing to argue that there may be continuities between Augustine's life and thought (hence admitting the validity and helpfulness of psychological probes), they also insist on the existence of discontinuities, a position that grants a privileged status to specifically religious forms of subjectivity and calls for a corresponding theological hermeneutic. In other words, to theologians, religion cannot be made a handmaid to psychology because there is an element to Augustine's life and teaching that lies beyond developmental determinism. For our purposes this translates into a search for psychoanalytic models (specifically, those of the psychoanalytic mystics) capable of dialoguing with the deepest recesses of Augustine's mystical teaching.

Structure: A Transformational Reading of the *Confessions*

My reading of the *Confessions* in this book departs from existing psychoanalytic readings by placing Augustine's visions at the core of his religious journey. It asks how a mystical work such as the *Confessions* can be reread and allowed to speak anew to psychoanalysis and a therapy-absorbed culture currently informed by a revived interest in things mystical. Thus, it embraces the need to articulate and converse with Augustine's mystical theology—his teaching on mystical ascents and mystical process in the context of his theological reflection—while simultaneously engaging the various historical, literary critical, and theological critiques of extant psychoanalysis. With the historian, it asks how meaningful shifts in the term "mysticism" play a role in both psychoanalytic understandings of mysticism in general and Augustine's visions in particular. With the literary critic, it seeks to understand exactly what Monica was doing at Ostia. With the theologian, it tries to discern the meaning of the ascents at Milan and Ostia in the context of other references to the mystical in the total Augustinian corpus while raising existential and epistemological challenges that demand a new psychoanalytic hermeneutic.

The multiple aims of this study are realized through five interrelated chapters, the conclusions of one leading to the investigations of the next. To facilitate this process, each chapter is structured around a theoretical problematic. Chapter 1, "Rhetoric," focuses on literary concerns, with the aim of deciphering the meaning behind the inclusion of Monica in the text. As we have seen, this inclusion has been construed as symptomatic, hence constituting a vital aspect of psychoanalytic theorizing on Augustine's mysticism. To open up a new reading of Augustine, this issue must be dealt with at the outset. Specifically, the argument revolves around the fact that many psychological analyses do not take into account the rhetorical structure of Augustine's narrative. Chapter 1 thus takes as its central problematic psychobiographical versus literary critical readings of the text, including the quest for the historical Augustine over against his rhetorically laced teachings.

By sifting through the rhetoric of the mystical ascents at Milan and Ostia, I hope to show how the presence of Monica at Ostia, understood as a symbolic literary construct, functions with respect to specifically Christian mystical ascents. Far from being a simple fantasy or free association, the presence of Monica implies a teaching about the nature of mystical ascents that goes beyond an understanding of Monica as symptomatic. This opens the door for further tasks, undertaken in subsequent chapters, of a full reconstruction of Augustine's deeper teaching concerning mystical ascents, the epistemology and interpretation of mystical modes of knowing, and the nature of the mystical process.

Chapter 2, "Vision," continues the analysis by taking as its central problematic the need to reconstruct Augustine's precise teaching on mystical vision. Assuming there is a Jamesian "More" to Augustine's mysticism, it starts by noting how extant psychoanalytic interpretations of the ascents at Milan and Ostia gloss over subtleties and nuances in the text, leading to a misreading of Augustine. Moreover, I show how extant psychoanalytic studies reflect the continued influence, a kind of emotional and aesthetic pull, of an embedded, developmentally based perennialism (the belief that there exists a universal common core to all mysticism) that has its roots in Freud's famous interpretation, in the introductory chapter of *Civilization and Its Discontents,* of the "oceanic feeling." Along the way, I expose how extant studies of Augustine's mysticism, indebted as they are to Freud, nevertheless misconstrue the latter's interpretative strategy—a strategy that, once revealed, offers considerable room for dialogue with Augustine's reconstructed teachings on mysticism. Psychoanalytic studies of Augustine's ecstatic mystical ascents, by focusing on the preoedipal, traverse a theoretical path that Freud not only would not choose but also did not choose. This thesis, which is documented with respect to Freud's correspondence with Romain Rolland, the man responsible for Freud's analysis of the oceanic feeling, opens the door for a new psychoanalytic approach to mysticism. Concurrently I will argue, in engaging contemporary academic debates on mysticism, that the psychoanalytic theory of mysticism must shift from a simple, naive perennialism to a more philosophically and textually sophisticated variant of constructivism.

Once the full reconstruction of Augustine's teaching has been presented and Freud's own approach clarified, the stage is set for a new task, set forth in chapter 3, "Vision Interpreted," which consists of a critique and constructive extension of extant psychoanalytic interpretations of Augustine's mysticism. The latter is accomplished by systematically addressing four central aspects of Augustine's teaching: the ascent of Amour/Eros, the epistemology of vision, the required physiological conditions of vision, and the place of theological formulation. The analysis proceeds historically and conceptually by first teasing out previously unacknowledged lines of psychoanalytic theorizing on mysticism in Freud's works and then judiciously applying selective formulations from that cadre of theorists I refer to as the psychoanalytic mystics. This also provides the opportunity to examine physiological and neurocognitive studies of mysticism. Indeed, a compelling case can be made that Augustine, who taught that apprehension of the Light requires a state of "virtual death," adumbrated modern understandings of near-death experiences. Although my analysis does not seek to corroborate Augustine's own theological teaching about the truth of his ontological assertions, for such a claim is beyond the constructivist reliance on a Kantian epistemology, it is possible to delineate psychoanalytic grounds for the *possibility* of mystical forms of noesis, and this delineation defines the limit of what psychoanalytic theory can do vis-à-vis Augustine's mysticism.

Chapter 4, "Therapeia," extends the analysis to include the vicissitudes of the mystical process. As suggested above, we can detect a distinct therapeutic effect of the visionary experience on Augustine's life, understood as an ancient form of therapeia. This effect, mediated through and shaped by the language of Neoplatonism and Christianity, instilled discernible shifts in Augustine's character and helped cultivate specific dispositions, virtues, and capacities, as well as occasional insights into the nature of the soul that anticipated psychoanalytic theory. While Augustine never articulated anything like a developmental theory of mysticism, enough material can be distilled from his ruminations to essay what the mystical process meant to him.

After explicating Augustine's thoughts on mystical process, the analysis turns to offering psychoanalytic keys to its meaning and value. The latter consists in adducing Winnicottian "transitional" modes of experiencing, while ascertaining their relevancy to recent psychoanalytic advances detailing the adaptive value of belief (or "God representations"). Specifically, the latter must be qualified with respect to the many recent critiques that construe psychoanalysis as an ethnopsychological system that can be applied cross-culturally and historically only if it becomes cognizant of the normative developmental trajectories implicit in its theory. Taking such critiques into account helps us to discriminate between psychoanalytic therapy and Augustine's mystically toned therapeia, a difference that can be not only articulated but also, with respect to psychoanalysis, valorized and embraced. The net result of this analysis is to affirm that whatever the "*x*" was that Augustine "saw" (or thought he saw), the meaning of his visions, for all intents and practical existential purposes, resides in how those visions were bound up with his emerging mystical theology, a theology that included what I have referred to as a process element. In other words, when dealing with Augustine's mysticism we should pay attention not only to the singular, episodic event but also to the kinds of capacities and dispositions that accrue during a lifetime. Indeed, it is the notion of a mystical life that provides the broader context within which we can make sense of singular experiences or events.

The first four chapters touch on a broad array of interdisciplinary studies: those animating the psychological reception history of the *Confessions* and its critique, the issues and debates found in the contemporary academic study of mysticism, and the multiple perspectives and dialogical projects that dot the landscape of the history of what has been dubbed the psychology-and-religion movement.[60] These include the classic psychology *of* religion approach, the dialogue between psychology and theology, psychospirituality, and what I will call the psychology-comparativist dialogue.[61] Taken together, they try to do justice to Augustine's own way of configuring his mystical soteriology while keeping the modern, psychological reader in mind.

The concluding chapter, on the other hand, can be conceived of as an attempt to reframe the argument. It does so by going beyond the confines of the case-history approach, linking the present study to a wider social base and to the various cultural concerns represented in this book's subtitle as "the culture of modern spirituality." Admittedly, treating this broader subject in a definitive manner lies well beyond the conceptual boundaries of the present study, but a good conclusion is a good beginning. In this particular case, I suggest that my analysis of Augustine is part of a significant cultural shift that has implications for both psychoanalysis and the modern appropriation of religious wisdom.

The concluding chapter develops and links together three interrelated themes, the psychological reception of Augustine, developments in the psychoanalytic theory of mysticism, and the contemporary interest in mysticism and spirituality as found in the psychology-and-religion movement. To do so, it attempts to contextualize the last with respect to relevant sociological and psychosocial concerns and perspectives. The first section concentrates on the changing nature of the psychoanalytic scholarship on Augustine, attributing it (and hence the genesis of the book) to a Weberian shift from the inner-worldly ascetic to the inner-worldly mystic. The second section, drawing on recent psychosocial theories concerning the process of individual and cultural forms of mourning, focuses on the origin, development, and cultural ascendancy of psychospirituality. I argue that psychospirituality, like modern spirituality in general, reflects a mourning for the mystical element in churched forms of religion, such as Augustine's mystical theology. In the course of this analysis I examine the degree of fit between Augustinian mysticism and the definition of mysticism advanced by the proponents of modern spirituality.

Finally, in the last section I turn to another dialogical project within the broad scope of the psychology-and-religion movement, the psychology-comparativist dialogue and its role in fermenting Western appropriations of the mystical in Buddhism and Hinduism. I aim to show, on the one hand, how the nature and scope of that dialogical enterprise have also been affected by the rise of the social base comprised of inner-worldly mystics, and on the other, its complicity in the development of modern spirituality, psychospirituality, and the psychoanalytic theory of mysticism.

The contemporary renewed interest in the mystical has directly affected psychoanalysis in numerous ways. I believe that the dialogical, constructivist, transformational approach developed in this study is the most suitable way for psychoanalysis to become a bona fide partner in the interdisciplinary study of mysticism. In place of the reductionist and pejorative views of Augustine and his mystical theology, this book offers a corrective approach grounded in psychoanalytic theory and attuned to the shifting consciousness of the culture itself.

one

RHETORIC

Psychoanalytic explorations of the *Confessions* have led to the emergence of a major interpretive divide over whether the work is a predominantly biographical memoir or a predominantly rhetorical text intended to teach and instill belief. This interpretive divide in turn reflects differences in methodological persuasion.

A central and often unchallenged assumption of psychoanalytic studies of the *Confessions* is that the subject of the psychological inquiry is none other than the historical Augustine. It is certainly possible to uncover the various complexes, fixations, and neurotic tendencies that animate the flow of Augustine's narrative, just as one can do with analysands' narratives in the clinical setting. If we assume that in some sense, human nature is universal, it is possible, by drawing on knowledge of clinical case-history material, to make reasoned judgments about the role developmental vicissitudes played in Augustine's religious journey, and indeed, this is a modern pursuit of inestimable worth. It is advantageous to note the extent to which the bishop's teachings on sexuality, for example, are not inscribed in a heavenly realm but are, at least to some extent, the product of sociohistorical and family determinants. What parades as essentialist religious teaching, if it is found to consist in part of projections rooted in a psychosocial matrix, can be successfully decomposed and altered.

A different perspective, one most readily associated with literary-theological studies, holds that the narrative of the *Confessions* is not a case history, an autobiographical recollection imbued with fantasy material that, when rightly interpreted, reveals unconscious content. On the contrary, the *Confessions* is a literary and theological construct that reveals less the historical Augustine than a series of idealized character types and rhetorically elaborated (if not wholly fictional) events, all designed to portray a religious teaching about the nature of being human and the need for a God and savior beyond human comprehension and control. At its extreme, this view holds that the historical Augustine, the man behind the text, cannot be ascertained to the kind of determinative degree needed for legitimating a psychoanalytic evaluation. What we have here is what Diane Jonte-Pace calls "a quest for the rhetorical Augustine."[1]

In between these two quite different approaches lies the possibility of a third kind of reading of Augustine, one that acknowledges the constructed nature of the text yet holds out the possibility that the psychobiographical enterprise, as one means of casting light on the shape of Augustine's life and thought, may in some way be validated.[2] The issue is how this intermediate position can be successfully described and implemented. It is to these three positions, the debates they prompt, and their impact on psychoanalytic interpretations of Augustine's mysticism that this chapter is devoted.

I will begin by taking a specific example, Augustine's use of Virgil's *Aeneid,* to illustrate the first two positions in detail. Then, focusing exclusively on the literary-theological perspective, I turn to exposing the constructed aspects of the mystical texts in the *Confessions.* In particular, I will scrutinize Augustine's rhetoric in relation to the figure of Monica in the mystical ascent at Ostia. There is good reason for addressing this specific issue: reductive psychoanalytic analyses of Augustine's mysticism center their evaluations on the presence of Monica in the text. It is on the strength of her presence that psychoanalysts are able to build their case for oedipal and preoedipal understandings of Augustine's mysticism. To map out a line of argument that opens up a new psychoanalytic reading of Augustine's mysticism, then, we must first clear the way for a more nuanced understanding of the role played by Monica at Ostia. The analysis undertaken in this chapter is thus foundational to the argument developed in the chapters to come.

The *Aeneid* and Oedipus

In book 1 of the *Confessions,* Augustine recounts the significant events of his early years. After making a few salient observations about the state of his soul in infancy, Augustine moves on to the embattled years of his childhood. It is these years, important as they are to human development, that have been of particular concern in psychological studies. A case in point is a recollection revealing sexual content—one that, given other supporting evidence, could be interpreted as determinative for the course of Augustine's sexuality and eventual conversion to Christianity. The recollection occurs in *Confessions* 1.13, where the young Augustine is presented as unable to focus on his studies, a distraction he attributes to the "disordered" state of his soul. What the boy Augustine found attractive were the tales of Virgil, specifically the wanderings of Aeneas. The *Aeneid* includes an account of the Trojan prince landing in Carthage and having an affair with the widowed queen Dido. The relationship ends when Aeneas, reminded of his task by the gods, secretly leaves Carthage at night for Rome. Dido, heartsick at his departure, commits suicide.

This story, Augustine tells us, fed his disordered soul:

> What indeed can be more pitiful than a wretch with no pity for himself, weeping at the death of Dido, which was caused by love for Aeneas.... Against you [God] I committed fornication.... I wept for dead Dido.... And if I were forbidden to read these things, I would be sad at not being allowed to read what would make me sad.... I sinned, therefore, in my boyhood when I showed greater affection for these empty studies than for the others that were more useful.... At that time "One and one makes two; two and two makes four" was a horrible kind of singsong to me. What really delighted me were spectacles of vanity.

What makes this event significant is that it prefigures a later episode during Augustine's young adulthood. In *Confessions* 5.8, Augustine recounts how God acted on him in such a way that he was moved to leave Carthage for Rome, the ostensible reason being that in Rome he could find better students and a more prestigious teaching position. Of interest is how Augustine describes the precise manner in which he left Africa, and how this affected Monica:

> But you, God, knew why it was that I was going from one place to the other, and you did not reveal the reason either to me or to my mother, who was most bitterly distressed at my going away and who followed me right down to the seacoast. She clung to me with all her force, begging me either to return or to take her with me, but I deceived her and pretended that I had a friend whom I did not want to leave until the wind was right for him to set sail. So I told a lie to her, my mother, and such a mother, and I got away from her.... Still she refused to go home without me, and I had

> much difficulty in persuading her to stay that night in a place near the ship where there was an oratory in memory of St. Cyprian. That night I stole away, leaving her behind; she stayed there weeping and praying.

The resemblance between Aeneas's surreptitious departure and Augustine's own sailing for Rome is striking. What are we to make of Dido's suicide, of Augustine weeping for the dead Dido, of Monica's weeping for Augustine, and of the parallel, right down to the leaving by night, between Augustine's departure for Italy and that of Aeneas?

The standard psychoanalytic line is that it is precisely here that the unconscious can be found irrupting through the text. Charles Kligerman treats Augustine's recollection of his boyhood infatuation with the Dido of antiquity as a "screen memory" (a false memory that represses unconscious conflict)—one that reveals the dynamics of his oedipal configuration. On the one hand, Augustine identified with Aeneas and the power and prestige of Rome—themes reflective of his wish to follow the path of his pagan father. On the other, Augustine's sorrow on reading of the way Aeneas left Dido and her subsequent grief and suicide can be interpreted as indicating a displacement of his feelings toward Monica. His response, in this interpretation, reveals his oedipal attraction and the rage, frustration, and guilt engendered in him by a powerful and controlling mother. Kligerman concludes that a kind of "sadistic" sexuality ruled Augustine at this stage in his life.[3]

Augustine's departure for Italy, insofar as it recapitulates that of Aeneas, supports this analysis. An incestuous bond between Augustine and his mother, betraying issues of control and rage, is captured in Monica's watchful eye and Augustine's need to lie to her and steal away by night. Other evidence buttresses this thesis: Monica's strongly advising Augustine against fornicating with another man's wife (*Confessions* 2.3), her subsequent role in the dismissal of Augustine's concubine (*Confessions* 6.15), her many fits of weeping, her attempts to control her son through her "prophetic" dreams (*Confessions* 3.11–12), and finally the strange pilgrimage in which she followed her son all over the Mediterranean seaboard only to end up as a den mother to Augustine and his friends (*Confessions* 6.1ff.). The operative assumption, in the standard psychoanalytic view, is that Augustine is faithfully recounting actual life events of the sort that one typically finds in the modern genre of autobiography.

On the other hand, there is ample evidence that Augustine's narrative combines elements of historical facticity with fictionalized, theological, and literary elements. Karl Weintraub, for example, observes that Augustine "sought to present his own life story as the typical model for any Christian life," hence diminishing "the value of historical specificity."[4] Anne Hawkins, David Burrell, Sandra Dixon, Diane Jonte-Pace, and others have similarly noted that the *Confessions* is a highly crafted narrative and work of art.[5] Indeed, as Augustine himself relates, and as Sabine MacCormack, Robert McMahon, John O'Meara, and others have carefully documented, the *Aeneid* was a popular work during Augustine's lifetime, and the works of Virgil commanded an especially powerful influence over Augustine's understanding of self, world, and other.[6] For a teacher like Augustine, well versed in the art of rhetoric, the use of the *Aeneid* as a means to convey theological teachings is a virtual certainty.

When applied to the episodes Augustine narrates, such a view prompts a very different understanding of the two passages considered above. From the perspective of the text as a rhetorical project, Augustine consciously drew on and transformed elements of the *Aeneid* to promote a more specifically Christian teaching. For example, while Augustine, like Aeneas, is called to Italy, only Augustine casts off pagan values and, through the guidance and calling of God, is regenerated through conversion and mystic vision. In this movement, as Eric Ziolkowski notes, one can discern elements of the philosophical and religious narratives Augustine utilized throughout the *Confessions:* the parable of the prodigal son and the Neoplatonic return or "flight" to the fatherland.[7] Further, both texts leave a grief-stricken woman on the shores of Carthage: just as Dido is left by Aeneas, the weeping Monica is left by Augustine. But whereas Dido commits suicide, the pagan response to grief and loss, Monica not only renounces her grief and successfully crosses the dangerous ocean in her mission to convert her son (an example of Monica as an instrument of God), she also, through her prophetic visions, consoles the hardiest of sailors during the turbulent journey. As Augustine writes in *Confessions* 6.1:

> By this time my mother had joined me. Her piety had given her strength and she had followed me over land and sea, confident in you throughout all dangers. In the perils of the sea it was she who put fresh heart into the sailors although as a rule it is for the sailors to reassure the passengers who are inexperienced on the high seas. But she promised them that they would get safely to land because you had promised this to her in a vision.

In sum, then, the notion that Augustine rhetorically wove the figure of Monica with the narrative of the *Aeneid* implies that Augustine's report of feeling sad as a boy reading the fate of Dido functions less as a straight autobiographical recollection than as a tale designed to illustrate the effects of sin, the state of those whose desires are disordered. Augustine used this recollection in a rhetorical fashion to illustrate how certain forms of "carnal" (that is, earthly) attachment can lead to hopelessness and despair. Here the question of historicity is transcended. Theological insight, autobiographical recall, and literary motifs are sublated in the service of a teaching that is not simply about Augustine the person but about human beings in general.

Similar points could be made about other episodes that are adduced to support a psychoanalytic reading of the *Confessions*. An example is the famous bath episode of *Confessions* 2.3:

> In the sixteenth year of my age . . . the brambles of lust grew right up over my head, and there was no hand to tear them up by the roots. In fact when my father saw me at the baths and noticed that I was growing toward manhood . . . he told my mother of it . . . [she] was seized with a holy fear and trembling. . . . For it was her wish, and I remember how privately and with what great anxiety she warned me not to commit fornication and especially not to commit adultery with another man's wife. . . . But, though I did not know it, these warnings came from you.

Psychoanalytic studies tend to see this account as a significant memory that helped shape the young Augustine's attitudes toward sexuality. God the "Father" is depicted as warning against oedipal desire. Episodes like this are used to argue that Monica cultivated an erotically toned relationship with her son. Monica did, after all, play a significant role in ending Augustine's sexual relationships and lived with him as his spiritual companion in Italy. Moreover, Augustine did choose celibacy, one of an array of options available to him in his culture. One wonders whether an incestuous relationship with his mother played a role in such a significant decision.

Commentators working from a literary-theological perspective, on the other hand, point out the rhetorical nature of this passage. The teaching to be conveyed in this passage, as Garry Wills notes, plays on the contrast between nudity (being nude at the baths) and being clothed. Augustine's concern in this episode, according to Wills, is with the mysterious linkage connecting grace, the baptism of water, salvation, and the "old" and "new" Adam: the young Augustine in the baths is an example of "a fallen Adam, not yet clothed in Christ's grace—as he will be when Ambrose immerses him in the *spiritual* bath of baptism. The two pool scenes form a kind of diptych, one concerned with care of the body under a worldly father's gaze, the other cleansing the soul with a recognition of God's paternity."[8] Wills further rejects psychoanalytic analyses ("his modern readers are indulging their own fantasies about a hyperactive penis"[9]) by noting that they misread the Latin text (reading, for example, the adjective *inquieta* in wholly sexual terms) and fail to appreciate the sociohistorical realities about the nature of the Roman baths (which were in actuality public gathering places that demanded strict decorum).[10]

To take a final example, psychoanalytic studies note the neurotic dimensions of the famous pear-stealing episode of book 2. What is foregrounded as symptomatic is Augustine's language of remorse and intense self-reproach—language that scholars such as Donald Capps, E. R. Dodds, and Leo Ferrari have located in the developmental vicissitudes of the *Über-Ich*.[11] Again, literary-theological perspectives counter, can we really assume that the pear-stealing episode took place? While the historicity of the latter remains controversial, what remains undeniable is that Augustine patterned this story on another familiar biblical one, the theft of the forbidden fruit in the Garden of Eden, in order to rhetorically convey the nature of the human condition, mired in original sin. The point, as Jonte-Pace notes, is that the inclusion of the story reflects a desire to present "a theologically motivated biblical allegory of human sin and disobedience," and not the need to recount "a personal memoir."[12] Again, existential event, theological insight, and rhetorical embellishment are sublated in a way that individual biography is transcended in the service of a teaching that speaks to the universal condition of humankind.

Monica: The Biography

The dichotomous interpretations, hovering between factual account and rhetorical construction, can be extended as well to the biographical details of Monica's life. Augustine does refer to Monica in other texts, notably in his *Dialogues* written at Cassiciacum and in some letters, perhaps even devoting a (now lost) text to a short life of her.[13] The problem, from a literary perspective, is that such texts, and in particular the *Confessions,* are not designed to offer a biography of Monica. Although it seems reasonable to hold that *some* biographical facts Augustine recounts about Monica are valid—for example, that she was born around AD 331 in

Numidia, that she was most likely a Berber, that she came from a fairly wealthy family—the *Confessions* provides only selective details about Monica's life. Some chapters in her life history are gone over in great detail, while others, notably the time Augustine spent away from her during his years as a young teacher in Africa, are entirely omitted.[14] Again, the reason is that the figure of Monica functions in the text to promote a specific kind of religious teaching. The historical Monica and the rhetorical Monica are intertwined to such an extent that it is difficult to put into perspective Monica's role as mother to Augustine.

Two episodes recounted in book 9, where Augustine does give us biographical depth about Monica, are cases in point. In *Confessions* 9.8, Augustine relates the story of how Monica as a youth had an "excessive fondness for wine." Only the taunting of a servant, who called her a drunkard, awakened her to her problem and spurred her to overcome it. Augustine uses this story at the outset of his history of Monica much as he used biographical details of his own life. There is a conversion motif apparent here: Monica moves from giving in to a disordered desire to the formation of a bad habit. Only the intervention of grace, in the form of a servant's taunt, redirects the young Monica's desire.[15] Also in *Confessions* 9.9, Augustine's description of how Monica dealt with her husband Patricius can be taken as an attempt to uphold her as a role model for Christian women in marriage.[16]

Augustine's account of his relationship with Monica similarly moves from historical actuality to rhetorical design in a manner that undercuts a simple psychoanalytic rendering. What appears to be total dependence on Monica and perhaps an incestuous bond may be an overinterpretation if placed in relation to a plausible alternative, Augustine's rhetorical strategy of promoting an equivalence between Monica as an instrument of God's grace and as an instrument of the church. From the perspective of the latter interpretation Monica becomes not only a model Christian mother who, through visions and dreams, conveys God's grace to her son but also a symbol of the Mother Church that saves humanity through the body of Christ. The "dependence" is on Christ, grace, and the establishment of the church as his saving "body."[17]

Monica: The Ascent at Ostia

The mutating function of Monica suggests it behooves readers at least to consider what Augustine the rhetorician had in mind when he included the figure of Monica in the mystical ascent scene at Ostia. In taking up the task of trying to understand Augustine's rhetorical intent in the specific instance of including Monica in the ascent, it is important to note that most modern psychologists are unaware that their understanding of the meaning of the term *mysticism* is not the same as Augustine's. Theologians are apt to tell us that what we call the mysticism of Augustine engages an important intellectual project (which is but one within the broader academic study of mysticism): that of mystical theology. The latter term has a specific meaning tied to the origin and development of the word *mysticism.* As Louis Bouyer's essay on the genealogy of the term reveals, *mysticism* is a Western term that is first found in the Greek Mystery religions.[18] At first *mystikos,* derived from the verb *muo* (to close), lacked any direct reference to the transcendent, referring only to the hidden or secret elements of ritualistic activities. Once picked up by the early church fathers, however, it migrated in a new direction, becoming defined with respect to three interrelated contexts: biblical, liturgical, and spiritual. Implicit in the Christian terms *mystical theology* and *mystical contemplation* was the notion that mystical experience brought one into contact with a transcendent reality, and further, that such experiences could be accessed only through the auspices of church and tradition. For Christians, a mystical experience referred to the presence of an objective reality above and beyond the wholly subjective. Mysticism was "the experience of an invisible objective world: the world whose coming the Scriptures reveal to us in Jesus Christ, the world into which we enter, ontologically, through the liturgy."[19] Contrary to modern Western psychological expectations, early Christians' interest lay not in championing the individual and depicting the deeper recesses of their own personal religious subjectivity but in promoting the teachings of the church. In following this line of argument Bernard McGinn, in his wide-ranging historical and theological study of the history of Christian mysticism, is willing to accept the use of the generic word "mysticism" as a "term of art." But he cautions against losing sight of the numerous other terms Christian mystics have utilized to describe their experiences, terms that are rooted in church and tradition and integrated into a wider context of the religious life. In other words, mysticism must be continually qualified, depending on the mystic and the tradition in question.[20] For McGinn, Christian mysticism in all its varieties is best qualified with respect to the notion of the presence of God: "we can say that the mystical element in Christianity is that part of its belief and practices that concerns the preparation for, the consciousness of, and the reaction to what can be described as the immediate or direct presence of God."[21] Further, as I indicated in the introduction, the meaning of mystical experience must go beyond the episodic, for the latter is inexorably bound up with "mysticism as a part or element of religion" and "mysticism as a process or way of life."[22]

Augustine's own preferred vocabulary for designating the mystical reflects a churched understanding of the divine. Like his fellow church fathers, Augustine, bishop of Hippo, wished to convey to his flock not simply his own experience but more, the teachings of the church. As McGinn notes, Augustine's use of specific terms and linked qualifiers (such as *contemplatio, sapientia, veritas,* and *amor-dilectio*) with respect to the *visio Dei* was always in reference to Christian beliefs, practices, and scripture. The vocabulary of Christian mysticism often reflects important meanings glossed over by modern studies of mysticism.[23] John Peter Kenney, in also noting that the modern appropriation of the term mysticism from James onward can shortchange the full meaning of the word, stresses that for Augustine, the term invariably had a communal import: the ascent to the divine is with one's fellow believers through Christ.[24]

This background is crucial for understanding why Monica is included in the ascent at Ostia. We know that in conveying to us his mystical ascents, Augustine utilized literary styles as popularized by the Platonists. By this he meant not simply the works of Plato but, more important, his follower Plotinus. These Greek figures had bequeathed to ancient culture a lasting and deeply influential way of thinking about the nature of the soul, God, and the way to access the vision of God. As I shall present in detail later on, early Christian figures who influenced Augustine, most notably Bishop Ambrose, had included Platonic concepts in their sermons as a way of conveying the deeper, mystical meaning of scripture. So it is that Augustine writes in book 7 that God "brought to my notice some books written by the Platonists" (7.9). This is because Augustine had been introduced to Platonic ideas in the sermons of Ambrose and, as a result, had read at least two major works of Plotinus ("On the Three Divine Hypostases" [*Ennead* 5, treatise 1] and "On Beauty" [*Ennead* 1, treatise 6]) in the translation of his fellow rhetorician, Marius Victorinus.[25] Whatever it was that Augustine really experienced at Milan, it was undeniably constructed in a style typical of the Plotinian ascent motif.[26] One ascends to the divine by degrees, first surveying the beauty of the external world, then proceeding inward to the soul and its powers, and then, paying heed to the need to go beyond the senses, the "tumult" of the flesh, the powers of dreaming and of imaginary visions, still deeper inward, beyond the soul to the "One" who lies above it. As Paul Henry observes, the "total forgetfulness of the sensible world, the impulse towards the world of spirit, repose in the world of ideas where all is truth, eternity, and satiety, the very brevity of this moment of union, and finally the disenchanted return to the inferior realm of the senses and of human speech"—all of these are key notions that Plotinus would have embraced.[27] Indeed, this ascent motif is equally apparent in the mystical passage at Ostia (*Confessions* 9.10). As Andrew Louth, André Mandouze, and others have noted, there are multiple references to Plotinus in this text, most notably Augustine's stress on *sileat* ("So we said: if to any man the tumult of the flesh grew silent [sileat], silent the images of earth and sea and air . . . the heavens . . . the very soul"), which is directly influenced by the *hesychon* of Plotinus in Ennead 5.1.2 ("Quiet let the earth be, quiet the sea and the air, and the heaven itself").[28] The influence of Plotinus is corroborated by Augustine, who, among other things, draws parallels between the Plotinian "Nous" and the Johannine "Word," and claims that the Platonists taught him to see God as incorporeal and evil as privation (7.10–17).

At the same time, it would be misleading to state that Augustine was at any time wholly converted to the philosophical views of Plato and Plotinus. Certainly Augustine was influenced by the Greeks and, while clearly indicating that they did glimpse the light of God, was equally critical of their soteriological agenda. Even in the account of the vision at Milan there are references to scripture, to God's grace, and recourse to a metaphor involving food and eating ("and you shall feed on me . . . [and] will be changed into me") reminiscent of the consumption of the Eucharist.[29] And while Plotinus would agree with Augustine that the mystical experience is transient, Augustine's stress on grace (God as helper) and sin (which accounts for the "weight" drawing one downward) would be foreign to the Greek manner of thought.[30] But insofar as the two mystical ascents, at Milan in book 7 and at Ostia in book 9, are strategically and rhetorically separated by Augustine's conversion to Christianity (in book 8), we need to examine in more detail how the Ostia vision differs from the mystical ascent at Milan, and in particular how the rhetorical inclusion of the figure of Monica at Ostia functions to highlight Augustine's desire to promote a specifically Christian mystical teaching.

While Plotinian and scriptural references can be found in both mystical passages, the vision at Milan gives more rhetorical weight to metaphors of sight, is more intellectual in tone, and has a pessimistic, driven-back quality to it.[31] This is in line with what one might expect from someone versed in Plotinus. As Eugene TeSelle has noted, Augustine's reading of Plotinus led him to believe that he could have a permanent vision—a kind of beatific vision and the leading of the "happy life": a life "led in true happiness, which in turn meant virtue, which in turn meant wisdom—in other words, a life in which his consciousness would be constantly bathed in the light of this higher realm."[32] But Augustine was to be disappointed. It was his inability to maintain the vision, his "sad weight" and "carnal habit," that pulled him down from whatever momentary vision he was able to muster. This is the existential reality that lies behind his critique of the Platonists and their "pride." Augustine became convinced that the Platonist idea of a permanent union with God that could be attained through human efforts was both arrogant and misguided.

In the account of the ascent at Ostia, on the other hand, there is a preponderance of affective language. Metaphors (for example, "we did, with the whole strength of our heart's impulse, just lightly come into touch with her") are given rhetorical weight, as are references to scripture (particularly the epistles of Paul and the Psalms). More important, unlike the experiences at Milan, one does not find at the summit of the ascent the language of being driven back. This is in part a result of Augustine's emphasis on his newfound distinction between ecstatic experience and the beatific vision. This is apparent in his description of the summit of the ascent at Ostia, where Augustine describes the ascent as a foretaste of the life to come:

> supposing that this state were to continue . . . so that his life might forever be like that moment of understanding which we had had and for which we now sighed—would not this be: *Enter into thy Master's joy?* And when shall that be? Shall it be when *we shall all rise again,* though we *shall not all be changed?*

Moreover, as Kenney points out, it is important to recognize that what may appear to a modern reader to be an episodic mystical experience at Ostia cannot be divorced from the wider canopy of a contemplative act, one that focuses on the articulation of the "architecture of the spiritual universe."[33] In the narrative of the ascent at Ostia Augustine is careful to describe how he and Monica, in the course of ascending upward, moved beyond the mind, but before coming into contact with the uncreated Wisdom they encountered a "region of inexhaustible abundance where you feed Israel eternally with truth for food." The latter reveals Augustine's meditations on scriptural references to the *caelum caeli* (the "heaven of heaven," which is the initial, primordial form of creation, existing outside space and time and holding created beings capable of continuous contemplation of the Holy Trinity). This architecture includes the notions of a specifically Christian monotheism, the reality of grace, the need for confession, the role of memory, and the personal nature of God's love for particular fallen souls.[34] Kenney notes that such an architecture was rhetorically inserted to distinguish the contemplation Augustine and Monica were engaged in from Augustine's Greek predecessors': "The structure of the transcendent world, the power and metaphysical depth of the soul, the method and practice of contemplation all differ from the theology of Plotinus and his school."[35]

This line of argument can be further developed to include the distinctive Christological and ecclesiastical nature of Augustine's mystical teachings. As I noted earlier, one of Augustine's major criticism of the Platonists was their "pride," "presumption," and unwillingness to humble themselves before the Word made flesh. It is important to stress that for the bishop of Hippo, the mystical journey began in the earthly tabernacle below. It was in the church that one was introduced to the presence of God and one's will and emotions stood the best chance of becoming "rightly ordered." While God's grace might eventuate in the elevation of experiencing that presence (as in the case of intellectual visions) as well as help purify one's heart, the journey was not completed until one entered the afterlife. The church, which both represented Christ as the head of its mission (the way and goal) and served metaphorically as the body of Christ, thus played an indispensable role in the bishop's mystical theology. In his *Homilies on John* and *Homilies on the Psalms,* Augustine makes clear the indispensable role of the church in spiritual progress.[36] For example, in his commentary on Psalm 41.7–10, Augustine, once again looking at the question of the *visio Dei,* recapitulates the Plotinian ascent motif found in the mystical passages at Milan and Ostia. To the question "Where is Thy God?" Augustine surveys "every corporeal nature" and "my own soul," but finds God only when he "pours forth" his own soul "above myself" (in ecstasy), finding God in his heavenly "dwelling place" (41.7). But this manner of finding God is possible only through the church. It is here that one can find the grace, teaching, and models of saintly life that propel one upward. The ascent is depicted as communal and as taking place between the earthly tabernacle and the heavenly dwelling place of God.

When placed in this context, the inclusion of Monica at Ostia becomes rhetorically meaningful. Monica's presence gives the ascent at Ostia a social, communal dimension entirely lacking from Augustine's ascent at Milan. If the latter can be said to resemble the Plotinian mystical dictum "the flight of the alone to the Alone," then Augustine's and Monica's communion with God at Ostia emphasizes that the beatific vision is invariably social. This point is buttressed by the setting in which the ascent at Ostia takes place. Augustine notes that he and Monica "were standing alone, leaning in a window which looked onto the garden inside the house where we were staying, at Ostia on the Tiber" (*Confessions* 9.10). As McGinn points out, this garden would have been a walled (enclosed) one. Since Augustine linked the church with the "enclosed garden" of the Song of Songs, it seems reasonable to conclude that Augustine's rhetorical inclusion of a walled garden was meant to emphasize the role of the church in the mystical ascent to God.[37]

This line of reasoning achieves further sophistication when it is noted that Monica takes an active role in the ascent upward. That is, Monica and Augustine were engaged in conversation—conversation that led them eventually to "touch" the One. As McGinn, Kenney, and others have noted, the notion of not only a communal ascent but one in which an unlearned woman is taking an active part would have been foreign to Plotinus.[38] Indeed, in the *Dialogues* written at Cassiciacum (*De ordine, De beata vita*), Monica is portrayed as actively engaging in religious discussions. In *De ordine* Augustine goes so far as to portray himself as Monica's disciple, exclaiming that her thoughts are so profound that he seemingly forgot her gender. Most significant, in *De beata vita* Monica is presented as having the key to philosophy not so much because she is learned (rather, as relatively unsophisticated with respect to knowledge about philosophy) but because she is completely devoted to God. Faith, hope, and charity are the theological virtues that lead to happiness—happiness that in its fullest sense is reserved for those in the afterlife. In contrast to the Plotinian stress on the learned, intellectual life, then, Monica is presented as one who is capable of coming to the deepest truths of wisdom by reliance on faith in and the study of scripture.[39] In sum, one can discern in these *Dialogues* two models of spirituality: the elite, learned, male, and philosophically sophisticated way of Plotinus and the humble, devotional way of Monica and the common Christian. As Kim Power notes, it is in the vision at Ostia that the two are both present and reconciled:

> By the time he wrote the *Confessiones,* Augustine had resolved his conflict between philosophy and faith, coming to the conclusion that the life of faith and the experience of God could illuminate the mind as brightly as philosophy. Monica is the exemplar of the faith route to God, as Augustine is of the philosophic. The Ostia vision is irrefutable proof of the resolution of his conflict. . . . This experience of joint ecstasy erases all distance between mother and son . . . the fact that Monica and Augustine shared the same joy suggests he is intending to convey a Christian rather than philosophic vision.[40]

This makes a certain amount of sense for, in his capacity as the bishop of Hippo, Augustine would have wanted to emphasize the communal, Christocentric, and ecclesiastical dimensions of a mysticism that reflected a specifically Christian ontology. By stressing the role of a relatively unlearned but wholly devoted woman in the communal ascent upward, Augustine accomplished his aim in a sophisticated, rhetorically elegant, and edifying manner.

Revisiting Rhetoric and Psychoanalysis

It cannot be seriously entertained that Augustine was entirely exempt from those vicissitudes of development that affect the rest of the human species, or that such developmental themes did not have an impact on his thought in some manner. The Monica of the *Confessions* may well have been a condensed version of Augustine's actual relationship with his mother, as well as a presence used rhetorically for strategic purposes. Yet the constructed nature of the text, along with historical and theological concerns, rightly calls into question the extent to which the psychobiographical project can be implemented. At the very least, the psychobiographer must take literary considerations into account in attempting to draw a convincing portrait of Augustine.

It is that challenge that animates the project of Diane Jonte-Pace, who, while sympathetic to psychoanalytic probes, grants that the *Confessions* portrays a "fictionalized self, an allegorically and rhetorically constructed self, rather than a literal self."[41] The issue, if one insists on the psychobiographical enterprise, is how to engage the problems of the constructed subject and what is clearly the use of borrowed literary units in narrating a life history. In addressing this problem, Jonte-Pace turns to Freud and his brief paper, "The Relation of the Poet to Daydreaming." In it Freud speaks to the appropriation of borrowed units of literature when he says that he "will not neglect to refer also to that class of imaginative work which must be recognized, not as spontaneous production, but as a re-fashioning of ready-made material."[42] He then states that the presence of such borrowed material is hardly uninterpretable. This, thinks Jonte-Pace, points to a new mode of psychobiography vis-à-vis the *Confessions:*

> The fact that Augustine borrowed from traditional genres, or even that he borrowed narrative units to recount his own life story, does not make psychohistory impossible. The *Confessions* may well be both rhetorically constructed and psychologically determined. While Augustine may have integrated themes and episodes from the literature of his time into his autobiography, one might use psychology to interpret the choices he made and the way he narrated the stories he chose. As Freud suggests, Augustine's choice of material, his style of embellishing a traditional text, and his manner of constructing a narrative out of traditional patterns, may be a valuable focus of interpretation. But at the very least, a psychohistory sensitive to the question of the subject requires a new approach: rather than asking why Augustine stole away from Carthage leaving Monica sobbing on the shore, one might inquire why and how Augustine borrowed and embellished that particular story from the *Aeneid;* rather than asking why he felt so guilty about stealing pears one might inquire into his unprecedented descriptions of the agonistic, conflictual, inner states described in the aftermath of the sin. One might even approach the text as Freud approaches a dream, viewing the borrowed text as the "day residue" and tracing the construction of "manifest content" through the condensation and displacement (metaphor and metonymy in Lacanian vocabulary) of dreamwork narrative.[43]

Applied to Augustine's visions, Jonte-Pace's project distills, at one level, to the conclusion that one can legitimately argue for the presence of Eros in the text. Indeed, the developmental themes that marked Monica's relation with her son are evident in the narrative. At the same time, in creating theoretical space for a "both-and" reading, Jonte-Pace's project also undermines a simple, reductionistic reading of the text as free-associative. There is a religious teaching here, and one must pay respect to what we earlier referred to as the Jamesian "More" that Augustine champions.

We have arrived at the possibility, then, of finding reasonable grounds for acknowledging the value of even the most reductive of extant psychobiographical analyses. In other words, at this juncture it suffices to say that the presentation I have offered so far does not necessarily undermine a psychoanalytic investigation of even the constructed character of the text or foreclose speculation concerning how the relationship between Monica and her son led to discernible developmental conflicts surrounding sexuality, male narcissism, and individuation. Similarly, it does not preclude discerning continuities between Augustine's life and thought. Insofar as this is the case, the earlier psychoanalytic studies I canvassed in the last chapter tally well with more recent feminist and feminist psychoanalytic analyses (drawing on theorists such as Lacan and Irigaray) that attend to the link between mystical ideology and practice, on the one hand, and the role of patriarchy and gender privilege in fermenting social inequality and abuse of power on the other.[44] In other words, there could well be, as noted in the Introduction and what Capps and Dittes refer to as a real "basement," to Augustine's mystical formulations, especially with regard to gender and sexuality. This point (which I explore in more detail in chapters 4 and 5) should not be overlooked. At the same time, theorists like Lacan (as we shall see in chapter 3) provide an expanded view of Eros, a *jouissance* and "winged Eros," that serves as a psychoanalytic foundation for a more nuanced understanding of a desire that "goes beyond" to the "More." If the event at Ostia was in part a literary construct, and if Augustine included it as part and parcel of his emerging mystical theology, then the rhetoric of Augustine's narrative behooves us to look further. It asks us once again to take a detour with respect to linked texts in which he expounds on the conditions and nature of vision and contemplation. It asks us to be open to the possibility that there exists a spiritual wisdom in Augustine's narrative that, while hardly precluding the presence of unconscious ideation, also admits of a depth that goes beyond the bounds of developmental determinism. If it is possible to draw a psychoanalytic portrait of Augustine fit for the modern psychospiritual imagination, then the task of ascertaining the precise nature of his teaching on mystical ascents needs more work. It is to that task that I now turn.

two
VISION

The discussion in the previous chapter prompts two interrelated lines of inquiry. First, we have concluded that Augustine's inclusion of Monica in the ascent at Ostia speaks to the rhetorical complexity of the text. If this is the case, then it is of interest to know the extent to which such rhetorical complexity is also linked to a sophisticated teaching about the nature of mystical ascents—one that can be used to mount an epistemological challenge to the psychoanalytic view that all mysticism be reduced to the developmental cycle. In order to ascertain this a full textual and theological reconstruction of Augustine's teaching on mystical ascents and visions—one that includes works well beyond the *Confessions*—must be undertaken, for such a task would help disclose the precise nature of the psychoreligious phenomena presented in the ascents at Milan and Ostia. Once this aim has been accomplished we will be in a better position to embark on the second line of inquiry, namely, that of evaluating the adequacy of extant psychoanalytic interpretations of Augustine's mysticism.

Psychoanalytic interpretations of Augustine's ascent are, as already noted, predictably simple, neglecting Augustine's precise teaching on mysticism and focusing instead on what commentators take to be a description of a transient unitive mystical experience, which they then interpret in terms of developmental forces. This hermeneutical strategy is based on a tradition of psychoanalytic theorizing of mysticism, a history that began with Freud's attempt, in *Civilization and Its Discontents,* to unravel the origin and nature of what he called oceanic feelings. As a prelude to the two interrelated tasks I have set out for this chapter, a look at the nuances, context, and consequences of Freud's analysis is in order. This investigation, while it may initially seem to be a detour, is nonetheless indispensable to the task of dissecting and reconstructing psychoanalytic forays into mystical phenomena.

A starting point is to unravel the sociohistorical context that informed Freud's understanding and analysis of mysticism. In the previous chapter I surveyed the origin and history of the term mysticism and its relation to the academic project known as mystical theology. Mystical theology dates from the era of Augustine and the church fathers, but the psychoanalytic foray into mysticism was heir to a new approach to the subject that developed in the sixteenth and seventeenth centuries. As Michel de Certeau has noted, it was during the latter period that *mysticism* appeared in the language as a substantive (*la mystique*) and became associated with subjective experiences divorced from church and tradition. This usage ultimately led to the investigation and interpretation of such experiences from a scientific perspective. This modern approach reconceptualized ecstatic and contemplative religious figures as social types within a particular tradition ("the mystics") while redefining the mystic's "Absolute" in generic terms "as an obscure, universal dimension of man, perceived or experienced as a reality [un réel] hidden beneath a diversity of institutions, religions, and doctrines."[1] These two moves allowed for another, namely, the psychologization of mystical experiences and states. The net effect of this historical shift was a new relation to religion. The psychological study of mysticism made "a nonreligious exegesis of religion possible."[2] Leigh Schmidt extended Certeau's initial observations through his own survey of religious texts in Great Britain and North America during the eighteenth and nineteenth centuries. Schmidt delineates the influence of numerous factors, most notably liberal Protestant thought, in both securing the widespread use of the substantive *mysticism* and inventing its modern form, understood as "ahistorical, poetic, essential, intuitive, and universal."[3]

Both Schmidt and Certeau observe that the interpretative efforts of the central psychological figures of the late nineteenth century and early twentieth century reflected developments in this new understanding of the term mysticism. The paradigmatic case is that of William James, who defined mysticism in a way diametrically opposed to that found in Bouyer's survey of the early church fathers. For example, James states in his *Varieties of Religious Experience* that he was "treating personal experience as the exclusive subject of our study,"[4] defining religious experience, of which mysticism is the deepest form, as "the feelings, acts, and experiences of individual men in their solitude, so far as they apprehend themselves to stand in relation to whatever they may consider the divine."[5] Tradition and its accoutrements, by which James meant theology, philosophy, liturgy, ritual, and the various aspects of church organizations, all crucial for access to the presence of God for the church fathers, were understood by James to be secondary phenomena, derived from the primary experiential matrix located in the individual, and thus essentially unessential for access to the divine. James's construal of mysticism as an experience that is not only divorced from church and tradition but is the original source for all church accoutrements—these are the premises that psychologists not only uncritically accepted but championed.

Schmidt also thinks that modern construals of mysticism have paved the way for the popular contemporary conflation of the terms "mysticism" and "spirituality."[6] There is much evidence to support this assertion. The Pauline *spiritus* (breath) characterized a person guided by the spirit of God (as against the carnal man, who turned toward materiality). It was growth in the spirit, which included the development of virtues, dispositions, and ideals in the striving toward Christian perfection, that was emphasized.[7] To be sure, through the centuries there were deviations along the way (at one point, spirituality came to denote ecclesiastical property and persons who exercised ecclesiastical jurisdiction), but in the main, spirituality held fast to its moral, psychological, and religious meanings.[8] Adhering to its biblical roots, much of current spirituality in the theological literature refers to religious growth in a particular tradition (such as the spirituality of Saint Teresa of Avila). In this way, "classical spirituality" (as some call it) and what I refer to as "mystical theology" are commensurate: both refer to growth and mystical experiences within a total religious matrix.

Going further, Mary McDonald has pointed out that alongside classical spirituality one can find what she calls a form of "modern" spirituality" that, like modern mysticism, is nontraditional or unchurched.[9] Modern forms of spirituality, like classical spirituality, are fixated on religious experience and the development of the self. The major dividing point between modern and classical forms concerns allegiance to a particular religious tradition. Conforming to the well-known public versus private split, the new, modern spirituality often portrays institutional religion as inimical and a locus of authoritarianism, mendacity, and dogmatism, which have replaced authentic, living religious experience. Adherents are notably eclectic, adopting a supermarket approach to religious traditions and practices, constructing a highly individualized private spirituality that is decidedly psychological and hews to a conception of the divine as innate and within. Understood in this way, one can see how modern mysticism and modern spirituality have become interchangeable terms (mystical experiences are seen as part of, indeed the culmination of, the spiritual path). Many people (recent estimates are as 21 percent for the general population and as high as 70 percent for those ages eighteen to twenty-nine[10]) now prefer to express their religious sentiments along the lines of an unchurched mysticism and spirituality divorced from religious institutions and their accoutrements. As the saying goes, "I'm spiritual but not religious." This unchurched or modern spirituality is highly individualized, very psychological, and predictably capitalistic in its stress on human potential and techniques for growth.[11]

To sum up, early twentieth-century psychology came to see mysticism as an innate feature of the subconscious (James), the unconscious (Freud), or the collective unconscious (Jung). It certainly helped that one reigning form of academic discourse about mysticism at that time was infatuated with the idea that there existed core characteristics of mysticism, not least of which was "unity." Specifically with respect to psychoanalysis, while the link between feelings of unity and mysticism was certainly extant before the birth of Western psychology as a science, some credit for the understanding of mysticism as episodic feelings of unity must be accorded once again to William James. In James one clearly sees the development from the church fathers' emphasis on mystical theology, which they understood only with respect to a total religious matrix, to a more generic view of mysticism as innate and universal. This view espoused an episodic experience located in the subconscious (or unconscious) that was capable of being activated through a variety of unchurched means. Moreover, in the case of James, such an experience became defined with respect to four specific marks: passivity, transiency, noesis, and ineffability. One could certainly add unity as a fifth mark, as James himself intimated:

> This overcoming of all the usual barriers between the individual and the Absolute is the great mystic achievement. In mystic states we both become one with the Absolute and we become aware of our oneness. This is the everlasting and triumphant mystical tradition, hardly altered by differences

> of clime or creed. In Hinduism, in Neo-Platonism, in Sufism, in Christian mysticism, in Whitmanism, we find the same recurring note, so that there is about mystical utterances an eternal unanimity which ought to make a critic stop and think, and which brings it about that the mystical classics have, as has been said, neither birthday nor native land. Perpetually telling of the unity of man with God, their speech antedates languages, and they do not grow old.[12]

The Jamesian rendering of unity (*unio mystica*), increasingly problematic for proponents of not only mystical theology but also of multiple Eastern traditions, has become canonical for psychoanalytic interpretations of mysticism. This is reflected in Freud's understanding and interpretation of the oceanic feeling. As the received view of the psychoanalytic theory of mysticism would have it, the oceanic feeling, as a paradigmatic illustration of the transient unitive mystical experience, has become linked with a form of perennialism (the view that all mysticism can be reduced to a common core). Interpreted psychoanalytically, mysticism became understood as a regression to the empirically verifiable feeling of unity and limitlessness characteristic of the developmental phase Freud called primary narcissism. If all mysticism is but a regression to the developmental stage of primary narcissism, then the varieties found in mystical texts can only reflect religio-cultural overlays and variations of an empirically based fundamental developmental fact.

It is unfortunate that this view of Freud's interpretation of the oceanic feeling has become the orthodoxy that has guided psychoanalytic understandings and interpretations of mysticism since is not only misleading but an outright error that has little basis in the texts and letters that constitute Freud's correspondence with Romain Rolland, the man responsible for the original psychoanalytic interpretation of the oceanic feeling. It is particularly unfortunate because this history has affected extant psychoanalytic interpretations of Augustine to no small degree. Indeed, the latter seem to have been held fast by an idealized bond, for it is the aesthetic and emotional pull of Freud and his analysis of the oceanic feeling in *Civilization and Its Discontents* that is clearly reflected in this literature.

Deconstructing Orthodoxy

In light of the above, a brief detour through the details of the debate between Freud and Rolland on oceanic feelings is in order.[13] The debate began in 1927, when Freud, who admired Rolland particularly for his artistry (Rolland won the Nobel Prize in Literature in 1915) and ethics (Rolland was dubbed the "conscience of Europe" for his public stance against anti-Semitism and his attempts to broker a dialogue at the outset of World War I), sent him *The Future of an Illusion*—the primary text establishing Freud as a reductionist and an enemy of religion. Most theologians and those sympathetic to religion focus on Freud's central assertion that religion is something akin to a cultural dream in which the projection of unconscious ideation, particularly that determined by Oedipus, becomes the central content as well as the determinative reason behind the creation and sustained popularity of religious symbols, myths, and narratives. While acknowledging the historical adaptive value of religion, such as its role in constituting the "cultural superego" and its ability to protect civilization from man's innate destructive tendencies, Freud's book was designed to facilitate humanity's move beyond a religious mode of adaptation to something he construed as more realistic. Ultimately, Freud condemned religion for promoting regression, defensiveness, and a reliance on wish fulfillment while forestalling a more mature, reflective, and psychoanalytic-humanistic mode of gaining insight into the unconscious and educating the instincts.

The power of Freud's argument, sociologists have observed, was based on his view of the trajectory of history. Freud was convinced of the rise of science, the inevitable march of secularization, and the corresponding decline of religion. This meant the coming collapse of the cultural superego and the corresponding rise of anomie, increasingly aggressive behavior, and social dislocation. Freud thought that the "masses," a social type he characterized as constituting the great majority of believers, were so in only a nominal sense, being hypocrites lacking cultural adaptability and the power to sublimate. Freud favored that social type (of which Rolland was one) that he referred to as the "vehicles of civilization," the "brainworkers" and "culture elite." Their task historically was to help keep civilization intact. The uneducated, hypocritical masses, on learning of the inevitable decline of civilization, would pose a direct threat to civilized behavior. Thus it is in these terms that Freud presented the major sociohistorical knot of his book: "either these dangerous masses must be held down . . . or else the relationship between civilization and religion must undergo a fundamental revision."[14]

Freud's solution to the problem was to address the cultured elite, those sympathetic to religion but also capable of being swayed by reason. To this end he employed the rhetorical strategy of creating an interlocutor who, in embodying the characteristics of the cultural elite, was cast as being slowly "converted" to Freud's way of thinking. To counter the inevitable decline of religion and the rise of the masses, Freud suggested, in a way reminiscent of Weber, that the cultural elite could help him in his quest to create a social space for a psychoanalytic practice offered, as he once stated to the lay analyst and Protestant pastor Oskar Pfister, as a "secular cure of souls."[15] It was psychoanalysis that would help offset *das Unbehagen* (unease) *in der Kultur.* Freud, then, had an ulterior motive in sending Rolland *The Future of an Illusion.* As a valued and well-placed member of the cultural elite, Rolland was ripe for facilitating Freud's project.[16]

Rolland's response to Freud's gift, in a letter dated December 5, 1927, became the impetus for the two men's debate over the nature of the oceanic feeling. In his letter he genuinely affirmed his sympathy for the thesis of what he called Freud's "lucid and spirited little book."[17] In an earlier letter he had written Freud to laud him for being the "Christopher Columbus of a new continent of the spirit."[18] But while Rolland entirely agreed with Freud's analysis of the "common-man's" religion, he went on to contrast the latter with the oceanic feeling. Like James, but not like the church fathers, Rolland described the oceanic feeling as a primordial religious datum, an essentially contentless feeling of the eternal that was the "true subterranean source" of all churches, creeds, and scripture. The oceanic feeling, wrote Rolland, is "totally independent of all dogma, all credo, all Church organization. . . . [It is] the true subterranean source of religious energy which subsequently has been collected, canalized and dried up by Churches to the extent that one could say it is inside the Churches (whichever they may be) that true 'religious' sentiment is least available."[19] Rolland confessed that he was familiar with the feeling, stated that it was often absent from institutionalized religion, and indicated that empirical examples of it could be found in literary figures and philosophers. Moreover, Rolland made it clear that he thought the oceanic feeling was amenable to psychological analysis. While Rolland was also searching for a way to create and maintain social cohesion, his solution was the advocacy of a religious psychology, an unchurched form of mystical psychoanalysis. This project was in part a result of his religious proclivities. Socialized into the Catholicism of his family, Rolland had been subject to a series of episodic mystical experiences that, following R. C. Zaehner and the academic nomenclature of comparative mysticism, could be called "nature" or "pan-eh-henic" experiences (which is to say, nontraditional or unchurched). For example, Rolland speaks of such extrovertive mergings of unity with nature as follows:

> I had, between the ages of 15 and 20 . . . several brief and staggering contacts with the Unity. These obscure illuminations were the key to the spiritual world where I lived for the next forty years. . . . I was possessed by nature like a violated virgin. For a moment my soul left me to melt into the luminous mass of the Breithorn. . . . Yes, extravagant as it may sound, for some moments I *was* the Breithorn. . . . In this sensation, past and future meld into one, as into an eternal present. Billions of sensations, little droplets that grow, come closer together, and disappear in order to come back again to the Ocean of Being.[20]

Years later, as a result of what he saw as the complicity of Catholicism in fermenting the Great War, Rolland, in a state of utter disillusionment, turned east, to the writings of Gandhi, Tagore, Ramakrishna, and Vivekananda. It was there, he said, that he found anew the mysticism of his youth and a source for the vital renewal of Western culture. Rolland was convinced that integrating the resources of East and West was the pivotal task of the future, and he eagerly accepted the challenge of helping to forge a new cultural whole. In so doing, Rolland drew from both the comparative study of mysticism, where, following Rudolph Otto, he unapologetically held fast to a basic, unsophisticated form of perennialism (which can be counted as one factor that helped align psychoanalysis with the perennialist school) based first on his own mystical experiences, and only then on an uncritical reading of comparative mystical texts. He then turned to psychology and its resources—resources he thought would help to constitute what he would come to call a "universal science-religion." It was this "religion," thought Rolland, that would be the salvation of mankind. So when he received Freud's little gift he, too, had a social agenda in mind—one commensurate with the nature of modern spirituality, much closer to the psychospirituality proposed by Jung, and thus quite different from the social project proposed by Freud.[21]

The full consequences of Rolland's entry into the emerging climate of nontraditional, unchurched modern spirituality for the psychoanalytic theory of mysticism are important and will be addressed later in more detail. What is of immediate relevance is that when one looks at Rolland's letter in the context of his ruminations on mysticism as found in his total corpus, the true character of the oceanic feeling does not match that found in the received view. What Rolland conveyed to Freud was that the oceanic feeling was not so much a transient feeling of unity, a mystical experience, but a constant, enduring mystical state. An examination of Rolland's letters, journals, and novels reveals that he distinguished between his early transient nature mystical experiences and the developmentally later statelike oceanic feeling. Rolland's transient mystical experiences exhibited an implicit teleology. Initially serving to "render the veil," they further enjoined one to a lifelong ethical and existential struggle that could (although not necessarily did) culminate in the more permanent statelike oceanic feeling. In other words, it is possible to distinguish a form of process mysticism in Rolland.[22]

When he initially wrote to Freud in 1927, Rolland talked of how he thought mysticism, and not Oedipus, lay at the root of all religion. Echoing James, he thought the mystical element was an innate part of the unconscious, that it was accessible to scientific probes, and that it constituted the generic oceanic source out of which religious dogma, scripture, ritual, and religious social institutions emerged. Moreover, to validate his stance, he was undertaking a study of the major figures of mysticism of both East and West (which eventually led to his biographies of Ramakrishna and Vivekananda).[23] Then, becoming autobiographical, Rolland referred to this "direct fact of the feeling of the eternal," which, he said, may well not be eternal so much as "without perceptible limits, and like oceanic, as it were." He continued:

> I myself am familiar with this sensation. All through my life, it has never failed me; and I have always found in it a source of vital renewal. In that sense, I can say that I am profoundly "religious"—without this constant state (like a sheet of water which I feel flushing under the bark) affecting in any way my critical faculties and my freedom to exercise them—even if that goes against the immediacy of the interior experience. In this way, without discomfort or contradiction, I can lead a "religious" life (in the sense of that prolonged feeling) and a life of critical reason (which is without illusion).[24]

In this passage, Rolland refers to his understanding of the oceanic feeling as a constant state. To be sure, the notion of a mystical state is not unheard of among theologians or comparativists of religion. For example, Saint Teresa's notion of spiritual marriage is a mystical state posited as the apex of the spiritual life and prepared for by a host of episodic mystical phenomena, including locutions, visions, and transient unitive experiences with God.[25] In Hinduism, the Hindu sage Sri Ramana Maharshi distinguished between two related mystical phenomena, *nirvikalpa samadhi* and *sahaja samadhi.* The former is understood to be a transient mystical experience and is compared to the episodic lowering of a bucket into a well. *Sahaja samadhi,* on the other hand, is understood as a more advanced mystical phenomenon. Indeed, it is the denouement of the mystical path, being described as a river merging into an "always present" feeling of a limitless, eternal ocean.[26] In other words, without arguing for exact equivalence, if one had to point to which mystical phenomenon in the comparative study of mysticism Freud was analyzing when he took up the enigma of the oceanic feeling, it would not be transient oceanic experiences of unity but the more advanced, statelike mystical phenomena found in such mystics as Saint Teresa and Ramana Maharshi.

That Freud also understood the oceanic feeling as a continual religio-psychological presence and not as an episodic mystical experience is corroborated by the second paragraph of the first chapter of *Civilization and Its Discontents.* There Freud, in summarizing Rolland's letter, characterizes the oceanic feeling "as consisting in a peculiar feeling, which he [Rolland] himself is never without." Surely this is not the episodic mystical experience made so accessible to psychologists by James. Indeed, Freud gives ample evidence of knowing what episodic mystical experiences are throughout his corpus. But the oceanic feeling was a different phenomenon, one that, Freud said, "caused him no small difficulty," in part because, as he put it, "I cannot discover this 'oceanic' feeling in myself."[27] For this new mystical phenomenon Freud needed a new explanation. The model he offered was not one that emphasized regression, as if Rolland's oceanic feeling were episodic, as if one were dipping a bucket into the well of oceanic primary narcissism, but rather the *preservation,* alongside the more sharply demarcated sense of being an individual ego (characteristic of post-infant subjectivity), of the more inclusive and continuous feeling of oceanic oneness or eternity characteristic of primary narcissism. In other words, empirically and developmentally speaking, we all originally have an enduring feeling of a constant state of the eternal. It's just that in some people it is preserved alongside the natural developmental tendency of the ego to sharply demarcate its borders:

> Our present ego-feeling is, therefore, only a shrunken residue of a more inclusive—indeed, an all-embracing—feeling which corresponded to a much more intimate bond between the ego and the world about it. If we

> may assume that there are many people in whose mental life this primary ego-feeling has persisted to a greater or less degree, it would exist in them side by side with the narrower and more sharply demarcated ego-feeling of maturity, like a kind of counterpart to it. In that case, the ideational contents appropriate to it would be precisely those of limitlessness and of a bond with the universe—the same ideas with which my friend elucidated the "oceanic feeling."[28]

The distinction between experience and state, between the episodic and process, is corroborated from yet another direction in Rolland's letter to Freud of July 17, 1929. This letter was written in response to Freud's request (in a letter to Rolland dated July 14, 1929) to use Rolland's letter of December 5, 1927, as a starting point for his yet to be published *Civilization and Its Discontents* (which appeared in 1930).[29] In his letter, Rolland, addressing the phenomenon of mysticism, raises the intuitive, noetic element that characterizes transient mystical experiences. Freud's response to that letter came in the form of a late added passage to the first chapter of *Civilization and Its Discontents,* where he acknowledges the noetic dimension of mysticism and offers a quite different model for its interpretation. Significantly, he does not simply tweak the preoedipal thesis, a move that would have verified the thesis according with the received view. On the contrary, he emphasizes mystical intuition as noesis and writes of the similarity between mystical practices, as well as the primordial depths of knowledge they unearth, and the aims and practices of psychoanalysis. In other words, Freud knew the difference between the oceanic feeling as a constant state and transient mystical experiences, and offered two different models to account for them. One model interpreted a constant mystical feeling of the oceanic as the preservation of the limitless ego-feeling of primary narcissism; the other model interpreted episodic mystical experience as the product of an introspective practice that, not unlike psychoanalysis, offered the practitioner glimpses of the unconscious—a model to which I return in the next chapter in formulating a new psychoanalytic line of analysis better equipped to engage with Augustine's visions.

Psychoanalysis, Perennialism, Constructivism

The received view of Freud and the oceanic feeling is based on a misreading of the text, and other lines of psychoanalytic inquiry might be better equipped to deal with Augustine's mystical theology. I turn now to the first task mentioned at the start of this chapter and do what theologians would ask of us: take a detour through the mystical passages of the *Confessions* in the light of other crucial texts in the Augustinian corpus. In this way a more accurate understanding of the exact nature of Augustine's teachings concerning mystical ascents and vision may be had. Once this task is concluded, a more appropriate psychoanalytic line of investigation can be broached.

The new task requires that we entertain the possibility that Augustine's visions were not a mere variation on Rolland's oceanic feeling. The traditional psychoanalytic approach to mystical texts, as I have noted, has been a rather simple perennialism: the oceanic feeling as the manifestation of a core, transient, unitive mystical experience has become synonymous with "mysticism everywhere." All mysticism becomes a regression to the developmental stage of primary narcissism; the varieties found in mystical texts merely reflect religio-cultural overlays and variations on an empirically based fundamental developmental fact. This is exactly how extant psychoanalytic studies of Augustine have treated the ascent at Ostia. In contrast, proponents of mystical theology claim that any attempt to isolate Augustine's episodic visionary ascent from the wider context of Augustine's views on what I have called the mystical process departs from the deeper meaning (if not the essence) of his mysticism. The narratives of books 7 and 9, in which the visions are embedded, articulate a specifically Christian conception of what Kenney refers to as the "spiritual architecture" of the universe: the fallen nature of humans, the nature of truth, the limits of vision in this life, the stress on the afterlife, and the means necessary for such salvation. All aspects of this spiritual architecture were specifically designed to cater to Augustine's congregation and respond directly to Platonic and Manichaean worldviews.[30] As Kenney notes, "it is an act of some exegetical violence to extract . . . an identifiable 'experience' . . . [because] the text itself is much more than an embellished record of an experience, whose outlines are recoverable beneath layers of philosophy and scriptural allusions."[31]

In light of the fact that Augustine's mysticism cannot be wholly divorced from a Christian worldview and its attendant practices, articulating Augustine's mystical theology is more fully commensurate with that contemporary academic perspective known as constructivism or contextualism. At the heart of this position is the thesis that all mystical experiences are mediated and constructed—that there are no pure or "raw" mystical experiences that constitute the perennial core. Steven Katz speaks to this when he says,

> *There are NO pure (i.e., unmediated) experiences.* Neither mystical experience nor more ordinary forms of experience give any indication, or any grounds for believing, that they are unmediated. That is to say, *all* experience is processed through, organized by, and makes itself available to us in extremely complex epistemological ways.[32]

For the constructivists, mystical experience, like all experience, is influenced by one's immersion in the language, concepts, beliefs, worldview, and values of a specific culture and religious tradition. Rufus Jones puts the point well when he writes,

> There are no "pure experiences," i.e., no experiences which come wholly from *beyond* the person who has them. . . . The most refined mysticism, the most exalted spiritual experience *is partly* a product of the social and intellectual environment in which the personal life of the mystic has formed and matured. There are no experiences of any sort which are independent of preformed expectations or unaffected by the prevailing beliefs of the time. . . . Mystical experiences will be, perforce, saturated with the dominant ideas of the group to which the mystic belongs, and they will reflect the expectations of that group and that period.[33]

As Katz emphasizes, the conditions of knowing are operative before the actual mystical experience (in the sense of conditioning the recipient as to how to interpret what is intuited), during the experience, and after it.[34] Because the terms used to describe the experience vary even within a religious tradition, as well as among traditions and from culture to culture, the concepts and terms (including a pervasive term such as "unity") do not have an essential, invariant, and cross-cultural core of meaning. Instead, they are defined with respect to the problems, the proscribed path, the metaphysical superstructure, and the expected solution generated by the specific religio-cultural tradition through which the mystic seeks deliverance. With respect to both experience and process, the constructivist argues for the acknowledgment of differences, a plea that calls for the mapping of a variety of incorporated interpretations of mystical phenomena. The thrust of this school, then, is pluralistic, valorizing the particularity of individual mystics and individual religious traditions.

Applied to the mystical texts in the *Confessions,* the constructivist view would hardly deny that something like a mystical experience or event took place. It would, however, deny that access to the original or raw experience behind the text can be had, for what we see is but the constructed version relayed in the text. Kenney echoes this position with respect to both the vision at Milan and that at Ostia when he states the following:

> As was the case in the ascension narratives of Book Seven, we do not find in this passage the language of direct description. Indeed Augustine tells us that he is giving an approximate account of their dialogue: "I said something like this, even if not just this way and with exactly these words" (IX.x [27]). The result is a meditation on the conditions under which souls can encounter the transcendent as well as a record of a particular religious experience. That process of meditation includes for Augustine an array of religious ideas and scriptural phrases. All are so deeply ingrained into the record of the event that none can be convincingly labeled as merely retrospective, as opposed to those which are original to the experience. Even the scriptural references might have been incorporated contemporaneously into the event, since they formed the shared and remembered religious vocabulary of Monica and her son. . . . There are no means at our disposal to pinpoint what was original to that interlude at Ostia, no way to discover the original characteristics of the experience itself, no discourse free from the religious language that Augustine uses.[35]

Restoring the Text: Augustine's Teaching on Mystical Ascents

It is crucially important to ask how Augustine characterized both the nature of and the conditions necessary for ecstatic ascent. This task requires considering multiple texts he wrote over the next two decades of his life, for Augustine's views on vision extend well beyond the confines of the seemingly autobiographical texts of the *Confessions.*

To start, Augustine's complex teaching on vision can be made accessible to those socialized into the nomenclature of the therapeutic understanding of the nature of the self in the following way. We know from book 10 that his inward search for God led him to the field of memory and to reflections on the will, where he elaborates on psychological phenomena that many commentators think prefigured later formulations of various psychological systems. These formulations include a description of memory as housing the "stomach" of the mind, the classic Augustinian divided will and chain of habit, the darkness and opaqueness of desire, and the problematic nature of sexuality in dreams. But we also know that in his ecstatic ascent he was led not only deep within himself but also above the summit of his soul, there to see the Light, being literally rapt, or enraptured, out of the body. As Andrew Louth notes, Augustine's ascent narratives are commensurate with his later, more detailed account of ecstasy, which is as follows: "the attention of the mind is wholly turned away and withdrawn . . . from the bodily senses . . . then whatever bodies may be present are not seen with the open eyes, nor any voices heard at all . . . this ecstasy is sudden and fleeting, and draws out the whole force of the soul."[36] As Kenney puts it,

> Contemplation is ecstatic in the *Confessions,* because the soul must be taken out of its fallen self in order to see the possibility of its salvation. And the fallen self is the only self there is. Thus the act of contemplation has a special power in the *Confessions,* since the soul of Monica is lifted up and out of its fallen self to encounter its author and savior. With neither the means to effect transcendence by itself, nor the power to insure its own salvation, the Augustinian soul must be brought out of itself and shown the conditions of its hope.[37]

The movement, as McGinn notes, is both *enstatic* and *ecstatic:* "Augustine taught that 'to go within is to go above,' that is, the enstatic movement into the soul's ground would lead to a discovery of the God within who is infinitely more than the soul, and hence to an ecstatic movement beyond the self—*Intus Deus altus est,* 'The God within is the God above.' "[38]

It is important to note that nowhere in Augustine's descriptions of the encounter with the Light does he use the term "union." As McGinn notes, the category of union, often seen as being the essence and goal of Christian mysticism, is absent from many Christian texts. Even in those that do utilize such a term one finds not one but multiple variants; one must "expand the notion of union, recognizing that there were several, perhaps even many, understandings of union with God held by Christians over the centuries."[39] Indeed, McGinn goes further, questioning the wisdom of placing the notion of union at the heart of Christian mysticism:

> The essential note—or, better, goal—of mysticism may be conceived of as a particular kind of encounter between God and the human. . . . This goal, essential characteristic, or defining note has most often been seen as the experience of some form of union with God, particularly a union of absorption or identity in which the individual personality is lost. If we define mysticism in this sense, there are actually so few mystics in the history of Christianity that one wonders why Christians use the qualifier "mystical" so often . . . it may also be argued that union with God is not the most

> central category for understanding mysticism. . . . I have come to find the term "presence" a more central and more useful category for grasping the unifying note in the varieties of Christian mysticism.[40]

McGinn observes that an absence of the language of union is particularly true of Augustine, who was perfectly aware of such terminology and its use in Greek texts (notably the Plotinian *henosis*).[41] But, contra Plotinus, Augustine's Christian teaching valorized the difference between God and the soul, as well as the need for God's grace in elevating the soul to the vision of its creator.[42] Moreover, while Augustine thought the direct experience of God was possible in this life, such an event was deemed to be indescribable. In other words, for Augustine God is, in his essence, essentially unknowable: there is an apophatic dimension to Augustine's mysticism. It is true that Augustine does make use of a variety of images and metaphors to point to (but not definitively capture) the nature of the *visio Dei*. Many of these are taken from the language of the senses (seeing, hearing, tactile sensations like touching, tasting, etc.). This form of synesthia and the smorgasbord of images were thus "strategies meant to suggest and not to circumscribe the inexpressible."[43] These "mystical senses," moreover, are operative in the ascent narrative at Ostia, where not union but the language of touching is favored.[44] As Augustine recounts in his ecstatic ascent at Ostia in 9.10: "as we talked . . . we did, with the whole strength of our hearts' impulse, just lightly come into touch with her." Kenney offers,

> That is what happened at Ostia. The finite souls of the contemplatives came into the presence of uncreated Wisdom. But the separation between them and the divine Wisdom was complete. It was breeched by divine initiative only to permit some contact between the finite and the infinite, and not to dissolve the former into the latter. Because Augustine seemed not to have shared the Plotinian doctrine of the One in his thinking before Ostia, it was never part of his conceptual field at Ostia, nor part of his retrospective interpretations thereafter. Union with the One is thus outside the bounds for a reading of the *Confessions*. It is another feature imposed on the ancient texts by nineteenth and twentieth century theorists . . . of mysticism.[45]

An orthodox psychoanalytic perspective may counter that such linguistic technicalities, being the wholesale product of a narrow-minded textology, do not trump the standard regressive thesis and the presence of the mother. Indeed, as is the case with many post-Freudian analyses, the issue simply becomes one of degrees of regression—degrees expressed in terms of the favored cultural nomenclature of the time. Nevertheless, these linguistic technicalities, in addition to the other evidence adduced here, make it increasingly difficult to subscribe wholesale to the orthodox psychoanalytic view.

A few specific features of Augustine's teaching on vision command our attention. Most important is his well-known threefold typology of vision as spelled out in later works (notably his Letter no. 147 to Paulina, Sermon 52, his Homilies on the Psalms, Homilies on the Gospel of John, and book 12 of his *Literal Meaning of Genesis,* in which he analyzes Saint Paul's ascent to the third heaven and Paradise in 2 Corinthians 12:2–4). Briefly summarized, the three types of vision are corporeal (or bodily), spiritual (or imaginative), and intellectual. The three are related in a hierarchical fashion (as Augustine puts it, "spiritual vision is more excellent than corporeal, and intellectual vision is more excellent than spiritual"),[46] and only in intellectual vision is there "no deception."[47] In corporeal visions one has the "vision" of external objects given by the senses. It is called corporeal "because it is perceived through the body and presented to the senses of the body."[48] Spiritual or imaginative visions, on the other hand, refer to an imaginative recollection or imprint (as in a dream): "the image of an absent body."[49] They thus refer to the imagination, and to corporeal images in the mind. However, in intellectual visions the knowledge gleaned is completely divorced from bodily sensations or imaginative visions.

Intellectual visions are of two kinds. The first pertains to incorporeal religious truths (such as the virtues: "charity, joy, peace, longanimity, kindness, goodness, faith, meekness, continency"[50]), which are not linked to sensation and physical objects but are "known" insofar as they are illuminated by the divine Light. In the second kind one sees the Light itself: "the brightness of the Lord is seen, not through a symbolic or corporeal vision . . . but through a direct vision. . . . In such a vision God speaks face to face to him whom He has made worthy of this communion."[51] In distinguishing between the two kinds of intellectual visions, Augustine once again utilized language reminiscent of the ascents in the *Confessions:*

> But distinct from these objects [of the first type of intellectual visions] . . . is the Light by which the soul is illumined, in order that it may see and truly understand everything, either in itself or in the Light. For the Light

> is God Himself . . . and when [the soul] tries to behold the Light, it trembles in its weakness and finds itself unable to do so. Yet from this source comes all the understanding it is able to attain. When, therefore, it is thus carried off and, after being withdrawn from the senses of the body, is made present to this vision in a more perfect manner . . . it also sees above itself that Light.[52]

This kind of direct intellectual vision is the highest vision granted to humans. Again recalling the *Confessions,* Augustine states that such a vision is necessarily brief (because of the existence of sin). For Augustine, this form of intellectual vision amounts to knowledge of heavenly things. It is important to note here (a fact I take up directly in the next chapter) that in speaking of this level of mystical insight, Augustine insists there is a physiological correlate. In *The Literal Meaning of Genesis* he teaches that in being raptured out of the self and in accessing this ecstatic level of vision one must be, at least for the duration of vision, in a state characterized by Kenney as "virtual death." In this regard Augustine cites scripture, Exodus 33.12ff., where it is stated that no one can see God's face and live.[53] It is only by dint of this partial (but not total) removal to the next life that this full and "highest" intellectual vision of the Light (God's substance) takes place. That is, in ecstatic experiences of God, one in a state of virtual death is raptured out of the self and its usual mode of knowing. An intellectual vision of the light and substance of God is thus much closer to an angelic mode of knowing. Theologically rendered, one needs the help of God to be lifted up to see this light, and in being lifted up one is removed from normal modes of corporeal sensing and knowing.

It is also important to note that, theologically speaking, Augustine teaches that intellectual visions involve not simply a cognitive element but also grace and love. Indeed, love, grace, and knowledge are intertwined in the ascent upward and in vision proper. It is God's love that initially grants us the limited knowledge that he is by inserting the bond of faith that creates the longing for vision. It is also God's love that later elevates the believer to that instant in which one is raptured out of oneself, to directly encounter the Light. Augustine speaks of seeing and touching God, but he also says that it is through the heart that one "sees" God; it is through acts of charity that one becomes more like God; and it is God's love that helps restore the "eye" of the soul. Moreover, it is clear that for Augustine, a certain moral preparation is needed to cleanse the eye of the soul in preparation for vision. Augustine is fond of quoting Matthew 5.8 ("Blessed are the pure of heart, for they shall see God") in this regard.[54] Augustine notes that God is always present; we fail to see him because the eye has not been sufficiently cleansed. And it is through becoming "like" him in goodness, love, and charity that we progress toward perceiving him. Citing 1 John 4:8, Augustine affirms that when one sees and touches God, one knows that God is love.[55] It is God's love in us that gives birth first to faith, then kindles our desire for him, eventually functioning as that new eye of the soul that sees God: "this new way of 'seeing' is in us, but it is not of us; it requires our cooperation, but its operation is from God himself."[56]

The question remains as to who is capable of accessing the highest levels of intellectual vision. Augustine holds that such a vision was attained by Moses and Saint Paul. Indeed, book 12 of his *Literal Meaning of Genesis* is devoted to how Paul, in his ascent to the third heaven and Paradise in 2 Corinthians 12:2–4, must have been, as Paul himself suggests, "out of the body" in a state of virtual death, there to see the substance of the Light. Certainly one could complain that Augustine was creatively misreading Paul here for, as more recent studies have suggested (a point I return to in the next chapter), the heavenly cosmology Paul references reflects more a Jewish mystical ascent motif than a Christian Platonism. As for Augustine, while there is general consensus that he experienced something at Milan and Ostia, theological debates (initiated, as André Mandouze has ably shown, as early as 1863[57]) have accrued over whether his reference to the Light indicates that he too attained the level of the highest intellectual vision of God's substance. The end of the debate, as may be predicted by its already being more than a century old, does not appear to be in sight. Although the present work supports those who think Augustine was privy to the highest level of intellectual vision, this conclusion is not a necessary condition of my argument. What is necessary is to ascertain Augustine's teaching and mystical theology: his views on the nature, aims, and conditions of mystical vision.

Bringing such textual considerations back into dialogue with issues entertained in the academic study of comparative mysticism, I note that Augustine's formulations are but one particular instance of a more general philosophical claim made by mystical authors in multiple traditions. John E. Smith aptly summarizes this mystical claim as follows (the emphasis is Smith's own):

> The point I want to underscore . . . is the idea, *and it expresses one of the truly universal features of all mysticism,* that day-to-day consciousness, shaped by ordinary needs, accompanied by habitual and familiar ways of responding to the world, has in some way to be suspended if some special insight into the nature of things, the true self, the purpose of life is to be gained. In short, there is the belief that the mystical truth is always there, but that ordinary experience stands in the way and must be put aside just as one removes a veil to reveal a treasure that existed all along. One key to unlocking the secrets of the many different forms of mysticism is an understanding of the various modes of preparation or discipline whereby the "eye of the soul"—to use a favorite mystical image—is cleansed and attains the proper vantage point from which to see.[58]

Again, speaking generally, and with the qualification that different mystical authors limn the nature of the eye that knows, the nature and conditions of knowing, and the object (or lack thereof) in various ways, one can illustrate Smith's point with respect to numerous and varied mystical texts. For example, an unchurched psychological and spiritual text can be found in the writings of R. M. Bucke, who notes that the experience of what he dubs "cosmic consciousness" involves an "intellectual illumination impossible to describe"—one in which, according to Bucke's personal testimony, he came to see that the universe is animated by "a living Presence."[59] This intellectual illumination, continues Bucke, places "the individual on a new plane of existence" and makes him "almost a member of a new species."[60] In making this claim, Bucke insists there are three distinct modes of knowing: simple consciousness (characteristic of animals), self-consciousness (characteristic of humans and denotes self-reflective awareness), and cosmic consciousness, which is not "simply an expansion or extension of the self-conscious mind . . . but the superaddition of a function as distinct from any possessed by the average man as self-consciousness is distinct from any function possessed by one of the higher animals."[61] Alternatively, one could take the example of Vivekananda, who, in commenting on the end and aim of Yoga practices, reflects that "the mind itself has a higher state of existence, beyond reason, a superconscious state, and that when the mind gets to that higher state, then this knowledge beyond reasoning comes."[62] So too the Sufi al-Ghazali stated that "just as the understanding is a stage of human life in which an eye opens to discern various intellectual objects uncomprehended by sensation; just so in the prophetic the sight is illumined by a light which uncovers hidden things and objects which the intellect fails to reach."[63]

Returning to Augustine's more specific formulations, then, one assumes that the Light, presented as the ground of reason and understanding, is not bounded by space and time and is of a different ontological substance. The encounter with God is perhaps best understood in an epistemological sense as one of "direct acquaintance."[64] Nevertheless, in the case of Augustine, and indeed with respect to similar claims by mystics as a whole, such modes of knowing are philosophically problematic. In relating this discussion to the previous section, we might ask how Augustine's claims would be rendered by the contextualist perspective I have chosen to champion.

Some forms of constructivism ("complete constructivism") are prone not simply to bracketing but to dismissing outright mystical claims to a privileged, intuitive knowledge of the divine. While this may be the case, Steven Katz's own view is much more subtle and tempered. For Katz, a constructivist/contextualist perspective would not necessarily disavow Augustine's assertions about humans, at least in principle, as being capable of knowing the Light. As Katz puts it,

> It is *not* being argued either that mystical experiences do not happen, or that what they claim may not be true, only that there can be no grounds for deciding this question, i.e., of showing that they are true even if they are, in fact, true . . . one would be both dogmatic and imprudent to decide *a priori* that mystical claims are mumbo-jumbo, especially given the wide variety of such claims by men of genius and/or religious sensitivity over the centuries as well as across all cultural divisions. Nor does it seem reasonable to reduce these multiple and variegated claims to mere projected "psychological states" which are solely the product of interior states of consciousness.[65]

> My view—and it is important that it be understood—is that while such transcendental realities or Reality may well exist, it (or He, She or It) can only be known by us in the way such metaphysical realia become available to us given the sort of beings we are.[66]

The constructivist stance, as I noted earlier, hinges on the notion of the constructed character of mystical experience. The levels at which mediation occur are many; the most fundamental engages the epistemological grounds of mystical knowing. With respect to that stage, many members of the constructivist school, as Anthony Perovich has pointed out, implicitly or explicitly adopt a Kantian epistemology.[67] The content of mystical "intuition" is given organizational form by the a priori structures or categories of the mind.[68] In Katz's view, however, the adoption of a Kantian epistemology does not affirm or deny the ontological assertions of mystics but brackets them on philosophical grounds as inaccessible. There are simply no philosophical or hermeneutical means for getting behind the text or establishing the veracity of the ontological claims, where made, of mystics. But this does not mean, as Katz states in the above quotation, that a constructivist position ipso facto rules such claims out of court. To establish the meaning of mystical experiences and states, then, one must examine a second level of conditioning, the religio-cultural surround, which further shapes the mystical experience. For the constructivists, mystical experience, like other kinds of experience, is not only subject to the a priori structures of the understanding but is also influenced by one's immersion in the language, concepts, beliefs, worldview, and values of a specific culture and religious tradition. It is here, then, that the constructivist tallies well with the project of mystical theology, for it is through the latter that the full meaning of the mystic's description of mystical experience and mystical process comes to fruition. Both the a priori categories of the mind and the language, concepts, beliefs, worldview, and values of a specific culture and religious tradition are operative before, during, and after the episodic ascent to the divine.[69]

Whether or not future philosophical efforts will succeed in going beyond the Kantian paradigm is open to question. Certainly there have been attempts to do so, and it is far from clear, as Perovich observes, that Kant himself was completely pessimistic with respect to the existence of non-ordinary forms of mystical intuition.[70] To be very clear about what stance I am taking vis-à-vis constructivism, I do not argue here that mystical experience is nothing but projected elements of developmental history, although such personal and cultural baggage (so to speak) will invariably be present in any imaginative religious or theological construction of what may constitute the More. In other words, we are not suggesting that psychoanalysis embrace a hard or "complete" form of constructivism that argues against the bona fide possibility of a mystical mode of noesis. On the contrary, the possibility remains that some form of unusual knowing that accesses profound levels of existence is operative in the mystical mind. Given the Kantian perspective presented above, it is not possible either to corroborate or to deny ontolological claims; one can only know that verification of such claims remains philosophically problematic. What I aim to show, in the next chapter, is that while psychoanalytic theory cannot establish the identity of any particular More the mystic may intuit, it can indeed offer meaningful formulations that provide psychological ground for the *possibility* that intuitive forms of mystical knowing may exist. Furthermore, the meaning of what that More may be in any specific case cannot be divorced from the entirety of the mystic's religious and theological reflections. And this broaches the issue of an episodic experience or event versus that of a process and a mystical life—a distinction that will prove to be quite important subsequently.

The task ahead, then, is to specify how psychoanalytic method can contribute to this more contextual view of mysticism. Extant psychoanalytic attempts, emphasizing as they do an erroneous understanding of even Freud's interpretation of the oceanic feeling, are surely insufficient. But there are other neglected avenues available—a "hidden history" of psychoanalytic theorizing about mysticism, as it were—that may prove more fruitful.

three

VISION INTERPRETED

With a more informed view of Augustine's teaching on the nature and conditions of mystical vision at hand, we are in a better position to return to psychoanalytic thought in an attempt to find common ground for dialogue. Lest the project be misunderstood, the aim is not to expand psychoanalytic thought to fully tally with Augustine's mystical theology. Such a pursuit clearly lies beyond the limits and self-identity of psychoanalytic theory. Rather, the aim is to open up new lines of argument, based on texts and teachings, where the two introspective traditions might have more to talk about than has previously been acknowledged. This chapter tacks through various formulations in an effort to arrive at a position that does more justice to the considerations advanced to this point. Specifically, the discussion concentrates on four elements of Augustine's teaching: the ascent of Amour/Eros, the epistemology of vision, the required physiological conditions, and the place of theological formulation.

Winged Eros

Extant psychoanalytic theorizing about Augustine's love of God has typically been reductionist, focusing on Monica as love object and the role of developmental determinism. To provide continuity with such views yet recognize the possibility of an Augustinian More, we must adopt a more inclusive approach. The issue then concerns how to acknowledge the unconscious "basement" yet ascend to upper floors, beyond the limits of sublimation. In other words, to what extent can psychoanalytic conceptions of Eros sprout wings?

What is demanded is a new approach—one that can be initiated through valorizing a particular reading of the Freudian corpus. Over the past century an array of different readings of Freud has appeared.[1] This outpouring in part owes to Freud's amalgamated thought: he was equally at ease citing the notable figures of the Western humanistic past as he was invoking developments in biology, neurology, and the social sciences. A reading of Freud as humanist would call attention to his deliberately citing such poets and philosophers as Goethe, Schiller, Shakespeare, Nietzsche, and Schopenhauer as prefiguring the insights of psychoanalysis. They were, he thought, "intuitive psychologists" who had unusual access to the truths of the unconscious and a special talent for portraying those insights in narratives, myths, and symbols that engaged even the common man's interests in nondefensive, ego-syntonic ways. To his contemporary Arthur Schnitzler he once wrote, "Whenever I get deeply absorbed in your beautiful creations I invariably seem to find beneath their poetic surface the very presuppositions, interests and conclusions which I know to be my own."[2] To the playwright Henri-René Lenormand he once confided that "the essential themes [of psychoanalysis] were based on the intuitions of the poets," while in an interview with the Italian writer Giovanni Papini he admitted that "psychoanalysis is no more than the interpretation of a literary vocation in terms of psychology and pathology. . . . Psychoanalysis was born . . . as a result of the scientific transposition of the literary schools I like the best. . . . In psychoanalysis you may find fused together though changed into specific jargon, the three greatest literary schools of the 19th century: Heine, Zola, and Mallarmé are united under the patronage of my old master, Goethe."[3] It is no accident that in 1930 Freud was awarded the Goethe Prize, usually reserved for outstanding novelists and poets.

This reading of Freud as eclectic fusionist in his thinking provides some background for the existence of what can be called a psychoanalytic ascent motif. In his monograph *Group Psychology and the Analysis of the Ego,* Freud, drawing once again on great thinkers of the Western past, and in rebuttal to those who sought to dismiss his views of sexuality as narrow and reductive, explained what he referred to as "the wider sense" of his use of the term Eros. This passage is important because it illustrates the nature of the psychoanalytic ascent motif in a way that recalls the figures that influenced Augustine:

> Libido is an expression taken from the theory of the emotions. We call by that name the energy . . . of those instincts which have to do with all that may be comprised under the word "love." The nucleus of what we mean by love naturally consists . . . in sexual love. . . . But we do not separate from this . . . on the one hand, self-love, and on the other, love for parents and children, friendship and love for humanity in general, and also devotion to concrete objects and to abstract ideas. Our justification lies in the fact that psycho-analytic research has taught us that all these tendencies are an expression of the same instinctual impulses. . . . We are of the opinion, then, that language has carried out an entirely justifiable piece of unification in creating the word "love" with its numerous uses. . . . By coming to this decision, psycho-analysis has let loose a storm of indignation. . . . Yet it has done nothing original in taking love in this "wider" sense. In its origin, function, and relation to sexual love, the "Eros" of the philosopher Plato coincides exactly with the love-force, the libido of psychoanalysis . . . and when the apostle Paul, in his famous epistle to the Corinthians, praises love above all else, he certainly understands it in the same "wider sense." But this only shows that men do not always take their great thinkers seriously, even when they profess most to admire them.[4]

Links between Freud's "wider sense" of Eros and Augustine can be forged in the following manner. We have seen that both Plato (through Plotinus) and Paul had a definitive impact on Augustine's teaching on mystical ascents. Throughout his works, and as is evinced in the above described psychoanalytic ascent motif, it is clear that Freud too was influenced by Plato. For example, Freud was fond of likening his structural model of the mind in works like *The Ego and the Id* to the chariot in *Phaedrus:* the rider (*Ich*) was always at pains to control the noble (*Über-Ich*) and ignoble (*Es*) horses.[5] And one hears echoes of the fundamental tenets of Plato's philosophy and his theory of anamnesis in psychoanalytic therapy—for example, in the structure of the end (self-knowledge), the means (asking questions), the assumptions (the answers are within), and the form (dialogue).[6] Surely Freud engaged in a creative misreading of Paul and Plato: he reimagined the two as intuitive forerunners of psychoanalysis to help legitimate his own thought. But such creative reworking of older thinkers is hardly a new phenomenon. If James Tabor is correct in reading Paul's ascent to the third heaven and Paradise as part and parcel of the cosmological world found in Jewish merkavah mysticism, then in his *Literal Meaning of Genesis* Augustine too is guilty, being ignorant of the religio-cultural context within which the ascent of 2 Corinthians was penned and creatively (mis)reading Paul in light of a Christian Neoplatonism.[7]

There are, of course, some real differences between Freud and Augustine with regard to the ascent of Eros. For example, we might observe that the psychoanalytic ascent motif is dependent on sublimation. The latter becomes the lever for redirecting sexual love to "higher aims," such as the love of abstract ideas. We might further observe that what limits Freud's ascent upward is the chain that ties sublimation to the downward pull of the instincts and the unconscious. In the latter, we find the psychoanalytic version of that doctrine so integral to the thought of Augustine, the doctrine of original sin. Unlike Plato's, Freud's steeds were neither winged nor capable of flight to the Platonic "Sea of Beauty." And here an important difference arises: with regard to the reach of love upward, Freud's theory is limited in comparison with those of Plato and Augustine. Freud's psychology is oriented toward the this-worldly concerns of alleviating neurotic suffering, facilitating adaptation to social reality, and increasing the capacity for *lieben und arbeiten* (to love and to work). Clearly, we must move beyond Freud to other psychoanalytic formulations—to what I referred to earlier as the "psychoanalytic mystics"—to create metapsychological space for winged Amour.

No single psychoanalyst has spoken more directly to this point than Jacques Lacan. In his inimitable manner, Lacan points to "something of the One," which he used in reference to Freud's Eros. This "One," in Lacan's thematic, has echoed across the centuries, as best evinced in the case of Neoplatonism. Moreover, this "One" is linked to an Eros or *jouissance* that "goes beyond." Lacan found such a *jouissance* in Christian mystics like Saint John of the Cross and Saint Teresa. In commenting on the latter's construct of a bridal mysticism, specifically her erotically charged "transverberation," and in linking this transverberation to Bernini's statue, *Teresa in Ecstasy,* Lacan notes colloquially that "she's coming, there is no doubt about it. And what is her *jouissance,* her *coming* from?"[8] Yet Lacan objected to reducing mysticism monocausally to sex. He stated that mystical utterances were the "best thing you can read," adding that his own work should be regarded as essentially "of the same order" as mysticism.[9] Indeed, as Webb and Sells have observed, Lacan has shifted psychoanalytic conceptions of language, the unconscious, truth, and healing toward a perspective commensurate with the mystics'.[10]

Turning to those psychoanalytic scholars who have explicitly looked to Eastern religions (what I have referred to as the psychology-comparativist dialogue), this avenue of exploration can be further developed. For example, the Indian psychoanalyst Sudhir Kakar has used Lacan's formulations to argue for a nonreductionistic psychoanalytic interpretation of the mystical intent to seek vision. Kakar's work defies easy categorization for, while a practicing psychoanalyst trained by Erik Erikson, he has integrated anthropological and religious perspectives into his clinical and scholarly work. Though hardly denouncing Freud's enlightenment agenda, Kakar has been influenced by those postmodern and postcolonial critiques of Western metanarratives that seek to deconstruct the hegemony of Western epistemologies, expose orientalism and colonialism where appropriate, and valorize other modes of non-Western and so-called archaic modes of knowing. Thus Kakar is fully aware of the tendency of applied psychoanalysis to be marred by unarticulated value judgments and hidden developmental norms, rejecting psychoanalytic theorists who have analyzed Eastern cultures—Jeffrey Moussaieff Masson, Géza Róheim, and George Devereux—on just such grounds. "Cultural judgments," writes Kakar, "about psychological maturity, the nature of reality, 'positive' and 'negative' resolutions of conflicts and complexes often appear in the garb of psychoanalytic universals."[11] Kakar insists that all attempts at applied psychoanalysis must be qualified by taking into account new information gleaned through specifically Indian case-history material and relevant ethnographic observations. As Kakar notes, the devaluation of non-Western modes of knowing can only "lend credence to the position of an increasing number of third-world intellectuals who maintain that the western sciences of man, including psychoanalysis, are in fact culture-bound ethnosciences whose claim to universality is both based upon and is an aspect of the global political and economic domination by the West."[12] In this sense, Kakar's anthropological and cultural sensitivity mirrors the historian's critique of extant psychoanalytic studies of Augustine: both caution psychoanalysis to become self-reflective enough to avoid projecting normative psychoanalytic notions of self, sexuality, life-cycle issues, visions of reality, and mental health onto the other, whether located in another culture or in the distant past. For Kakar, then, Vedanta mystical ideation and philosophy, far from indicating pathology and regressive states, often reveals a transformation of narcissistic structures and a subjectivity imbued with the delight of creative apperception.[13]

Similarly, Kakar argues that we must respect the mystic's intent to seek the divine:

> Lacan . . . has postulated that man's psychic life constantly seeks to deal with a primordial state of affairs which he calls the Real. The Real itself is unknowable, though we constantly create myths as its markers. Perhaps the principal myth involves the rupture of a basic union, the separation from the mother's body, leaving us with a fundamental feeling of incompletion. The fantasies around this insufficiency are universal, governing the psyche of both patients and analysts alike. In the psyche, this lack is translated as desire, and the human venture is a history of desire as it ceaselessly loses and discovers itself in (what Lacan calls) The Imaginary and, with the advent of language, The Symbolic order. Born of rupture, desire's fate is an endless quest for the lost object; all real objects merely interrupt the search. As the Barandes put it, "It is the task of the *neotenique* (i.e., immature, even fetalized being) being separated from its original union by its fall into life and into time, to invent detours for itself, deviations of object as well as means and aims. Its condition is inexorably perverse—if perversions must be." The mystical quest seeks to rescue from primal repression the constantly lived contrast between an original interlocking and a radical rupture. The mystic, unlike most others, does not mistake his hunger for its fulfillment. If we are all fundamentally perverse in the play of our desire, then the mystic is the only one who seeks to go beyond the illusion of The Imaginary and, yes, also the *maya* of The Symbolic register.[14]

Kakar's and Lacan's embrace of a psychoanalytic understanding of Eros that "goes beyond" the quotidian can be widened to create space for the integration of more reductive psychoanalytic studies of Augustine, many of which focus on his conflicted sexuality. In this both/and approach the motivational factors that determine mystical intent are overdetermined and cannot be captured by a simple recourse to the child's relationship with the mother as the explanatory root of all things.

An apt application of this both/and approach is found in Jeffrey Kripal's psychoanalytic portrait of Ramakrishna. In promoting a concept of Eros that is at once deeply psychoanalytic yet also (and here he draws explicitly on Plato) "harnessed and 'winged' for ecstatic flight,"[15] Kripal offers a psychoreligious rendition of the erotic, defined as "a dimension of human experience that is simultaneously related both to the physical and emotional experience of sexuality and to the deepest ontological levels of religious experience."[16] The erotic, claims Kripal, is a term in which "the horizons of religious experience and psychoanalysis can meet in the act of interpretation."[17] Thus it is that for Kripal, Ramakrishna's tantric form of mystical eroticism engaged both sexual conflict and divine ground:

> Lacan was clear enough about his own answer to where Teresa was "coming from". He rejected the notion that the mystical can be reduced to sexuality and instead speculated that such ecstatic experiences of "a *jouissance* which goes beyond" issue forth from our own ontological ground.... Ramakrishna in *samadhi,* not unlike Bernini's "Teresa in Ecstasy", is obviously "coming." But "what is his *jouissance,* his *coming* from"? . . . I have respected the religious world of Tantra and have chosen to interpret Ramakrishna's mystico-erotic experiences within that universe. I would argue, then, that the saint's experiences were "coming from" the ontological ground of his Tantric world. . . . I would insist, moreover, that such a realization be understood on its own terms, as a genuine religious experience.[18]

In bridging psychoanalytic and tantric notions of sexuality and vision, Kripal sees in the symbols and acts of Ramakrishna's erotic mysticism a progressive (cultural-mystical) as well as regressive (psychoanalytic) meaning. It is Gananath Obeyesekere's anthropological take on Ricoeur's dialectic between *arche* and *telos* that paves the way for providing a relation between the two.[19] It is important to note that Kripal's analysis is dependent on a tantric conception of the body in which sexual energies are a "lower" manifestation of the full spectrum of energy embodied in the Hindu term *shakti.* The Hindu "body" is one that "goes beyond" the Freudian body in its postulation of an innate energy that is at once biological, psychological, and religious. As such, the movement from eroticism to vision cannot be accounted for by simple sublimation but, in adopting Hindu terms, only through an alchemical transformation of bodily energies, which necessitates a move to a specifically Tantric worldview—one in which libido receives its definition in relation to erotic-mystical energy (that is, to shakti). Hence it is that Kripal distinguishes between sublimation and realization. So too must one note the very different view of development inherent in such a worldview. Echoing the thoughts of Romain Rolland, who in his study of Indian mysticism similarly insisted on the physiological basis of mysticism, Kripal observes that it is the opening of those psychophysiological structures known as cakras and the mystical understanding they bequeath that becomes the marker of development. From this postmodern perspective, libido-based notions of development are relativized and turned on their head. As Kripal points out, from the standpoint of the successful tantric, "Freud only got to the third Cakra."[20]

The both/and approach is useful to suggest how a successful dialogical, transformational psychoanalytic interpretation of Augustine's mystical ascent might proceed. The views of Lacan, Kakar, and Kripal allow us to admit the possibility of psychosexual tensions, such as in Augustine's relationship with Monica, while also allowing us to go beyond the Freudian ascent motif as found in *Group Psychology and the Analysis of the Ego,* thereby providing a new psychoanalytic justification for Augustine's position on the ascent of Eros.

This analysis, however, must be offered with a caveat. Lacan's *jouissance,* Kakar's use of the latter, and Kripal's definition of the erotic all have the advantage of being within the psychoanalytic tradition while also justifying the desire for the divine as irreducible and sui generis. At the same time, the theoretical model is religiously neutral and generic: such a formulation can be tailored to fit a number of mystical texts and figures. Lacan is equally at home citing figures as diverse as Plotinus, Saint John, and Saint Teresa. In the case of Kripal, what one finds is a postmodern position in which Freud's libido-based notions of development are relativized ("Freud only got to the third Cakra"), and the ontological source of his "coming" is understood in explicitly Hindu tantric terms. Applied wholesale to Augustine, this would be problematic, for the content of Kripal's dialogical efforts, pertaining as they do to a Hindu saint with Hindu conceptions of the body, cannot be imported without some qualification. In Augustine there is no articulation of cakras and shakti, and his views on the nature and content of vision—indeed, his entire mystical theology—is obviously different from that of Ramakrishna. One does not find in Lacan, Kakar, or Kripal specific Augustinian teachings about God's active role in imparting love and knowledge in the ascent upward. The latter belongs to Augustine's theology. A psychoanalytic approach to his visions, then, must also allow space for mystical theology and a constructivist approach to the latter—a point I return to shortly.

Freudian Navels

Augustine's mystical ascent was not simply about an expanded notion of Eros but also involved the acquisition of knowledge, in which physiological and empathic-cognitive elements play a role. While Lacan, Kakar, and Kripal have suggested ways to extend the dialogical reach of

Eros, they do not supply the theoretical formulations that could expand a bona fide dialogue with Augustine's teaching about the more cognitive-empathic elements apparent in mystical ecstasy. Again, as with the psychoanalytic ascent motif, we will not find here exact parallels with the formulations of Augustine's mystical theology. Rather, the aim of this work is, contra extant psychoanalytic studies of Augustine's visions, to uncover formulations that can serve to legitimate a psychoanalytic ground for the possibility of mystical modes of knowing.

Freud is a necessary starting point, if only to recognize that extant psychoanalytic analyses of ecstasy and vision, based as they are on a misunderstanding of Freud's interpretation of Rolland's oceanic feeling, have entirely neglected other avenues within the Freudian and indeed the long history of the psychoanalytic written corpus. Picking up a thread left unfinished in the previous chapter, I propose that, when faced with the phenomena of episodic, ecstatic mystical experience, Freud turned not to the preoedipal thesis but to something quite different. The paradigmatic example of this occurs in the last paragraph of the first chapter of *Civilization and Its Discontents,* where Freud, having finished with his analysis of Rolland's statelike oceanic feeling, turns to a related mystical phenomenon:

> Another friend of mine, whose insatiable craving for knowledge has led him to make the most unusual experiments and has ended by giving him encyclopedic knowledge, has assured me that through the practices of Yoga . . . by fixing the attention on bodily functions and by peculiar methods of breathing, one can in fact evoke new sensations and coenaesthesias in oneself, which he regards as regressions to primordial states of mind which have long ago been overlaid. He sees in them a physiological basis, as it were, of much of the wisdom of mysticism. It would not be hard to find connections here with a number of obscure modifications of mental life, such as trances and ecstasies. But I am moved to exclaim in the words of Schiller's diver: "Let him rejoice who breathes up here in the roseate light!"[21]

The reference to ecstasies indicates that we are on the right track in our quest to find a more appropriate Freudian line of argument as concerns the kind of mystical phenomenon Augustine spent so much time describing. Initially, it seems apparent that this text, insofar as Freud mentions yoga and physiology, is meant as a response to Rolland's letter of July 17, 1929. Rolland penned the latter in response to Freud's request to use his letter of December 5, 1927, and the perplexing phenomenon of the statelike oceanic feeling in *Civilization and Its Discontents:*

> I am much honored to learn that the letter I wrote to you at the end of 1927 has prompted you to new researches, and that in a new work you will reply to the questions I had posed to you. . . . Since 1927 I have been able to delve deeply into that "oceanic" sentiment, innumerable examples of which I find . . . in what I might call the ritualistic and multi-secular physiology which is codified in treatises on yoga. . . . At the end of my work, while reading, for comparison, some of the great mystics of Europe and particularly those of the Alexandrian epoch, those who lived in the West during the 14th century—not to speak of the considerable work of Abbe Bremond on French mysticism during the 16th and 17th centuries—I was surprised to observe once again, that it is not at all true that the East and the West are two worlds separated from each other, but that both are branches of the same river of thought. And I have recognized in both the same "river ocean."[22]

Freud responded by thanking Rolland for his permission to use his letter of December 5, 1927, in his upcoming work, adding, "it is easier for you than for us to read the human soul!" Anna Freud and, following her, Jeffrey Moussaieff Masson, the Vermorels, and Daniel Merkur indicate that the "another friend of mine" whom Freud refers to is Friedrich Eckstein.[23] Eckstein is less known in psychoanalytic circles than his sister, Emma, a patient of Freud who underwent, at his suggestion and under the care of Freud's famous confidant, Wilhelm Fleiss, an unsuccessful nasal operation, the latter becoming a prominent part of the famous "Irma's injection" dream described in *The Interpretation of Dreams.* Friedrich, who came to know Freud as early as the mid-1890s, was an advocate of the occult and spiritualism, helping to found the first Viennese Theosophical Society, becoming its president, and later introducing Rudolph Steiner to theosophy. In any event, "another friend" certainly has affinities with Rolland and, insofar as the letter of July 17, 1929, references yoga and the physiology of yoga, Freud's passage above can be regarded as exhibiting a condensation of Rolland and Eckstein.

Freud did not offer an explicit or detailed analysis of the deep mystical states as advocated by Rolland and Eckstein but instead deflected analysis in favor of adducing an excerpt from Schiller's poem "The Diver." Yet this reference, while not immediately apparent, contains an implicit working model for mystical ecstasy and trance. The poem portrays the plight of a lowly page who, on two successive occasions, dives into a feared "whirlpool" (described as an "ocean womb" that leads down "to the depths of hell") to retrieve a king's goblet, the reward being the king's daughter and, eventually, the crown itself. The depths of the whirlpool (a term Freud explicitly used to refer to the unconscious), being fearsome and gruesome, are depicted as difficult to navigate. The page emerges from his first attempt at retrieving the goblet exclaiming "let him rejoice who breathe up here in the roseate light!" On his second attempt, however, with the promise of the king's daughter's hand in marriage, the page succumbs to the depths, never to return. In "The Diver," then, we see a condensation of oceanic and oedipal imagery. It seems that Freud was drawing an analogy between the poem and psychoanalytic therapy. One "dives" into the oceanic whirlpool of the unconscious, there to gain insight into the terrors below. Further, the condensation of oedipal and oceanic imagery indicates what Freud thought to be the nature of that whirlpool. In other words, what we have developing here is a second model that corresponds not to the statelike oceanic feeling, unity, and preoedipal ideation but to transient mystical experiences, mystical noesis and intuition, and a similarity between the depths achieved by the latter and that of psychoanalytic therapy.[24]

Other linked texts and letters buttress this line of argument. For example, insofar as Freud not only utilized the "intuitive" insights of poetic and philosophers to make his points but did so with intellectual consistency, it is significant that twenty-five years earlier (during the academic year 1904–5), he had cited the same Schiller poem in conjunction with mysticism in a conversation with Bruno Goetz, later poet but then student at the University of Vienna. Goetz went to Freud for help with acute facial neuralgia, which he thought might be psychological in origin. That proved not to be the case, but the two struck up a friendship, and Goetz spoke with Freud on numerous occasions. In one meeting Goetz relayed to Freud his participation in the Sanskrit scholar Leopold von Schroeder's class on Indian thought at the University of Vienna and his enthusiasm for the Bhagavad Gita. Freud cautioned Goetz to "take care," as the Bhagavad Gita was "a profound poem with awful depths."[25] He then went on to state that the deep state of insight and of nirvana as presented in the Bhagavad Gita was "not nothingness . . . but an ice-cold, all-comprehending yet scarcely comprehensible insight."[26] He warned Goetz not to take such depths lightly or to fall prey to the European romantic fascination with nirvana. Indeed, he admonished him not to undertake this deep psychic surgery without adequate preparation. It is by way of warning the young Goetz about these awful depths that Freud alludes to Schiller's diver: "'Head first, head over heels into the abyss' is all very fine, but the enthusiasm which it has aroused in Europe is based on a sad misunderstanding. The *Bhagavad-Gita* is a great and profound poem with awful depths. 'And still it lay beneath me hidden deep in purple darkness there,' says Schiller's diver, who never returns from his second brave attempt."[27] In this text and in *Civilization and Its Discontents,* then, we see Freud referring to the primordial depths of mysticism, ecstasies and trances, and mystical practices as being commensurate with those mapped by psychoanalysis. Or perhaps it is more accurate to say that Freud was reading his emerging theory of the mind into the classic mystical texts and theories.[28]

The matter is settled in a series of texts and letters that make up the later portion of the Freud-Rolland correspondence. In 1930 Rolland sent Freud his biographies of Ramakrishna and Vivekananda, in which he had critiqued a well-known psychoanalytic book on mysticism, Ferdinand Morel's *Essai sur l'introversion mystique,* and Morel's thesis that mysticism was nothing but a regression to the intrauterine stage. In particular, Rolland not only advocated that mystical introversion and mystical intuition engaged contents of the Freudian unconscious (and here Rolland mentioned Freud by name), he went further, claiming that despite Kantian objections to the ability of mystical intuition to engage the Real as such, "Kant's analysis was familiar to Vivekananda," and further, that various Vedantic philosophers "had already predicated and even surpassed it."[29]

Freud's response to the biographies is telling. He first thanked Rolland "for the gift of your twin-headed, three-volume work!," then went on to address the problem of mystical intuition. He admitted that mystical intuition could reveal "instinctual impulse and attitudes" that admittedly could be "highly valuable for an embryology of the soul," but that it could not, as with Rolland's view of the mystics, be utilized to "teach them how to solve the riddle of the universe."[30] In fact, this line of argument had been prefigured in a "pre-Rolland" text, namely, in chapter 5 of his *The Future of an Illusion.* There Freud, in rebuking what he calls the "desperate efforts" of philosophers and theologians to defend the legitimacy of institutional religion," addresses the thought of Tertullian:

The "*Credo quia absurdum*" of the early Father of the Church . . . maintains that religious doctrines are outside the jurisdiction of reason—are above reason. Their truth must be felt inwardly, and they need not be comprehended. But this *Credo* is only of interest as a self-confession. . . . If the truth of religious doctrines is dependent on an inner experience which bears witness to that truth, what is one to do about the many people who do not have this rare experience? One may require every man to use the gift of reason which he possesses, but one cannot erect, on the basis of a motive that exists only for a very few, an obligation that shall apply to everyone. If one man has gained an unshakable conviction of the true reality of religious doctrines from a state of ecstasy which has deeply moved him, of what significance is that to others?[31]

Freud indicates that moments of religious ecstasy are far too subjective, rare, and inaccessible to empirical, scientific verification to serve as the basis for the defense of institutional religion. On the other hand, the passage is littered with rhetorical questions and defensive rationalizations, which gives one the impression that Freud is not denying that such altered states have some adaptive value for the "very few." Freud specifies the kind of knowledge that one might gain in such deep and rare states in the next chapter of *The Future of an Illusion* when, in returning to the epistemological status of mystical intuition, he concludes that it "can give us nothing but particulars about our own mental life, which are hard to interpret."[32] Nevertheless, as in his letters to Rolland, here we have Freud admitting that the knowledge gained through mystical intuition is akin to psychoanalysis in its inner trajectory and unearthing of unconscious content.

This position is echoed and extended in another, later text (in his *New Introductory Lectures on Psychoanalysis*) addressed to Rolland in which Freud expressly equates certain mystical practices and forms of knowing with those of psychoanalysis. The text is important, for it contains one of the most quoted of all psychoanalytic one-liners—a phrase that can be referred to as the "psychoanalytic motto":

It is easy to imagine, too, that certain mystical practices may succeed in upsetting the normal relations between the different regions of the mind, so that, for instance, perception may be able to grasp happenings in the depths of the ego and in the id which were otherwise inaccessible to it. It may safely be doubted, however, whether this road will lead us to the ultimate truths from which salvation is to be expected. Nevertheless it may be admitted that the therapeutic efforts of psychoanalysis have chosen a similar line of approach. Its intention is, indeed, to strengthen the ego, to make it more independent of the super-ego, to widen its field of perception and enlarge its organization, so that it can appropriate fresh portions of the id. Where id was, there ego shall be. It is a work of culture—not unlike the draining of the Zuider Zee.[33]

Here again we see Freud confirming the stance taken in his letters to Rolland, in his conversation with Bruno Goetz, and in the text of *Civilization and Its Discontents.* Mystical practices, trances, and ecstasies may "upset" the "normal relations" between the ego and id so that insight, psychoanalytic or mystical (as with mystical intuition), becomes possible. But such intuition is not able to solve the "riddles of the universe" or privy to salvific truth.

Evidently Freud was not satisfied with this emerging model of mystical ecstasy and intuition. Later in life he returned to the problem and offered a different if more fantastic hypothesis. The initial point of reference can be found in the twenty-third volume of James Strachey's mammoth *Standard Edition* of Freud's works, where one finds a lone speculative entry, but a sentence long, among a series of entries of similar nature and length, in a section titled "Findings, Ideas, Problems" (Freud's own title). The entry is dated August 22, 1938, and reads simply as follows: "Mysticism is the obscure self-perception of the realm outside the ego, of the id."[34] Once properly contextualized, this seemingly innocuous sentence leads one to think that in fact, Freud was in the midst of developing a new and important extension of his interpretative model of mystical ecstasy.

The major project concerning Freud's application of his psychoanalytic method to religious phenomena from 1934 on remains his contested work, *Moses and Monotheism.* There is a tangential but not entirely insignificant relation between the latter and Rolland. Freud had been asked by Victor Wittkowski to write something to celebrate Rolland's seventieth birthday—a gift that later eventuated in Freud's writing his paper on the Acropolis. However, before the birth of that essay Freud had responded to Wittkowski, in a letter dated January 6, 1936, that he was old, infirm, lacking in creative output, and thus unable to produce anything of worth for Rolland. Referring to his book on Moses, Freud went on to say, "As recently as a year ago I succeeded in writing something that would have been of special interest to R.R., but it suffered from one defect which prevented it from being published, and since then my ability to produce has dried up. It is probably too late for it to revive again."[35] Surely there are several reasons why Freud would have linked Rolland with his book on Moses, not least the Mosaic emphasis on renunciation, secondary-process thought, and truth and justice. But what is of special interest now is how the thesis of *Moses and Monotheism* holds the interpretative key to Freud's last theory of mystical ecstasy.

The pivotal point boils down to the explicit manifestation of Freud's later and more expansive view of the unconscious. One sees an inkling of this in his "Findings, Ideas, Problems," where Freud, in an entry dated July 20, 1938, barely a month before his entry on mysticism of August 22, states the following: "The hypothesis of there being inherited vestiges in the id alters, so to say, our views about it."[36] Clearly, then, his subsequent reference to mysticism of August 22 would include this latter view of the id. The notion of "inherited vestiges" refers to Freud's more cursory and Lamarckian views, outlined in works from *Totem and Taboo* onward, of the phylogenetic transmission of traumatic primal events. In *Moses and Monotheism,* Freud took this view much farther in speaking to the matter of the "development" of religion. In *Totem and Taboo* he had offered a dubious thesis concerning the origin of religion: that it was the repeated murder of the alpha ape father in the small, wandering primal hordes that resulted in totemic society, understood as the first organized and structured social community. The worship of the totem, with its attendant moral prohibitions against incest and murder, was the first, rudimentary form of religion. This traumatic "primal deed," as Freud was to call his psychoanalytic version of original sin, occurred so often and over so many generations that it became part of the id. In other words, as early as *Totem and Taboo* Freud was positing that alongside the normal developmental traumas unique to each individual was a deeper layer of universal traumatic events that was inherited and common to the mass of humanity. As he later put it in *Moses:* "the archaic heritage of human beings comprises not only dispositions but also subject-matter—memory-traces of the experience of earlier generations."[37]

Freud's embracement of phylogenesis and the theory of Lamarck led to increasing consternation among the most loyal of his followers. As Ernst Jones so politely put it, "It is not easy to account for the fixity with which Freud held this opinion and the determination with which he ignored all the biological evidence to the contrary."[38] Indeed, Freud's defensiveness seems irrational enough to suggest the influence of deep psychodynamic forces. Along these lines one might note two significant facts. First, Freud's postulation of an "archaic heritage" allowed him to retain, even if in a stunted and distorted form, his original and quickly discarded theory concerning the role of actual seduction in the life of neurotics.[39] This becomes clear in his discussion of "primal phantasies," the essence of which is to account for, by way of phylogenetic transmission, the seemingly excessive nature of some of the sexual and aggressive phantasies that he found to exist in the life of his present-day neurotics. While actual physical seduction may not have occurred in such a person, it definitely did occur many times over in the life of our ancestors. It is this fact that enables Freud to say the following:

> Primal phantasies . . . are a phylogenetic endowment. In them the individual reaches beyond his own experience into primaeval experience at points where his own experience becomes too rudimentary. It seems to me quite possible that all the things that are told to us to-day in analysis as phantasy—the seduction of children, the inflaming of sexual excitement by observing parental intercourse, the threat of castration (or rather castration itself)—were once real occurrences in the primaeval times of the human family, and that children in their phantasies are simply filling in the gaps in individual truth with prehistoric truth.[40]

The key phrase here is "beyond his own experience." Given the crucial nature of the role of Freud's abandonment of the seduction theory for the development of psychoanalysis and the debate that has raged over the extent to which he willingly or unwillingly did so, his formulation takes on added import. Freud is saying that one needs the influence of the archaic, phylogenetic deep past to supplement the more usual psychoanalytic focus on the ontogenic "developmental past" to account for the clinical data of neuroses.

This avenue of inquiry is supplemented by the fact that *Totem and Taboo* was published during a time when Freud's chosen heir, Carl Jung, had turned competitor and was developing his theory of the collective unconscious and archetypes. It may well be, as others have pointed out, that such ideas were "in the air" and that Freud's version of the theory was psychoanalytically specific and lacked the religious connotations linked to Jung's notion of a collective unconscious.[41] Yet it is hard to dismiss the thought that Freud felt the threat of Jung's formulations. In acknowledging the existence of a common, universal dimension of the unconscious beyond that of the personal unconscious, of the need of the individual to reach "beyond his own experience," Freud was saying to

Jung that, yes, there do exist things like archetypes, but one and only one: Oedipus.

Now that the context has been established, we can understand its impact on Freud's new understanding of religious ecstasy. In *The Future of an Illusion* Freud had spoken of such ecstasy in conjunction with Tertullian's *credo quia absurdum,* offering that such states could cough up the contents of one's personal unconscious. In the letters to Goetz, in his *New Introductory Lectures on Psychoanalysis,* and in letters to Rolland he likened mystical practices and the intuitive knowledge they uncovered to the practice of psychoanalysis. In *Moses and Monotheism,* Freud, in recalling the argument of *Totem and Taboo,* becomes more specific about the nature and extent of that intuitive knowledge. He begins by once again affirming that one's psychical life includes "not only what he has experienced himself but also things that were innately present in him at his birth, elements with a phylogenetic origin—an *archaic heritage.*"[42] He notes that "If we assume the survival of these memory-traces in the archaic heritage, we have bridged the gulf between individual and group psychology."[43] Freud is here unambiguously stating the existence of a common storehouse of archaic memories buried deep within the phylogenetic dimension of the unconscious.

Then, in speaking to the vicissitudes of group psychology, about the development of religion from totemism through matriarchy and then to monotheism, Freud insists on the determinative dynamic factor of our archaic heritage and especially the primal deed. The rise of Moses and the introduction of monotheism were successful precisely because both recalled the memory of the great primal father and the various impulses linked to him. In speaking to the latter, and again referencing Tertullian, Freud goes on to state that such archaic experiences exercise "an incomparably powerful influence on the people in the mass, and [raise] an irresistible claim to truth against which logical objections remain powerless: a kind of 'credo quia absurdum.'"[44] Here Freud is not referencing Tertullian and religious ecstasy, as he was in *The Future of an Illusion,* to speak of the particulars of one's personal unconscious but of the dynamic force of our common phylogenetic archaic heritage. The "core" of the historical truth that determined the charisma of Moses is the complicity we all have in the primal deed:

> The first effect of meeting the being who had so long been missed and longed for was overwhelming and was like the traditional description of

> the law-giving from Mount Sinai. Admiration, awe and thankfulness for having found grace in his eyes—the religion of Moses knew none but these positive feelings towards the father-god. The conviction of his irresistibility, the submission to his will, could not have been more unquestioning in the helpless and intimidated son of the father of the horde—indeed those feelings only become fully intelligible when they are transposed into the primitive and infantile setting.[45]

Freud adds that such intense awe and admiration, being feelings beyond the normal range of the personal unconscious, require a correspondingly altered state: "only religious ecstasy can bring them back."[46] In other words, what both motivates and is uncovered in religious ecstasy is the content of not simply the personal unconscious but that of the universal memory traces that define the content of our phylogenetically transmitted archaic heritage.

At this point we have reached the limits of the Freudian take on mystical intuition. The aim of this rather lengthy detour has been to add to our attempt to show not only that extant psychoanalytic interpretations of Augustine's visions are based on a misinterpretation of the Freud-Rolland debate over the nature of the oceanic feeling but also that they have entirely neglected another avenue of thought, one that Freud himself would have taken. Augustine was talking about intellectual visions, and significantly, Freud's response to the problem of ecstasy and the nature of mystical insight was *not* regression to primary narcissism. Where the most optimistic evaluation of Freud's earlier formulations would see the mystic "diver" as incapable of reaching "salvation" (though capable of reaching the deepest roots of Oedipus), a less optimistic but perhaps more balanced view is that Freud saw the mystic as having intuitive access to the unconscious (though prone to misunderstanding and misrepresenting the nature of unconscious forces). The essence of Freud's last and more dubious formulations reveals a Freudian version of the uprush of Jung's collective unconscious and archetypical material. In any event, what we see is a Freud who, even to the end of his days, struggled to find an adequate psychoanalytic explanation for mystical claims of noesis.

Certainly there remain problems, for it appears that Freud was hardly interested in looking at textual differences among mystics of various traditions concerning their teaching on mystical modes of knowing, such as trances and ecstasies, preferring instead to level all such distinctions, universalizing their psychological nature, and interpreting their meaning through Oedipus and a structural model of the psyche. Assuredly, Augustine's claims regarding salvific truth have no place in the Freudian scheme of things, but one can discern a new psychoanalytic line of reasoning that gives grounds for the possibility of dialogue based on the actual Augustinian teaching on vision. To explore this line of thought, I return to the subsequent theorizing on mysticism in the long history of psychoanalysis, that by the "psychoanalytic mystics."

Hidden Histories

The correspondence between Freud and Rolland took place during the originative, initial phase of the psychology of religion movement. Freud wrote his important works on religion during this time, while Jung was developing his theory of archetypes and the collective unconscious. Moreover, a number of scholars, some now forgotten, contributed to the study of mysticism, spirituality, and anomalous phenomena, among them R. M. Bucke, Théodore Flournoy, G. Stanley Hall and the Clark school, James Leuba, Karl Girgensohn and the Dorpat school, Joseph Maréchal, Frederic Myers, James Pratt, George Coe, and Georges Berguer.[47] Indeed, if the psychological study of religion is seen as coextensive with the founding of scientific psychology in the latter half of the nineteenth century, then the period from 1880 to 1944 encompasses the important, if not classic, texts in the field, including James's *The Varieties of Religious Experience,* Bucke's *Cosmic Consciousness,* Leuba's *The Psychology of Religious Mysticism,* Flournoy's *From India to the Planet Mars,* Myers's *Human Personality and Its Survival after Bodily Death,* and Maréchal's *The Psychology of the Mystics.*

Many of these theorists had what may be termed mystical or anomalous experiences, as well as familiarity with mystical techniques and practices. For example, Bucke, a valued correspondent of James, championed an early form of perennialism, advocating an evolutionary view of the human species based on his own mystical experiences of "cosmic consciousness." William James in turn was led to mysticism and the embracing of the "subliminal" and the possibility of the More not only by his Swedenborgian father but also by his own personal experiences. On one occasion, while hiking in the Adirondacks, James experienced a sense of heightened awareness. On another occasion, while under the influence of entheogens (in this case, nitrous oxide), he drew the conclusion that normal waking consciousness is but one type of awareness around which lie potential other forms of consciousness, some even contradictory, that are inevitably reconciled into a greater unity.[48]

Similarly, Carl Jung, after his break with Freud, was seized by a period of personal disintegration that led to a series of visions that he describes as a "confrontation with the unconscious" that gave him "the *prima materia* for a lifetime's work."[49] Later, in what is now known as his most clearly explicated treatise, *Two Essays on Analytical Psychology*, Jung gave theoretical sophistication to his earlier existential crises: the process of individuation, the notion of the collective unconscious and the delineation of its archetypes, the objectivity of the psyche, active imagination, and so on.

Less well known is the influence on Freud of Frederic Myers, who deeply influenced James, especially the latter's adoption of the concept of the subliminal. Myers was convinced that mankind was evolving and that paranormal phenomena such as telepathy were footprints, so to speak, of that evolution, and thus that great spiritual teachers were highly evolved creatures who embodied and communicated the higher reaches of the moral, physical, and psychical dimensions of human beings. For Myers, the key lay in hypnotic trance, for it was through trances that such deep states could be accessed. Of course, it was Freud's failure at hypnosis that led to the signature psychoanalytic technique of free association and to the gradual development of the structural theory of the mind. Myers, on the other hand, made hypnosis the signature practice of his work and, in so doing, developed a very different appreciation of the relation between the "subliminal" and mystical and anomalous phenomena. Among the latter Myers explicitly included what the contemporary mind would call near-death experiences and Paul's ascent to paradise.[50] That is, Myers thought that hypnosis led to trance and that trance was the gateway to ecstatic visionary ascents. This thesis has received added import in recent years with the work of Jonathan Garb, a noted scholar of Jewish mysticism, who, utilizing the work of the hypnotherapist Milton Erickson, argues for a link between hypnotic trance states and Jewish merkavah ascents—the same religio-cultural worldview that informs Saint Paul's ascent in 2 Corinthians.[51]

Even forgotten psychoanalysts of Freud's day were struck by the wisdom they found in mystical texts and figures. Paul Federn, vice-president of the Vienna Psychoanalytic Society, spoke highly of the knowledge gained in ecstasy and was critical of Freud's views on the oceanic feeling.[52] Trigant Burrow, whose notion of "contention," described as a "time-limited state of organic community with others and the world associated with a decrease in egocentric striving," represented a fundamental psychospiritual, holistic mode of human consciousness.[53] Later psychoanalytic interest in the mystical led to new avenues of theorizing. The ego psychologist Hans Loewald, who was influenced by Heidegger, saw in the unconscious a primordial nontemporal and nonhistorical source of wisdom and revitalization.[54] Erik Erikson valorized the German Christian mystical tradition and, in particular, Angelus Silesius, whose analysis of Luther emphasized the "unborn core of creation."[55] Indeed, Erikson was responsible for a sea change in the psychoanalytic view of the monastery, which for many heirs of Freud was but a socially sanctioned institution for the neurotic. Erikson, in his analysis of Luther and his early life in an Augustinian monastery, referred to monastic activity as a moratorium, thereby giving it adaptive value. For Erikson the monastery "offers methods of making a meditative descent into the inner shafts of mental existence, from which the aspirant emerges . . . with gems of wisdom."[56] And contrary to those psychoanalysts who equate pathology and narcissistic fragmentation with the renunciant monk, Erikson argued that the mystic must have a pretty strong sense of self to be able to lose it in the abyss of the godhead.[57]

One could similarly cite Wilfred Bion, the analysand of Melanie Klein and pioneer of advances in group dynamics, who advocated the state of "O," framed in mystical terms as the "absolute truth, the godhead, the infinite, the thing-in-itself. . . . It can 'become,' but it cannot be 'known.'"[58] This group also includes, as we have noted, the notions of *jouissance* and the Real as articulated by Jacques Lacan.

Perhaps most significant for our project is the religio-psychological concept of "cosmic narcissism" as developed by the self psychologist Heinz Kohut. Cosmic narcissism forms the mystical horizon of his psychology and functions as one of the ideal transformations of narcissism. Referring back to Rolland's oceanic feeling, Kohut insisted that cosmic narcissism is statelike, consisting in "a shift of the narcissistic cathexes from the self to a concept of participation in a supraindividual and timeless existence."[59] Cosmic narcissism "transcends the bounds of the individual," and one lives "*sub specie aeternitas,*" without elation or anxiety, bathed in a continual communion with a contentless, supraordinate self, participating in "supraindividual ideals and the world with which one identifies."[60] Cosmic narcissism, as an advanced form of transformed narcissistic structures, accounts not only for the statelike feature of Rolland's oceanic feeling but also for the ethical and existential dimensions Freud neglected in the analysis undertaken in *Civilization and Its Discontents*.[61]

Interestingly enough, in Kohut's psychology we have a position close to that advocated by Rolland: a mystical psychoanalysis suitable for the culture of modern spirituality. To this end, Kohut isolated a particular figure who he thought embodied such mystical awareness for the contemporary person: Dag Hammarskjöld, the former secretary-general of the United Nations. In his essay "On Leadership," Kohut suggests the need for a new, unchurched rational religion, "an as yet uncreated system of mystical rationality which could take the place of the religions of the past."[62] He then points to "instances of heroic men of constructive political action who have achieved a transformation of their narcissism into a contentless, inspiring personal religion,"[63] further commenting that humanity will have to produce such types in greater numbers in order to survive. It is here that Kohut points to Hammarskjöld: "Dag Hammarskjöld . . . an example of this type, describes his contentless mysticism in the following words: 'Faith is a state of mind and of the soul . . . the language of religion is [only] a set of formulas which register a basic religious experience.' "[64]

Thus it appears that, at the very least, psychoanalysis has not been blind to the significance of mysticism, and neither, for that matter, has it ventured to offer more positive models for its interpretation.[65] However, what is important for our purposes is to pick, from the wealth of models available to us, those that offer the most appropriate mode of dialogue with mystical processes of Augustine. To set the stage for such a dialogue, I note that to this point, we have seen Freud admitting that the "wisdom" of mysticism lay in accessing, through mystical practices, what he called primordial states of consciousness, and that he interpreted this move as commensurate with psychoanalytic thought and practice. As intimated in his reference to Schiller's "The Diver," mystical practices could, at their best, enable one to gain insight into the deepest knots of oedipal distress. In this sense, mysticism and psychoanalysis were seen as operating along similar lines. Alternatively, and less optimistically, mystical intuition could reveal "instinctual impulses and attitudes" and be valuable for an "embryology of the soul," but could not "solve the riddle of the universe" or eventuate in salvific knowledge. Rolland explicitly challenged Freud on this very matter. He argued that yogic practices and mystical intuition accessed an unconscious religious dimension that went beyond not only the oedipal formulations of Freud but also that of Kant's a priori categories in accessing "the Real" as such. The issue debated by the two men, then, comes down to varying introspective practices, the nature of the cognitive versus empathic modes of knowing they lead to, and the interpretation of the unearthed, "primordial" content.

Furthering this debate, especially as it informs a better psychoanalytic understanding of our earlier reconstruction of Augustine's teaching on mysticism, requires that we find those resources that are continuous with Freud's initial forays yet, like Lacan's or Kakar's and Kripal's extension of what I call Freud's psychoanalytic ascent motif, are capable of expanding Freud's cursory attempts to account for mystical noesis. Exactly such resources may be found in the ruminations of those I refer to as the psychoanalytic mystics. To show this, and to provide a better historical context for understanding such resources, I must again make a brief detour back to Freud, especially his reflections on "primordial states of mind" that have been "overlaid," and to that specialist in the paranormal, Frederic Myers.

Freud was familiar with Myers and the institution that he founded, the Society for Psychical Research, and knew of the various studies on telepathy, or instances of "thought-transference"—so much so that he wrote to the society that had he the ability to start his career anew, it would be precisely such anomalous phenomena that he would make the centerpiece of his research.[66] The reason for this interest lay in what Freud thought was clear clinical evidence of telepathy in the psychoanalytic session. Freud ended up penning six essays on telepathy and, in the end, not only became converted to its reality but also made it known that psychoanalysis had paved the way for what he thought would be its inevitable scientific verification. It is unfortunate that this episode in psychoanalytic theory and history, in taking a cue from biblical studies (appropriate in that there is a concordance with Freud's substantial oeuvre), has been relegated to the status of being apocryphal. Indeed, the term *apocrypha,* which literally means "things hidden away" and which designates texts of uncertain authenticity, those that fall outside the canon, or writings whose authorship is questioned, is an apt characterization for the treatment accorded to such texts by a majority of those within the psychoanalytic community today. Even strong defenders of Freud, such as Ernst Jones, were taken aback by Freud's "conversion." Jones's consternation was surely brought to a boil when, in confronting Freud about the matter, he was met with an intentionally mysterious reply intimating that thought transference was a step on the slippery slope to acknowledging the existence of "der liebe Gott."[67]

In theorizing about the manifestation of telepathy, Freud insisted that two general conditions were needed. First, telepathy was facilitated when two people were emotionally tied together, for example, parent and child. That is, empathy is conducive to the transmission of telepathic knowledge. Next, he recognized that receptivity to telepathic messages was enabled by having one's attention diverted from the rational consciousness of waking life, thus inducing alternative states of consciousness, of which sleep and the dream life are paradigmatic examples. Finally, in asking his readers to "have kindlier thoughts on the objective possibility of thought-transference and at the same time of telepathy," Freud offered a working theory to explain such phenomena:

> The telepathic process is supposed to consist in a mental act in one person instigating the same mental act in another person. . . . The analogy with other transformations, such as occur in speaking and hearing by telephone, would then be unmistakable. . . . It would seem to me that psychoanalysis, by inserting the unconscious between what is physical and what was previously called "psychical," has paved the way for the assumption of such processes as telepathy. . . . One is led to a suspicion that this is the original, archaic method of communication between individuals and that in the course of phylogenetic evolution it has been replaced by the better method of giving information with the help of signals which are picked up by the sense organs. But the older method might have persisted in the background and still be able to put itself into effect under certain conditions. . . . It is a kind of psychical counterpart to wireless telegraphy.[68]

Freud's reference to an "original, archaic method of communication" that can become operative under specific conditions (that is, altered states) recalls my earlier analysis of his characterization of mystical practices such as yoga and of trances and ecstasies as capable of excavating the primordial depths of the unconscious. The fact that this is not an isolated observation is confirmed in the bold claim by Heinz Kohut that among the altered states found in the analytic session is a deep form of empathy that results in "thought-transference." For Kohut, empathy is innate but increasingly overlaid by other, nonempathic modes of knowing during the course of development. In deliberately citing exactly those Freudian texts surveyed above, Kohut claimed that psychoanalytic practices, physiologically speaking, required both a certain level of somatic relaxation and, with respect to mentation, the "intentional curbing of the usual cognitive processes."[69] These conditions allowed the manifestation of empathic modes of communication that could rightly be termed telepathic.

One could object that the formulations canvassed to this point have hardly arrived at Augustinian intellectual visions. Indeed, one could complain that our brief detour, having wavered into the realm of the anomalous, has taken us too far afield. On the contrary, such a detour is crucial, for it continues to ground historically an important psychoanalytic strand of theorizing willing to admit the value of altered states and the possibility of buried, archaic modes of knowing. Moreover, the above, in conjunction with Freud's ruminations on mystical noesis as found in his debate with Romain Rolland, provides that theoretical foundation for a line of reasoning taken up in the works of the psychoanalytic mystics.

Foremost among the latter is Kakar's notion of an amplified empathy. The latter is understood to be a mode of mystical knowing—one that can be framed as the psychoanalytic version of the epistemological term so familiar to philosophers and theologians, knowledge by direct acquaintance. Kakar observes that for Freud, the "mechanistic" ego is not the personality but an agency that mediates between and among the unconscious, the superego, and reality through various defensive maneuvers. The Eriksonian self, however, is different from the Freudian ego, for it is preconscious, can be made conscious, and designates one's social roles and personality. The "I," on the other hand, is more problematic, for it is neither the ego nor the self but that which reflects on both. For Hindus, this "I" is pure consciousness, the *atman* whose counterplayer is *brahman*. In Kakar's rendition of Upanishadic thought, the Hindu term *moksha*

> can be understood to mean that a person living in this state has an all-pervasive current of "I". "I" is the centre of awareness and existence in all experienced situations and in all possible selves. . . . *Moksha*, however, is not limited to gaining this awareness of "I" in a composite self. Rather, it is held that this ultimate "man's meaning" is not realized until a person also has a similar feeling of "I" in the selves of others, an *empathy amplified* to the point of complete identification.[70]

By valorizing the buried, archaic modes of knowing that we have seen in Freud and Kohut, and by going one better than the Freud of *Moses and Monotheism,* Kakar achieves a new theory of the phylogenetic unconscious:

> In the Hindu ideal, reality is not primarily mediated through the conscious and pre-conscious perceptions, unconscious defenses and rational thought processes that make up the ego; it emanates from the deeper and phylogenetically much older structural layer of personality—the id, the mental representative of the organism's instinctual drives. Reality, according to Hindu belief, can be apprehended or known only through those archaic, unconscious, pre-verbal processes of sensing and feeling (like intuition, or what is known as extra-sensory perception).[71]

It is the aim of Hindu mystical practices to empower one to access such modes of knowing.

Arthur Deikman has carried this line of reasoning forward by utilizing empirical data on subjects in contemplative meditation in conjunction with the textual evidence of mystics from multiple traditions. Deikman uses the formulations of psychoanalytic ego psychology, specifically the concept of deautomatization, as initially coined by Hartmann and elaborated by Merton M. Gill and Margaret Brenman, to account for the diminution of ego functions during, of all things, hypnosis.[72] In other words, mimicking Myers, for Deikman the processes of meditative trance and hypnosis have much in common. Significantly, it was Freud's failure at hypnosis that led him away from those case histories of hypnosis and trance that could have provided the clinical grist for a theory of those altered states and archaic modes of knowing valorized by the mystics.

Deikman's view of deautomatization holds that as human development proceeds, our perceptual, motor, and behavioral systems undergo a slow process of automatization until they operate on a "second-nature" or "automatic" level. For example, seemingly unconscious or preconscious phenomena such as perceptual focusing or audio processing, infant and childhood tasks such as walking and talking, or learned routines such as tying one's shoes and driving are all functions that, while once requiring attentional energy and concentration, are considered at the adult level to be routine. As one matures, one invests less intentional energy on such functions, allowing the energy thus saved to be reallocated to new and more complex tasks, such as abstract reasoning. In first learning to drive an automobile, one's attention is entirely devoted to steering, but later one can engage in abstract problem solving to the extent that miles on the highway pass without notice.

A potential drawback of the process of automatization is that certain "archaic" modes of perceiving and relating may be left in a nascent state or entirely abandoned in favor of a socialization process that sanctions the cultivation of cognitive modes of operation actively engaging the sense world. In other words, the kinds of cognition favored by a culture of rampant capitalism could well be different from those preferred and cultivated in a monastic setting. One such archaic mode of cognition, thinks Deikman, is awakened as a result of practices that facilitate detachment from and renunciation of the sense world in conjunction with contemplative techniques that both deautomatize cognitive-perceptual processes and restore and cultivate buried, archaic modes of knowing. In summing up this process, Deikman writes,

> Development from infancy to adulthood is accompanied by an organization of the perceptual and cognitive world that has as its price the selection of some stimuli and stimulus qualities to the exclusion of others. If the automatization underlying that organization is reversed, or temporarily suspended, aspects of reality that were unavailable might then enter awareness.[73]

With specific reference to the experiences of the mystics that he dubs "trans-sensate," Deikman goes on to suggest the following:

> Such experiences are the result of the operation of a new perceptual capacity response to the dimensions of the stimulus array previously ignored or blocked from awareness. For such mystics, renunciation has weakened and temporarily removed the ordinary objects of consciousness as a focus of awareness. Contemplative meditation has undone the logical organization of consciousness. At the same time, the mystic is intensely *motivated* to perceive something. If undeveloped or unutilized perceptual capacities do exist, it seems likely that they would be mobilized and come into operation under such conditions.[74]

Deikman's "ascent motif," then, proceeds as follows: detachment and removal of ties to the sense world, a return inward and contemplation (which leads to deautomatization, a prominent feature of which is the silencing of thoughts), and the opening and cultivation of new modes of knowledge—modes that become operative in part because the mystic is intensely motivated. In other words—and here the intersection with Lacan's *jouissance* is evident—the mystic desire for the Jamesian More facilitates the cultivation of alternative modes of knowing. This also recalls both

Freud's and Kakar's views that there exist archaic, empathic modes of knowing that can become operative during altered states.

This progression of thought is ripe for dialogue with the ascent narratives penned by Augustine. His ascents speak of returning from the external world: a turn inward that, in being rhetorically embellished with passages from the *Enneads* (5.1.4, 5.1.2), emphasizes *sileat* and *hesychon* (which is to say the silencing of normal sense-based knowledge and of thoughts), then a movement above the soul where, with the "soul's eye," one perceives the divine light. At the same time, while Augustine's ascent may well have involved the process of deautomatization, and while his contemplative activity may well have opened a new capacity for knowing deep in the unconscious and with respect to an "amplified empathy," Augustine's specifically Christian teaching on the latter goes well beyond that of any psychoanalytically conceived process. Returning now to a theoretical point I made at the end of the section on the ascent of Eros, Augustine's teaching on vision involves explicit theological assertions about the nature of faith in the turn inward, the role of God's active love, the formation of the eye of the soul, and the knowledge gleaned through that eye. These theological formulations clearly cannot be incorporated wholesale as part of psychoanalytic theory. Again, all that can be suggested here are genuine psychoanalytic grounds for the possibility of alternative modes of mystical knowing—grounds that seem to make more sense than the simple recourse to preoedipal functioning. As was the case in the above discussion on Augustine's ascent, then, another way must be found to account for the integrity of Augustine's mystical theology without sacrificing the neutrality of psychoanalysis. I return to this point later.

Seeing the Light: Near-Death and Virtual Death Experiences

Augustine's reflections on the psychophysiological conditions of intellectual visions provide some common ground between his mystical theology and Freudian theory. Indeed, as we have seen, the Freud-Rolland debate referred, however tangentially, to the role physiology plays in accessing "primordial states of mind." It has been noted, if only colloquially and informally, in both the culture of academia and that of the psychoanalytic institute, that were Freud alive today, he might have lunch with Paul Ricoeur and humanistic psychoanalysts like the late Bruno Bettelheim, but the rest of his day would be spent talking with Sullowayian "biologists of the mind." As recently documented by Kelly Bulkeley,

Freud's engagement with neuroscience is evident from his very first attempts at theorizing about the mind.[75] It is no coincidence that contemporary psychoanalysts and neuroscientists have evinced a mutual interest in each other and in things mystical. Even Deikman's efforts, while indebted to psychoanalytic ego psychology, were informed by the then existing state of neurocognitive science, much of which focused on bihemispheric (right brain/left brain) functioning.

Bulkeley notes that recent studies of the psychophysiology of mystical experience by neuroscientists tally with the conclusions of Freud, Kohut, Kakar, and Deikman, namely, that contemplative practices produce discernible shifts in conscious awareness.[76] For example, James Austin made a study of Zen Buddhism using the methods of cognitive neuroscience, combined with introspection on his own mystical experience of timelessness and eternity in which the "insinuations of selfhood" vanished. He agrees with Deikman that contemplative activity functions to "desynchronize habitual states of consciousness and open the brain-mind system up to the creation of new modes of awareness."[77] He calls for establishing what he calls, going one better than Aldous Huxley, a "perennial *psychophysiology*."[78] Eugene D'Aquili and Andrew Newberg used SPECT imaging (single-photon emission computed tomography) to monitor the brain activity of subjects in meditation in an attempt to establish what they refer to as a "photograph" of God. They hypothesize that prayer and meditation shut down the brain areas responsible for sense perception and orientation while exciting (as a result of intense concentration) the prefrontal cortex, a combination that results in a feeling of endlessness and unity.[79] In further entering the domain of religious studies, they offer an essentialist view of mysticism, a "core" experience, located in the frontal cortex, which they call absolute unitary being (or AUB):

> Neurobiologically and philosophically, there cannot be two versions of this absolute unitary state. It may *look* different, in retrospect, according to cultural beliefs and personal interpretations—a Catholic nun, for whom God is the ultimate reality, might interpret any mystical experience as a melting into Christ, while a Buddhist, who does not believe in a personalized God, might interpret mystical union as a melting into nothingness. What's important to understand, is that these differing interpretations are unavoidably distorted by after-the-fact subjectivity. . . . There is only absolute unity, and there cannot be two versions of any unity that is absolute.[80]

Kelly Bulkeley, one of the few scholars of religion who have endeavored to bring brain science studies and their conclusions into dialogue with academic thinking on mysticism, takes issue with the notion that cognitive neuroscience research corroborates a psychophysiological version of perennialism. He adduces contrary studies that show that different meditative techniques engage different portions of the brain, activate different brain-mind patterns, and lead to different modes of consciousness. As a result, Bulkeley insists that the conclusions of his preferred neurocognitive studies are more consistent with Katzian constructivism:

> Writing well before the "Decade of the Brain," Katz did not have the CN [cognitive neuroscience] resources we now possess to bolster his constructivist argument. Nevertheless . . . where Katz speaks in philosophical terms of the "synthetic operations of the mind," we can speak in CN terms of the neural systems involved in processing, evaluating, and storing perceptual information. Where Katz speaks of "reconditioning consciousness," we can speak of decentering and recentering the dynamic relationship between different neural systems (e.g., via dreaming, sexuality, and creativity). The Kantian view that "there is NO unmediated experience" is confirmed by CN research on the constructive powers of the brain-mind and its subtly creative role in shaping our experiences. Katz's rejection of the allegedly universal mystical achievement of "pure consciousness" is supported by a growing CN literature on the functional anatomical differences between different forms of contemplative practice. . . . No one supreme state of mystical awareness exists toward which all practices strive; rather, multiple modes of extraordinary consciousness are produced by a variety of techniques, each of which is deeply rooted in the unique soil of a distinctly psychological, cultural, and religious context. . . . As Katz suggests, what religious devotees experience is not the universal "ground" of consciousness but rather the creative *outcome* of a particular kind of contemplation, practiced by a particular individual, in a particular life historical context. I believe we are at the beginning of a new research era in which the rich historical and cross-cultural resources of RS [religious studies] will combine with the ever-expanding application of brain imaging technologies by CN to explore these manifold mystical outcomes, discovering previously unimagined complexities and open-ended developmental potential in the exquisitely chaotic workings of the human brain-mind system.[81]

These reflections are also pertinent to another branch of cognitive neuroscience research, namely, near-death experiences. We have already noted that Augustine's teaching on the *visio Dei* required not only a turn inward and the gradual silencing of all images but also a distinct physiological condition, that of virtual death. While Moody's initial attempt to establish core characteristics of virtual death experiences has been challenged over the past three decades, giving rise to an ever-changing laundry list of what qualifies as a near-death experience, one constant has been the experience of a bright light, often interpreted as divine or emanating from a world beyond.[82] Thus, Augustine was not alone in juxtaposing divine light with an experience of virtual death, and there is now a substantial comparative literature corroborating the physiological condition of near death with mystic vision.[83] In this regard it is relevant, given Augustine's interpretative gloss on Saint Paul's heavenly journey, that Paul Badham (who is oblivious of Augustine's interpretation of the Pauline text) also sees 2 Corinthians 12 as indicative of someone who had a physiological condition of virtual death, and as such experienced something at least analogous to contemporary near-death experiences.[84]

But positioning the mystical experience within the framework of the virtual death experiences has not been a panacea. Not only do the purported characteristics of near-death experiences change constantly but numerous theories have been proffered to account for them. These theories range from physiological explanations, such as the effects of hypoxia or hypercarbia, katamine, and endorphins, to neuropsychological explanations that span the spectrum of that discipline: the role of states of depersonalization or derealization, limbic lobe stimulation, and dying-brain syndrome, as well as studies on the effect of virtual death on the visual cortex, nervous system functioning, and hallucinatory activity. The list quickly lengthens as religious studies, philosophy, sociology, literary studies, and history are thrown into the mix.[85]

It is not my intent here to provide an overview and critique of what is now a wide-ranging and multidisciplinary exploration of the nature of near-death experiences. Rather, a few summary points must suffice. First, the fact that Augustine insists that virtual death is a physiological prerequisite of intellectual vision, that the essence of the latter is the encounter with a divine light, and that empirical studies conclude without any reasonable doubt that a condition of virtual death has discernible brain-mind effects argues for the necessary inclusion of such studies in any consideration of the relation between psychology and Augustine. Second, while one school of research, paradigmatically illustrated by the work of Susan Blackmore, insists that near-death experiences can be wholly accounted for by naturalistic causes, one cannot, as Carol Zaleski notes, entirely rule out other causes, even religious ones. Indeed, the plethora of explanations and counterexplanations is by now so expansive and contested that it is reasonable to conclude, with Zaleski, that "the final outcome will be a draw."[86] Third, even for those who champion a religious perspective it is difficult to use the near-death experience literature to buttress the claims of perennialism. In this respect, anyone advocating a religious perspective is best advised to adopt a thoroughgoing constructivism. As Zaleski (echoing Bulkeley) puts it,

> We cannot simply peel away the literary wrapper and put our hands on an unembellished event. Even when a vision actually did occur, it is likely to have been reworked many times before being recorded. The vision is a collaborative effort . . . one cannot point to the moment when the vision changed from a matter of personal confession into a public project; rather, it is built up in layers placed over one another like a series of transparencies . . . even the hypothetical bottom layer—the visionary's own experience—has a collective aspect. . . . His very experience of the other world is shaped by expectations, both conscious and subliminal, that he shares with his peers, and he draws upon a common treasury of images from scripture, folklore or literary tradition, and religious art.[87]

In other words, a constructivist take on the near-death experience literature can hold that any claim to seeing a divine light, as with Augustine, is not necessarily indicative of a common core. At the same time, without denying the noumenal claim of a mystic like Augustine, such an approach, as a result of its decidedly Kantian stance vis-à-vis the noumenon, can simply bracket any notion of an *ontos* as both inaccessible to empirical confirmation and philosophically problematic.

The Developmental Infrastructure of Constructivism

The formulations offered so far go well beyond the reductive emphasis on the preoedipal nature of Augustine's visions that characterized so much of post-Freudian psychoanalytic theory, but they cannot corroborate the claims of Augustine's Christian mystical theology. The lines of argument I have offered are instead generic: how Eros might include a movement beyond self toward the divine, how there may exist buried potentialities in the self that are capable of that form of cognitive-empathic knowing valorized by mystics, and that there are commonalities between the mystical vision and cognitive neuroscience findings regarding the experience of virtual death. The specific manner in which mystics both within and between traditions may qualify such general formulations indicates that a dialogical tension must always hold between psychology and religious mysticism. All psychoanalysis can do is articulate reasonable ground for the possibility of such visions. Again, the stress on a constructivist Kantian epistemology renders the actuality of any *ontos* inaccessible (which is not to deny or, for that matter, establish its truth). Augustine, of course, went much further: his mystical teaching made specific ontological and theological claims. The matter before us now is how to make psychoanalytic sense of his explicit theological rendering of mystical ascents, knowing, and loving without blurring the line between psychoanalysis and theology.

The short answer lies in the Winnicottian notion of transitional objects, transitional experiences, and transitional modes of being. Simply and summarily put, transitional modes of experiencing are the psychoanalytical, developmental infrastructure of constructivism and, consequently, of Augustine's mystical theology. This initial formulation is in need of further exploration and elaboration. In preparation for the latter, it is important to note the distinction, upheld throughout this study, between episodic vision and mystical process. Without this distinction and its illustration with respect to Augustine, no accounting of his mystical theology is complete. In the task that now lies in front of us, then, we need to bring together mysticism as episodic and as process with constructivism and transitional modes of being.

four
THERAPEIA

In exploring how the academic term *mysticism* can be profitably utilized to probe the history of Christian mysticism, Bernard McGinn is adamant that its interpretation and meaning cannot be divorced from the total matrix of Christian ideation, practice, and accoutrements. Moreover, McGinn is careful to distinguish between mysticism rendered in terms of an episodic experience and what he refers to as "a process or a way of life."[1] Although a distinction can be drawn between mysticism as experience and mysticism as process, McGinn holds that ultimately, the two are inseparable:

> Mysticism is always a process or a way of life. Although the essential note—or, better, goal—of mysticism may be conceived of as a particular kind of encounter between God and the human, between Infinite Spirit and the finite human spirit, everything that leads up to and prepares for this encounter, as well as all that flows from or is supposed to flow from it for the life of the individual in the belief community, is also mystical, even if in a secondary sense. Isolation of the goal from the process and the effect has led to much misunderstanding of the nature of mysticism and its role as an element of concrete religions.[2]

Reformulated in the nomenclature of modern depth psychology and applied more narrowly to the spiritual growth of the individual, the notion of mysticism as process evokes the general term *development.* Mysticism conceived of as a process shifts the emphasis from the mystical experience per se to mystical transformations of character, set in the broader context of a religious life. Without diminishing the importance of singular epiphanies or deep meditative intuitions about the nature of self and reality, mysticism as process asks that the episodic be evaluated in relation to the cultivation of a specific set of dispositions, capacities, virtues, and lasting elevations of consciousness. This is crucial, for it is commonplace in the post-Jamesian psychological understanding of mysticism to confine its parameters to an episodic, ecstatic encounter with the divine.

It is possible to accept the general notion of process or development without universalizing or essentializing it. Indeed, mystical traditions, authors, and texts treat process elements in quite diverse ways. Thus, a process view of mysticism is implied in the Zen ox-herding pictures, in Sri Ramana Maharshi's distinction between *nirvikalpa samadhi* and *sahaja samadhi,* in the Sufi notions of stages and stations, and in Saint John's and Saint Teresa's language of "mansions" and "stages" (purgation, illumination, union). Saint Teresa's classic work, *The Interior Castle,* is particularly illuminating in this regard. On the one hand, it could be read as a book of guidance enumerating an impressive array of Christian mystical encounters: three different kinds of union (the episodic union of the fifth mansion, the union of wills, and the continuous presence of the Holy Trinity characteristic of the spiritual marriage of the seventh and final dwelling place); multiple forms of locutions; various forms of corporeal, imaginary, and intellectual visions; raptures; and associated phenomena. On the other hand, all these encounters may be understood as gaining their true meaning for Saint Teresa when operationalized to cultivate specifically Christian virtues, capacities, and dispositions. From this perspective, increasing one's capacity to love God and one's neighbor was Saint Teresa's true mystical aim.

Such an understanding is hardly absent from depth psychology, for the long transformative struggle of analysands in psychoanalytic therapy cannot be reduced to the episodic, to a singular insight or epiphany, even though such events unquestionably occur and often mark important moments in the course of a successful therapy. Moreover, different developmental trajectories in the psychoanalytic tradition evince different normative therapeutic aims and ideals. Thus, while Freud endeavored to create a social space for a humanistic "secular cure of souls" designed to heighten the ability to love and work (*lieben und arbeiten*), Erik Erikson's life-cycle theory formulated the ideal of "generative man," while Heinz Kohut valorized the figure of Dag Hammarskjöld and his unchurched form of spirituality. In Erikson's system, psychic development proceeds through a European series of stages, each with characteristic crises, and, when adequately resolved, increases a person's capacity for faith, hope, and love. For Kohut, the archaic structures of narcissism are transformed into humor, empathy, creativity, wisdom, and the ability to tolerate transience. Such different formulations provide grist for the anthropological view of psychoanalysis as an ethnopsychological system complete with religio-ethical horizons of meaning.[3]

With respect to the culture of modern spirituality, I have already suggested that Romain Rolland was the initial instigator of a move toward a mystical psychoanalysis that had as its goal the achievement of a statelike oceanic feeling. Rolland distinguished between his earlier transient mystical experiences in nature and the developmentally later statelike oceanic feeling. Initially serving to "render the veil," the former enjoined one to a lifelong ethical and existential struggle that could (although not necessarily did) culminate in the more permanent oceanic feeling. Rolland did say that his transient mystical experiences, these "brief and staggering contacts with the Unity," as he put it, "were the key to the spiritual world where I lived for the next forty years."[4] In his *Mémoires,* Rolland observes that his notes were full of such experiences during the 1880s. In one such note he recalls he "was possessed by Nature like a violated virgin. For a moment my soul left me to melt into the luminous mass of the Breithorn. . . . Yes, extravagant as it may sound, for some moments I *was* the Breithorn."[5] Rolland also described these experiences in terms that prefigured the account he gave to Freud: "The entire universe is one unique, immense sound from which burst, like a ripe pomegranate, billions of harmonics, all composing one same oceanic harmony."[6] Yet, as he put it in his poetic manner, any episodic experience is a "ray of sunlight" that, while capable of splitting asunder "the protective covering of the clouds," cannot "keep the fields bathed in light. . . . That is the work of a lifetime. No one accomplishes it in one attempt."[7] It was the "repeated blows and wounds of life" in accordance with the purposeful (teleological) nature of the "subconscious" that could, if one were attentive and persistent, lead to a more permanent transformation (the statelike oceanic feeling).

While Rolland insisted that transient mystical experiences had an implicit teleology, the desired outcome was far from certain. This was one reason why he was so interested in the research of the early psychologists of religion, including Freud, Jung, Morel, and James. The disjunction between episodic experience and a more permanent, transformative mystical consciousness required, Rolland thought, engagement with the unconscious. As he once put it, mystics of all stripes "did not wait for Dr. Freud to teach them that the best cure for the mind is to make it look its deeply hidden monsters straight in the face."[8]

Therapy, Therapeia

Our discussion in the previous chapter concluded that one cannot assume a common core (i.e., the doctrine of perennialism) with regard to episodic mystical experience. Similarly, our discussion in this chapter has indicated that it would be equally fallacious to assume, with respect to the wider definition of mysticism seen during the course of a life, what could be called a process perennialism. Here, as with mystical experience, it behooves us to do the hard work of reconstructing and contextualizing the text of the mystic in question, in this case Saint Augustine. Unlike Saint Teresa, Saint John, and many other mystics, Augustine never formulated a stage approach or a systematic progression of the process of development. Nevertheless, we can try to tease out such a pattern, one that intersects, at least to some extent, with what modern psychology calls therapy.

In fashioning his therapeutic system Augustine was dependent on the Christian nomenclature and concepts of his era. Thus, at the foundation of his project was the assumption that humans are fallen creatures mired in original sin. The complexity and depth of this psychic and ontological reality were worked through over and over again in the *Confessions,* animating episodes from the jealous infant of book 1 to the inability to sustain vision apparent in books 7–9 and the search through *memoria* of book 10. At the same time, because humans were created in the image of God, there was an optimistic counterpoint: humans are capable of responding to God's love in terms of faith—faith that, once kindled, could lead to ascent, vision, and transformation.

The problem for Augustine was the inability of humans to sustain vision. In early works like *De quantitate animae* (*The Greatness of the Soul*), Augustine was optimistic in thinking that the sustained enjoyment of the eternal was in principle possible. However, he quickly tempered that optimism, for the thrust of the *Confessions* is precisely to deny the permanence of vision. In this Augustine was like Freud, who initially thought cures were possible, only to conclude later that analysis was "interminable." The observation of the weight of sin, of falling from the light of vision into the Platonic "region of unlikeness"; his divided will; the power of sexuality and the opaqueness of desire: all these spoke to the fallen nature of human beings and the need for a Therapist beyond our control. To be sure, Augustine's life was marked by occasional echoes of the inward and upward ascent that betokened what the life beyond might hold. Thus in 10.40 he remarks as follows:

> When have you not walked with me, O Truth . . . With my outward senses I surveyed, to the best of my ability, the world. . . . From these I entered into the recesses of my memory. . . . And I heard you teaching me and commanding me. . . . And sometimes working within me you open for me a door into a state of feeling which is quite unlike anything to which I am used—a kind of sweet delight which, if I could only remain permanently in that state, would be something not of this world, not of this life. But my sad weight makes me fall back again; I am swallowed up by normality; I am held fast and heavily do I weep, but heavily am I held. So much are we weighed down by the burden of custom!

These echoes are of interest because they indicate that vision gave rise not to a single but to a repeated ("sometimes") elevation of consciousness, a heightened inner dispositional sensibility characterized as "a state of feeling . . . a kind of sweet delight" that was "not of this world." But again, Augustine remarks that it is the fallen nature of humans that prohibits the permanence of such a state. It is because Augustine came to see mystical experiences and their echoes as intermittent and the Neoplatonic aim of continuous vision as presumptuous, arrogant, and unattainable that he shifted the emphasis of the mystical life from striving for an episodic encounter with divinity to striving for a process, and reforming the *imago Dei.* In other words, whatever one makes of the philosophically problematic insight Augustine achieved in his visions, the multiple effects they had on his awareness of his inner world and the need for transformation seem undeniable.

We have come, then, to Augustine's *therapeia:* a mode of healing that is understood as lifelong, that assumes original sin (fallenness) and the *imago Dei* within, in which vision informs the ultimate aim, and which is understood religiously as a soteriology. Margaret Miles writes about the difference between modern therapy and ancient therapeia in the following:

> The *Confessions* was catharsis for Augustine both in the sense of recall, reevaluation, and reinterpretation of old personal dramas—"past history

as present meaning"—and in the sense of catharsis as "the vision of completion, the experience of unification and . . . transformation. . . ." [But] Augustine does not simply construct a "case-history"; the *Confessions* is primarily therapy in the Platonic sense of a methodical conversion from a "misidentification of reality," to recognition of the reality, the patterns of behavior, that has been implicit but unidentified within one's most intimate and pressing experience . . . the *Confessions* is therapy in the modern sense of retracing of events . . . but it is *therapeia* in the ancient sense when Augustine gives this story of his life a cosmic setting and significance. The task of Platonic therapy is the construction of an articulated orientation to a final, authoritative, and implicit reality. It is only in the light of this reality . . . that he can see himself accurately.[9]

But we can be more specific about the nature of this "articulated orientation to a final, authoritative, and implicit reality"—that sacred canopy and model of and for reality, as the anthropologist Clifford Geertz would have it—in which Augustine came to understand his life. Kenney speaks to this point when he notes that a discernible "spiritual architecture" informs Augustine's contemplative practice:

> The idea of an infinite, eternal, and immutable first principle is at the core of the depiction of contemplation in the *Confessions*. This is the still center from which the whole of reality emerges through creation and to which it seeks to return.[10]

> God, while remaining in himself, also engages in an outflow, first to create the world, second to know and appreciate it, and finally to save souls fallen from their proper state. Contemplation is the sight of God directed outside himself in creation and then back upon himself through contemplation. God's contemplative presence is the active force holding reality in existence, and the Christian soul can come to connect up with that divine intellection.[11]

It is this understanding of self and cosmos that is reflected in the ascent at Ostia. As the constructivist position would have it, vision is linked to this overarching contemplative scheme. At the same time, while vision reveals a glimpse and foretaste of the life to come, it also informs the this-worldly aims and means that make up the linked elements of therapeia. With regard to the latter, several interrelated characteristics need emphasizing. First, because the Christian spiritual architecture advocated by Augustine recognized the energetic inflow back to God and also the inability of human beings to both attain and sustain vision, it proclaimed the need to ride, as it were, the power made available through the Word. It is Christ who allows us to restore the image tarnished through Adam's sin. Moreover, insofar as Christ was seen as the head of the church, understood as a collective body and "living soul," the indwelling spirit catalyzed through Christ was effected through membership, through baptism and Christian practices. The process of deification, completed only in the afterlife, starts collectively with others in that shared communal bond that is the Body of Christ. Vision is episodic, and embracing Christ is the path to that inner transformation that accords with vision.

Second, this inner transformation necessarily requires the practice of confession. As Kenney notes,

> Contemplation is effective only when it is conjoined to confession. Only then does the soul contact God and grasp the true nature of its present condition. . . . For confession is a distinctively Christian practice—admission of the fallen and culpable state of the soul, recognition of the reality of God's presence, and finally, submission to the saving power of Christ. Contemplation serves to prepare for this practice. . . . But contemplation is only completed by confession. Contemplation without confession is futile and empty.[12]

Moreover, contemplation and confession are guided by the wisdom contained in scripture, understood as the authoritative voice on the human condition and its hope for salvation. Indeed, confession for Augustine is an essentially scriptural practice, a practice reflected in the scope of his citations: from the oft-cited Romans 1:20 ("from the invisible things of him from the creation of the world are clearly seen, being understood by the things that are made"), which serves as the basis for the turn inward and ascent upward, to the multiple citations from Genesis and Exodus through the Psalms and gospels. Inner work is guided by reflection on the truths contained in scripture—an act that displaces the Platonic reliance on mere dialectic. It is important that for Augustine, the practice of confession could not be successfully implemented without the search through memory. As Louth observes, memory for Augustine "means the whole mind, both conscious and unconscious."[13] It is through this prayerful, meditative descent into the depths of memory that one finds one is more than simply a being determined by the material order. One is intrinsically spiritual, and while God is the creator of the mind and thus not in or contained by *memoria,* he nevertheless "deigns to dwell" in it through love.[14] Faith is the response to that love, felt as an initial longing for something more and then later, at least in principle, actualized in terms of ascent and vision and integrated through confession.

Third, the search through memory aided by the wisdom of scripture led Augustine to understand that the *imago Dei* within was triune in nature. As was fully explored in his later *De trinitate,* it is through knowing, willing, and remembering relative to the divine light and the truths of scripture that we ascend. So it is that Kenney notes,

> Augustine discerns a trinitarian dimension to contemplation. . . . The contemplative soul . . . is inhabited by the Spirit and knows "the things of God" only through the Spirit. Renewed in its mind, the Christian soul has an ability to understand and "judge" created things, since such a "spiritual person" begins to grasp "the Trinity in Unity and the Unity of the Trinity." Even aspects of human psychology are indicative of the inner life of God. Being, knowing, and willing are functional analogues of the trinitarian life of the Godhead. . . . It is this divine contemplative motion, out into creation and back through the "things of God," that establishes the great rhythm of creation. It is this majestic spiritual movement that spiritual persons discover in contemplation.[15]

Interestingly enough, along the lines I have proposed, McGinn refers to this process as a spiritual therapy: "the supreme mystery of the Christian faith is a spiritual therapy designed to help restore the image of God in us so that we can more fully share in the experience of the divine presence in this life."[16]

Finally, the aim of Augustine's mystical process was similarly informed by vision. Eugene TeSelle speaks to this point when he notes that ecstatic vision, often seen as the aim of the mystical path, is neither foreign nor undesired in Augustine's mysticism. However, because it is episodic and, in Augustine's mystical theology, points beyond itself to the more continuous presence of God found only after death, the nature of life must necessarily seek a particular regimen—a task TeSelle refers to as a "journey of the affections":

> The ecstatic vision, which plays such an important role in much mystical literature as the principal goal that is sought . . . is important to Augustine as well; but it is not the central issue. To him neither the reality of God nor the ability of the mind to apprehend God was seriously in question: the Light is always there, and one always has the mental eyes with which to see. The central problem is rather that the eyes of the mind must be purified by the right affections. To him the beatitude, "Blessed are the pure in

heart, for they shall see God" (Matthew 5:8) is not only a promise of *what* can occur, but prescription of *how* it must occur if it is to occur at all.[17]

The ideal aim of this process of reformation, as TeSelle's psychologically informed analysis concludes, constituted something akin to an angelic form of being:

> The ideal kind of personality development, for Augustine, is not that seen in human life, which is fallen but has possibilities for repentance . . . but that of the faithful angels, who freely respond to the divine light and love, are given certitude about remaining in unity with God, and who as a result constitute the "city of God," God's true dwelling place, which has been in the heavens from the first moments of creation and to which all faithful souls are in pilgrimage. They represent what finite spirit could and should be, an "ego ideal" which can be imagined and hoped for.[18]

In this process of reformation Augustine cited Matthew 5:8 ("Blessed are the pure of heart, for they shall see God") to emphasize the need for moral purification, the destruction of the vices, and self-discipline. For Augustine, God is always present but hidden by the inability of the soul to act lovingly in word and deed. Vision is perfect when there is perfect likeness of the *imago Dei* to God, and this happens when the soul is reformed in and through love. It is carnal habit (earthly attachment) that must eventually be extinguished. Indeed, for the modern psychological mind, it may be hard to stomach the extreme ascetic regime needed to realize such aims. For example, at the core of Augustine's therapeia was not only recognition of the depth of sexual desire but also its radical solution, celibacy. And while celibacy may have been rooted in the aim of freeing oneself from carnal habit, it was far from the only requirement. There were others that formed chains to worldly attachment: the allure of food and gluttony (10.31), the enticement of the senses (10.32), the lust for spectacle (10.35), the pitfalls of ambition, praise, and blame (10.37, 10.8, 10.17, 10.14, 10.25/27, 10.11), and even the power of misplaced curiosity (10.35).

Mystical Process, God Representations, and Constructivism

This brief introduction to Augustine's therapeia accomplishes the general aim of sketching the trajectory of Augustine's understanding of mystical process without exegetical violence or the unnecessary imposition of modern psychoanalytic categories. Moving forward, we can now add that Augustine's mystical process has been of interest to psychologists precisely because in his efforts to survey and reform his inner world he made observations that resonate with many similar ones as noted in the history of depth psychology. At the same time, there are some clear divergences, summed up in the linked yet different terms *therapy* and *therapeia*. As with Augustine's formulations of vision, we may ask how to make psychological sense of Augustine's attempt at using the cultural ideation, narratives, and practices of his era to fashion a rudimentary mystical soteriology. Any attempt to do so must bring together psychoanalysis, mystical experience, mystical process, mystical theology, and constructivism. I have also suggested that the overarching psychoanalytic conceptual framework holding these diverse projects together is erected on the concept of transitional modes of being and experiencing. In effect, the latter is the developmental infrastructure of Augustine's constructivist mystical theology.

The terms "transitional objects" and "transitional phenomena" originated in the work of the British psychoanalyst D. W. Winnicott.[19] Winnicott worked out such terms from his clinical observations of infants and children to explain what happens in their inner world during the developmental process of separation and individuation. The crucial observation for Winnicott lay in the emergence in the child's life of an object, such as a blanket or stuffed animal, to which the child developed an intense bond and from which it received nurturance. Such objects seemed to aid in the process of individuation and the mastery of the world "out there." Understandably, Winnicott suggested that transitional objects symbolized the absent mother, enabling the infant/child to receive sustenance and cohesion from a felt and remembered internal nurturing maternal presence. The latter, moreover, facilitated the child's developing the self-cohesion and confidence necessary to creatively master and integrate external reality. Such objects, even if not theorized as such, were familiar to the everyday person and even those in the world of literature and film: the little boy's relationship with the alien in the film *E.T.*, the tiger in the comic strip *Calvin and Hobbes* (a simple stuffed tiger when the parents are around but a living co-creator of a world of fantasy when alone with Calvin) and Linus's blanket in *Peanuts* are all cultural examples of the presence and power of transitional objects.

For Winnicott, the emerging mastery of the world, illuminated by the capacity to find and use transitional objects, is just the beginning. The ability to creatively master reality occurs throughout the life cycle. Initially illustrated by the child's finding and developing attachments to transitional objects, such capacities are expressed and developed in the play of school age, and later in the adult capacity for theorizing about the external world in the cultural arena of the arts, science, and religion.

Sociologically speaking, the transitional object points to an area of experience to which both inner psychological and outer cultural reality contribute: Hobbes, insofar as he is an object of play given to and not created by Calvin, is constituted by culture. Yet Calvin also creates Hobbes, breathing life into him and investing him with meaning in their joint efforts to playfully engage and master external reality. For Winnicott there exists an unchallenged third area of experiencing, both real and unreal, that undercuts Freud's simple opposition between inner and outer reality and their correlates, the pleasure and reality principles. Winnicott refers to this third area as the "substance of illusion"—an inner/outer space illuminated by transitional objects, play, the arts, religion, and science. Illusion, in this Winnicottian sense, is not so much delusion but the more accurate and necessary psychological rendering of man's being-in-the-world. Epistemologically, then, and moving away from Freud's firm marriage to a strict empiricism, Winnicott would say that we never get to the "*x*" that defines the "real" of external reality: we are forever moving toward it, and the task of "reality acceptance" is lifelong.[20] Michael Eigen notes that this is a new psychoanalytic view of what lies at the ground of personhood, individuation, and health when he states that "what is at stake in transitional experiencing is not mainly a self or an object (mother) substitute, but the creation of a symbol, of symbolizing experience itself."[21] The primary object of creative experiencing is not simply mother or father and various interpersonal relationships but more, "the unknowable ground of creativeness as such."[22] For Winnicott, the initial capacity to form transitional objects is also the first attempt at symbolizing: it denotes not only the child's first use of a symbol but also the capacity to symbolize. Winnicott's theory, then, is really a theory of the individuating imagination.

This would, of course, include the specifically religious imagination. No one has modified Winnicott's clinical formulations for application to the Judeo-Christian tradition better than Ana-Maria Rizzuto.[23] Contra Freud, Rizzuto thinks that belief "is an integral part of being human, truly human in our capacity to create nonvisible but meaningful realities capable of containing our potential for imaginative expansion beyond the boundaries of the senses."[24] Turning Freud on his head, Rizzuto thinks that all persons have at least a rudimentary form of what she calls a "God representation," and that this is so enmeshed with the individuation process that "to stop believing in God is to cease to be oneself."[25] People can repress their God representation, but they are then shut off from the adaptive benefits that it can provide throughout the life cycle.

Rizzuto conceptualizes her "God representation" as being transitional in nature: "God, psychologically speaking, is an illusory transitional object."[26] Indeed, it is a "special" transitional object, one formed not from "plushy fabrics" but from those "representational materials" that find their source in the primary objects of infancy and childhood. Moreover, the God representation is an overdetermined quilt and "work of art" influenced by culture at large, incorporating sexual and nonsexual elements, both preoedipal and oedipal elements, and representational as well as ideational components; and it is capable of evolving with the life cycle to the extent that it can escape developmental determinism. Because of the child's naturally inquisitive nature and the inescapable fact of socially extant religious ideation and narratives, Rizzuto posits that even a rudimentary God representation is mediated for the child through the parents, and beyond them, through the culture at large at an early age. Developmentally, this rudimentary conceptual framework becomes unavoidably imbued with relational and developmental depth. Clinical studies show that the God representation, differing from Freud's conceptualization, can be composed of both paternal and maternal elements and may reflect preoedipal as well as oedipal developmental configurations: the God representation is an "object-related representational process marked by the emotional configuration of the individual prevailing at the moment he forms the representation—at any developmental stage . . . from oral to oedipal."[27] Secondary-process thought also contributes to the formation of the God representation. Here Rizzuto distinguishes between the "concept of God" (the God of the theologians and philosophers, fabricated at the level of secondary-process thought, which follows the rules of philosophical inference, argumentation, and theorizing) and the "images of God" (which find their source in the developmental vicissitudes of the representational process of identification, internalization, and structural conflict). Finally, in adopting Erikson's notion of epigenesis, Rizzuto holds that the God representation is available for evolution, transformation, and use throughout the life cycle. Epigenesis means that the God representation need not be subject to the determinism of the archaic infantile past but can be reworked, refined, and transformed. Crucial to the latter is the integration of the conceptual aspects of the God representation with the deeper, developmentally and interpersonally based images of God. A dialectical process between the two is posited as taking place through significant experiences, idealized mentor figures who elicit transference (from a psychoanalyst to a pastor), and the individual psychical work of self-scrutiny and self-reflection. Through such auspices a process akin to the analytic session takes place, resulting in the integration and transformation of the conceptual and image-based aspects of the God representation:

> Integration of the conceptual component of the God representation and some of the images that contributed to it requires a persistent psychic work of soul searching, self-scrutiny, and internal reelaboration of the representation. This is analogous to what happens in the analytic process, where many of the sources that have provided elements for the formation of a particular representation or experience are reconsidered and divested of some of their real and imaginary danger or appeal. These considerations explain how many analyses that have not dealt with religious issues have, however, modified the God representation and religious beliefs.[28]

Conversion, then, is understood by Rizzuto to be the "ego-syntonic release from repression in a given individual of an earlier (or even present) parental representation linked to a God representation."[29] Moreover, Rizzuto thinks that a God representation, being a collage and a work of art to which multiple sources contribute, can express deep mystical insights as well: "The developmental process of forming a God representation is exceedingly complex and is influenced by a multitude of cultural, social, familiar, individual phenomena ranging from the deepest biological levels of human experience to the subtlest of spiritual realizations."[30]

Sudhir Kakar elaborates a specifically mystical dimension to the God representation. Speaking to the psychological terrain of the Indian inner world, he refers to a "cluster of ideas," the "heart" of which consists of the religious notions of *moksha, dharma,* and *karma.* The latter, thinks Kakar, provides "a coherent, consistent world image in which the goals of human existence, the way to reach this goal, the errors to be avoided, and the obstacles to be expected along the way" are offered to the individual.[31] When explicating how this world image is internalized and functions, Kakar becomes Winnicottian:

> Above and beyond the objective world of phenomena capable of validation which we term "real", and the individual distortions and denials of

> these phenomena which we are accustomed to calling "unreal", such world images (in any culture) constitute a third distinct category, both "real" and "unreal", a meta-reality which is neither deterministically universal nor utterly idiosyncratic but which fills the space between the two. It is culturally specific and harbored or accepted, often unconsciously, as the heart of a community identity. Like the evidence of the senses which more often than not goes unquestioned, the meta-reality of a culture is also rarely summoned for conscious examination; yet it exercises an influence on individual thought and behavior that is somewhat comparable to the working of the reality and pleasure principles.[32]

Kakar provides an important expansion of Rizzuto's views by offering a culturally sensitive, postmodern view of how an overtly mystical God representation can offer a valid, if different, kind of religious orientation. Given that the "goal" of Hindu thought is the Upanishadic notion of moksha, Kakar laments the strong tradition within psychoanalysis that tends to render it in pathological terms. The latter, for Kakar, reveals the implicit ethnopsychological value system and unfortunate colonialist tendencies of psychoanalysis. Indeed, Kakar thinks that the Hindu worldview, with its introspective discipline of yoga and aim of moksha, offers a vision of reality that is simply different from, if not in some sense more profound than, that offered by Freud. It is these varying "visions of reality," as he calls them, that he sees as responsible for the "mutual misunderstanding" between the two healing systems:

> The psychoanalytic vision of reality, for example, is primarily influenced by a mixture of the tragic and the ironic. It is tragic in so far as it sees human experience pervaded by the ambiguities, uncertainties and absurdities where man has little choice but to bear the burden of unanswerable questions, inescapable conflicts and incomprehensible afflictions of fate. Life in this vision is a linear movement in which the past cannot be undone, many wishes are fated to be unfulfilled and desires ungratified. Fittingly enough, Oedipuses, Hamlet and Lear are its heroes. The psychoanalytic vision is however also ironic in so far as it brings a self-deprecating and detached perspective to bear on the tragic: the momentous aspects of tragedy are negated and so many gods are discovered to have clay feet. It tends to foster a reflective adaptation and deliberative acceptance. The tragic vision and its ironic amelioration are aptly condensed in Freud's offer to the sufferer to exchange his unbearable neurotic misery for ordinary human unhappiness. On the other hand, the yogic (or more broadly

> the Hindu) vision of reality is a combination of the tragic and the romantic. Man is still buffeted by fate's vagaries and tragedy is still the warp and woof of life. But instead of ironic acceptance, the yogic vision offers a romantic quest. The new journey is a search and the seeker, if he withstands all the perils of the road, will be rewarded by exaltation beyond normal human experience. The heroes of this vision are not the Oedipuses and the Hamlets but the Nachiketas and the Meeras.
>
> These different visions of reality . . . combine both the objective and the subjective. Their aim is to impose a meaning on human experience and not the discovery of an absolute truth. Inevitably they set up ideals and goals of life which may converge in some respects yet diverge in others. To call such deviations "pathological" or "ignorant" is to confuse a vision of reality with *the* reality and thus to remain unaware of its relativity.[33]

Kakar's Winnicottian conceptual lens is generic and psychoanalytic enough to supplement Rizzuto's concept of an evolving God representation, and both can be tailored to provide a working theory to conceptualize anew Augustine's therapeia. In the following discussion I seek to unpack the changing, evolving nature of Augustine's God representation, including its image-based and conceptual facets, with an eye to understanding the impact of the visions at Milan and Ostia on his growing interest in his inner world and the articulation of his therapeia. What is offered, then, amounts to snapshots of the evolution of Augustine's God representation. The analysis proceeds by way of linked vignettes, starting with Augustine's boyhood (books 1–2) and moving on to his flirtation with Manichaeism (books 3–6) and the impact of his visions (books 7–10).[34]

Boyhood: "Limited Capacities" and a Disordered Soul

In his *Soliloquies,* Augustine remarks that what he seeks to know are two things: God and the soul. As far as the evolution of his God representation is concerned, these are inexorably allied. Put psychologically, his life stage and personal circumstances were determinative for both the state of his soul, his inner apprehension of it, and his subsequent conceptualization and knowledge of God. Indeed, in the *Confessions* Augustine all but tells us what such life circumstances were, the state of his soul and his knowledge of God linked to them, and why, in some instances, he finds his evolving understanding of the latter problematic.

Certainly Augustine's narrative of the determinative events and episodes of his infancy and youth are selective. More to the point, they are so because Augustine chose events that enabled him to rhetorically weave his particular life story with the more universal themes concerning the nature of the soul and the human condition found in scripture. Paramount among the latter is the doctrine of original sin, or human sin present at birth. This is the foundation of his concept of the soul: we are created and fallen creatures whose desires are misdirected and disordered. Thus Augustine's narratives of, among others, the infant nursing at the breast (1.7), the pear-stealing episode (2.4ff.), the bath episode (2.3), the machinations of theater (3.2), and the wanderings of Aeneas and the death of Dido (1.13) are all designed to show the state of such a disordered soul. Of course, the hopeful counterpoint is Augustine's equally firm stance that we are made in the image of God and that we possess the gifts of reason, memory, will, and the capacity for faith—all of which speak to the possibility of healing and reformation.

Nevertheless, it is in the rudimentary psychological soil of the disordered state of boyhood that Augustine first mentions his exposure to the doctrines of Christianity. Thus it is that Augustine reflects on his early entry into the faith in *Confessions* 1.9–11, as follows:

> While I was still a boy, then, I had heard of an eternal life promised us through the humility of our Lord God stooping to our pride. My mother had great hope in you, O God, and as soon as I came out of her womb I was marked with the sign of the Lord's cross and was salted with His salt. (1.11)
>
> We saw, God, how men prayed to you and, with our limited capacities, we formed an impression of you as of someone great, who was able, even when not present to our senses, to hear us and to help us. For when still a boy I began to call upon you. (1.9)

Here Augustine confirms the centrality of his mother and surrounding community in conveying the Christian faith to him, the fact that he himself prayed as a young boy, and, most important, his conceptualization of God as "someone great." The latter corresponds to what Rizzuto calls the "conceptual" dimension of Augustine's God representation. Owing to his culture, Augustine's God representation was predominantly paternal. Again, as befitting his life stage, the conceptual dimension of his God representation was hardly sophisticated in a psychological, philosophical, or theological sense. One might surmise that most believers add sophistication to this conceptual dimension of their God representation as they proceed in life—but such is not always the case. Indeed, in *Confessions* 12.27 Augustine would come to retrospectively critique such rudimentary conceptualizations of the divine in stark but not wholly unforgiving terms:

> Some people, for example, when they read or hear the words which we are discussing think of God as though He were a kind of man or else like some great force associated with an enormous mass, and they imagine that by some new and sudden decision He made heaven and earth outside Himself. . . . And there are other such notions too, all due to the fact that some people are used to thinking in material terms . . . such people are still feeble little creatures. . . .

The key words here are "material" (in the above quotation) and "limited capacities" (in the previous quotation from *Confessions* 1.9). Time and again in multiple books of the *Confessions* Augustine remarks on how material conceptions of God are but figments of the imagination; how God, "corporeally conceived," renders belief "empty" and incapable of transformation (see 4.2–16 passim). Psychoanalytically conceived, the notion of materiality is, of course, that of projection: we are merely making God in our own image. And, as with Freud, this means that such a rudimentary paternal concept of God carries with it developmental baggage: we are projecting unresolved and conflicted psychic content onto a culturally valorized sacred worldview. Certainly Augustine, like Freud, understood that such rudimentary conceptualizations of the divine, if left there, carried with them a certain ethical and existential risk. Such corporeal conceptualizations of the divine were synonymous with a lack of spiritual depth and incapable of offering personal transformation. In other words, linked to his critique of this rudimentary conceptual dimension of the divine was a moral one. So it is that he notes how, as a boy, his prayers to God were more in the form of wish fulfillment—a form that did not entail self-transformation and which he describes as "foolishness" (1.9). One can, then, surmise that Augustine's later evaluation of his boyhood faith was that it too was disordered, even if it had the potential, through God's grace, of becoming less so through the vicissitudes of life and reflection. In this vein, those who are sympathetic to theology could find, and indeed have found, room for dialogue with psychoanalysis, which has its own version of the disordered soul. As has been mentioned, many extant psychoanalytic studies, which typically focus on narratives such as the impact of the *Aeneid* on the young Augustine, the theft of the pears, the bath episode, the beatings at school, and so on, are liable to see in these early books the beginning of the oedipal and preoedipal themes that exercised a discernible effect on Augustine. One can hardly disregard such insights or what they have to say about the nature of a God representation that is determined by, in some cases, wholly developmental forces. While this task is not undertaken here, I will later qualify how such studies can be integrated into the development of Augustine's God representation.

Adolescence: Moratorium, Dualism, and the Problem of Evil

Augustine tells us that books 3–6 spanned a nine-year period of his life, from age nineteen to twenty-eight—one that psychologists would refer to as late adolescence to early adulthood. Among other things Augustine relates are several life changes that, while not unexpected, are surely of significance. In book 3.4, for example, he mentions that his father died when he was seventeen—a fact likely to have had a strong impact. And, like many young men of his era, Augustine became attached to a concubine. Indeed, Augustine's rhetorically elegant description of the physical and emotional upheaval of puberty and adolescence in *Confessions* 3.1 has proved to be timeless: "I loved the idea of love. . . . Being in love with love I looked for something to love; I hated security and a path without snares. . . . I was fettered happily in bonds of misery so that I might be beaten with . . . the rods of jealousy and suspicions, and fears and angers and quarrels."

Alongside these important changes in family cohesion and sexual development was the establishment of a career trajectory. During these years Augustine toiled, first as student and then as teacher, in the rhetorical arts. Following Erikson, we could think of the academic years as a sort of a moratorium, providing a liminal social space that, much as a modern university might, gave the young Aurelius the time, leeway, and sufficient diversity of ideas to experiment and form a sense of identity and purpose. This training had an impact on another important area of his life, religion. We know that, with respect to his boyhood Christianity, his reading in humanistic and philosophical literature led to what can aptly be described as a de-idealization: "I therefore decided to give my attention to the study of the Holy Scriptures and to see what they were like. . . . They seemed to me unworthy of comparison with the grand style of Cicero" (3.5). And so it was, he goes on to say, that he fell in with the Manichaeans and became a "Hearer." Augustine tells us that what attracted him was their erudition, embodied in the figure of their wise bishop Faustus (a man he came to idealize as a true sage) and the intellectual power of their belief system. In particular, Augustine had been vexed, in a seemingly obsessive manner, by the problem of evil. And, as Brown notes, the "Manichean answer to the problem of evil is the core of the Manichaeism of the young Augustine."[35]

Augustine's retrospective critiques of his interest in the doctrines of the Manichaeans are very much in line with those he leveled at his boyhood conceptualization of the divine. He stresses that the dualism offered by the Manichaeans led him to make the continued mistake of materiality, for "God" and evil" became but "substances," and hence nothing more than projected figments of his imagination:

> When I wanted to think of my God, I did not know how to think of him except as a mass of bodies, for it seemed to me that what was not this was nothing. . . . Because of this I believed that evil was also some such a kind of substance, with its own foul and hideous bulk. . . . I came to the conclusion that there were two masses in opposition to each other, both infinite, but the evil one more contracted and the good one more expansive. (5.10)

> I did not know how to think except in terms of a kind of corporeal splendor. (4.2)

> I did not yet know that evil is nothing but a privation of the good . . . and how could I see this, when my eyesight could reach no further than bodies and the sight of my mind no further than a fantasy? I did not know that God is a spirit and not one with parts extended in length and breadth, nor one of whose being can be used such words as "size", "weight", "bulk." For every thing of that kind must have parts which are less than the whole, and even if it is infinite there will be less of it in a part defined by a fixed space than in its total infinitude, and so it cannot be wholly everywhere, as Spirit is, as God is. (3.7)

To this critique of the "conceptual" aspect of his adolescent God representation Augustine levels an existential, moral, and spiritual one. Specifically, such a conception was incapable of helping him in the required task of introspection and inner transformation. So it is he states in book 5.10:

> I was still of the opinion that it is not we ourselves who sin, but some other nature which is in us; it gratified my pride to think that I was blameless and, if I did something wrong, not to confess that I had done it, so that you might heal my soul, because my soul had sinned against you. Instead, I liked to excuse myself and accuse something else—something that was in me, but was not really I.

In trying to put together life stage, life circumstance, and the change of Augustine's God representation, psychoanalysis can help, for it would be easy to insert a developmental infrastructure that fits neatly with Augustine's own narrative. While anthropologists warn us that the life stage we call adolescence is not universal and, where present, is culturally variable, being next to nonexistent in some societies and certainly not as significant or as long as it is in our own, we would be justified in claiming that the hallmarks of adolescence, exacerbated by the absence of a father and the presence of an overweening mother, are found in Augustine: the struggle with sexuality, the need to form a personal and career identity, the existential grappling with the foundational questions of life. In this regard certain features of the text stand out. First, the idealization of and long wait for Faustus indicates the need, in object-relations terms, for a paternal, idealized cultural self-object capable of providing protection, nourishment, and guidance. Surely Augustine's reference to his father's death seems not only odd (being in parentheses) but oddly out of place (being in a passage referencing his first love of philosophy and desire to "fly back to God"). As Augustine puts it in book 3.4, reading philosophical texts

> altered my way of feeling, turned my prayers to you, Lord, yourself, and gave me different ambitions and desires. Every vain hope suddenly became worthless to me; my spirit was filled with an extraordinary and burning desire for the immortality of wisdom, and now I began to rise, so that I might return to you. I was in my nineteenth year (my father having died two years previously). . . . I was on fire then, My God, I was on fire to leave earthly things behind and fly back to you.

The seemingly odd parenthetical reference to his father makes sense when understood as part of a belated feeling of loss—a tone that marks the entire passage. Yet one does not need such interpretative evidence to surmise that the adolescent Augustine would have desired appropriate, culturally valorized paternal self-objects to guide and direct him in the throes of personal turmoil. A dualistic worldview that assuaged his obsession with evil would be attractive for similar reasons. Brown notes that "the need to save an untarnished oasis of perfection within himself formed, perhaps, the deepest strain of his adherence to the Manichees."[36] Psychoanalysis would supplement Augustine's ostensible conscious reason, the need to fashion a theodicy, as his sole motive by pointing to the role of unconscious forces. On the one hand, the tragic death of his father and the loss felt as a result was the real reason, however downplayed in the text, for his sudden interest in theodicy. On the other, Augustine's retrospective insight into how the Manichaean worldview enabled him to evade responsibility for sin is psychoanalytically understood as the need to repress the stage-appropriate emergence of strong, conflicted unconscious desires and tendencies—feelings undoubtedly exacerbated by the loss of a father who, with respect to oedipal and preoedipal issues, both constrained and guided. Indeed, it is noteworthy that Augustine's description in book 4.15 of the "evil" substance is an exact equivalent of the instinctual core of the unconscious: "I called the other a Dyad—anger as in deeds of violence, and lust as in sins of impurity." For Freud, the devil, through psychic splitting, is but the projected personification of repressed, unwanted unconscious instincts.[37] Augustine, in the throes of adolescence, had found the perfect myth, as well as an idealized paternal figure, for dealing with his unconscious and need for cohesion.

This is, of course, only a general framework—one that stresses the adaptive benefits of his Manichaean phase. Many other extant psychoanalytic studies have targeted more specific narratives of books 3–6 (such as the death of his friend, Monica and the dream of the ruler, the nature of his relation with the nameless concubine, etc.) with great insight, if at times more reductive and pejorative conclusions. These studies have their place and, as will be elaborated more fully later, can be made to fit into the Rizzutonian conception of an evolving belief system. At this juncture it is sufficient to note that books 3–6 show a dramatic change in both the image-based and conceptual components of Augustine's God representation. The latter can be described as resulting from several related factors: a change in life stage, the de-idealization of Augustine's boyhood Christianity, a growing intellectual sophistication, an enabling social space/liminal moratorium, the accessibility of cultural self-objects, an obsession with the need to defend against strong instinctual forces, and the need to fashion a working identity. Further, despite his retrospective critiques, such changes seemed to be enabling: they allowed him to navigate the vicissitudes and exigencies of a significant period of his youth until he was ready, as Augustine himself says, to search within.

In and Up: The Transcendent, Incorporeal Light

Augustine's tone shifts markedly when, in books 7–10, he engages Neoplatonism and returns to Christianity. It is this phase we looked at most closely in the preceding chapters. One significant result of the vision at Milan is that Augustine states how he came to know the "real God" for the first time (7.17). In other words, he now knew what it was to be properly "ordered" toward God. As a result, the conceptual component of his God representation shifted in a dramatic way. God was now conceived of as incorporeal, immutable, and transcending the ability of the material senses and imagination to conceptualize. This God Augustine would present as a paradox: "everywhere you are present in your entirety, and no single thing can contain you in your entirety" (1.3). Moreover, God was now "deeper than the deepest recesses of my heart" and above the summit of the soul (3.6). It was this inward and upward God he contrasted with the "empty," "phantasm" God of the "senses," of his earlier Manichaean period and the rudimentary concept of God he held with the "limited capacities" of boyhood. As we have seen, Augustine came to the conclusion that in rare cases of states of altered consciousness involving a virtual death (as with Moses and Saint Paul), one might glimpse the Light itself. In other words, it is here that our considerations in the previous chapters concerning Augustine's teaching on visions, or what we in the modern world call his episodic mystical experiences, should be inserted into the discussion.

The existential impact of these encounters was dramatic. Being unable to sustain vision, Augustine was torn away from the Light and plunged back into the Platonic "region of unlikeness." He was dragged down from the heights by his "weight," by which he meant all attachments to the sensory world and the desires that accrue as a result, in effect relegating the goal of the pilgrim to a this-worldly soteriological regimen. It is here, then, that we need to insert his ruminations on therapeia, or his mystical process. The realization of God as transcendent and immaterial, as not identified with the soul but the creator of it, was linked to the notion of evil not as material substance but as privation of the good—a notion directly relevant to the task of inner transformation. In contrast to his stay with the Manichaeans, Augustine was now forced to take responsibility for his own sins. So it is that he states: "And I asked 'What is wickedness?' and found that it is not a substance but a perversity of the will turning away from you, God" (7.16).

Earlier I noted the essential characteristics of this therapeia. To this can now be added, with respect to his evolving God representation, that its ultimate trajectory accords well with what Kakar refers to as a "tragic-romantic" vision of reality, its mystical base, and its attendant normative view of health and maturity. Augustine now aimed at the light of vision and TeSelle's "ego ideal" of angelic purity. What is of further import is how the introspective insights detailed by Augustine intersect with the map of the inner world offered by modern depth psychology. While it would be redundant to simply regurgitate what previous studies have already detected, it is a useful exercise to revisit the more pertinent observations in the context of how an evolving, mystically based God representation can illuminate the psychological dynamics of his efforts to create a healing system.

For example, both Augustine and psychoanalysis agree on the value of the talking cure. One seminal text with regard to the practice of confession is book 10.2, where Augustine says that before God, "the very depths of man's conscience are exposed, and there is nothing in me that I could keep secret from you, even if I did not want to confess it. I should not be hiding myself from you, but you from myself. . . . Whatever I am, then, Lord, is open and evident to you." This notion of God as the "innermost physician," as Capps has pointed out, reverses the meaning of the Garden of Eden story. Adam sought to conceal his shame from God; Augustine realizes that only through self-disclosure can one come closer to God.[38] In book 10.2 Augustine says that when he confesses, he does so "with the words of the soul and the crying out of my thought . . . [and] a clamor of feeling"—which can be taken as meaning that for Augustine, confession is not simply an intellectual exercise but one that involves elements of openness, inwardness, will, and catharsis. For Augustine, one becomes oneself by confessing: "For to hear from you about themselves is simply to know themselves" (10.3). This confessing involves not simply a recognition of one's past but an active catharsis of it and recognition of its determinative power. Thus the first nine books of the *Confessions* are retrospective and show Augustine tracing his past sins in a manner reminiscent of psychoanalytic therapy: the past determines present action. Augustine knew that people differed from one another in that the sum total of their past actions resulted in different habits: Alypius is celibate because of a bad experience with women (9.8); Monica would have been a drunk had it not been for an act of grace mediated through a servant (6.12).[39]

To take this further, "confessing" was a practice linked to the search through *memoria*. Like depth psychology, Augustine came to understand that the vast inner world is more than that which is available to the conscious mind. Without doing exegetical violence to the text, it would not be too much of a creative misreading to note, for example, the relation between Augustine's *memoria* and the psychoanalytic notion of the unconscious in passages like those of book 10.8 and 10.14:

> How great, my God, is this force of memory, how exceedingly great! It is like a vast and boundless subterranean shrine. Who has ever reached the bottom of it? Yet this is a faculty of my mind and belongs to my nature; nor can I myself grasp all that I am. Therefore, the mind is not large enough to contain itself. But where can that uncontained part of it be? Is it outside itself and not inside? In that case, how can it fail to contain itself? At this thought great wonder comes over me; I am struck dumb with astonishment. (10.8)

> This same memory also contains the feelings of my mind. It does not contain them in the same way as the mind itself has them when it is experiencing them, but in a very different way, appropriate to the nature of memory . . . the memory must be, as it were, the stomach of the mind. (10.14)

Certainly the depiction of *memoria* as a "vast subterranean shrine" is of great interest to the psychoanalyst, especially when it contains elements that act in relation to the conscious mind as a stomach. So too are Augustine's reflections on the darkness and opaqueness of that stomach—reflections that suggest the conflict and the power of repression:

> I may be deceiving myself. For here too there is a sad kind of darkness, the darkness in which the abilities that are in me are hidden from me, so that when the mind questions itself about its own powers, it cannot be certain that its replies are trustworthy, because what is inside the mind is mostly hidden and remains hidden until revealed by experience, and in this life, which is described as a continuous trial, no one ought to feel sure that, just as he has been worse and become better, he may not also, after having been better, become worse. (10.32)

Again, one cannot help but notice Augustine's recognition of the power of sexuality vis-à-vis reason. Augustine may well have thought that the move to chastity would cure him of his sexual desires. He soon learned otherwise. It is psychoanalytically meaningful that he uses the example of a dream to illustrate the depth of sexual habit:

> Certainly you command me to restrain myself from the lust of the flesh, the *lust of the eyes, and the ambition of the world.* You commanded me to abstain from sleeping with a mistress, and with regard to marriage you advised me to take a better course than the one that was permitted me. And since you gave me the power, it was done, even before I became a dispenser

> of your Sacrament. But there still live in that memory of mine, of which I have spoken so much, images of the things which my habit has fixed there. These images come into my thoughts, and, though when I am awake they are strength-less, in sleep they not only cause pleasure but go so far as to obtain assent and something very like reality. These images, though real, have such an effect on my soul, in my flesh, that false visions in my sleep obtain from me what true visions cannot when I am awake. Surely, Lord my God, I am myself when I am asleep? And yet there is a very great difference between myself and myself in that moment of time when I pass from being awake to being asleep or come back again from sleep to wakefulness. Where then is my reason which, when I am awake, resists such suggestions and remains unshaken if the realities themselves were presented to it? Do reason's eyes close with the eyes of the body? Does reason go to sleep when the bodily senses sleep? (10.30)

It is telling that Kenney, without acknowledging the psychoanalytic subtext that these ruminations convey, has this to offer with respect to the above passage:

> While Augustine distinguishes between the moral condition of the conscious and the sleeping self, he is nonetheless puzzled by the continued functioning of reason within the sleeper's mind along with the degree of consent and culpability involved. The impression conveyed is of a soul not yet purified of sexual desire and in need of divine grace to cure the "sickness of the soul." What distinguishes this text of Augustine is both the self-report of his condition and the palpable sense that there are opaque elements of the self that evade the power of reason. The self's conviction and conversion ride on the surface of deeper, unresolved energies. . . . Even after the most profound moment of contact with divine Wisdom, nothing seems to have changed in the depth of the soul.[40]

The focus on sexuality is linked to the most famous of Augustine's teachings, that of the divided self. Again, while Augustine expressly notes that it was his "personal experience" that led him to interpret Romans 7 in terms of inward conflict (however much exegetical violence, as noted in the previous chapter, that may have done to Paul's formulation), his final "working through" of this teaching may also be attributed to reflection and cultural-theological forces. Regardless, one cannot help but see his appreciation of Freudian ambivalence. Augustine realized that inner psychical space is defined with respect to a geometry of conflict:

> From a perverse will came lust, and slavery to lust became a habit, and the habit, being constantly yielded to, became a necessity. These were like links, hanging each to each (which is why I called it a chain), and they held me fast in a hard slavery. And the new will which I was beginning to have and which urged me to worship you in freedom and to enjoy you, God, the only certain joy, was not yet strong enough to overpower the old will which by its oldness had grown hard in me. So my two wills, one old, one new, one carnal, one spiritual, were in conflict, and they wasted my soul by their discord. (8.5)

Certainly the stomach of *memoria* and the opaque darkness of the mind, the acknowledged strength and depth of sexuality and desire, the divided will and the power of dreams, the inability of reason to will one's way out of the fallen state, and the need for healing and confession all have resonances in psychoanalytic thought. It shows that whatever else one may think of Augustine's turn inward, it is hard to contest that it was a bold attempt at mapping the inner world: an original, if ancient, mode of coming to grips with the power of desire, relationships with significant others, and the unconscious itself. Indeed, it is precisely Augustine's candid admission that he suffered from what TeSelle calls "unresolved conflicts" that justifies psychoanalytic interest in and theorizing about Augustine.

It is of further interest to discern what factors may be at least partially responsible for Augustine's newfound interest in and ability to traverse the depths of his inner world. Drawing on the salient features that can help transform the God representation as articulated previously, one can point to the interrelated interaction of a few pivotal factors: the availability of transference figures (such as Ambrose or Simplicianus) and idealized cultural self-objects (Saint Anthony), the integration of significant writings and texts (the books of the Platonists, Saint Paul), pivotal conversion and mystical experiences, and a long period of intense inner reflection and "soul-searching."

It is important to note here that Augustine's meeting with new figures and texts was occasioned by the de-idealization of Faustus and of the Manichaean worldview. One can envision a slow process of growing into young adulthood in which enough self-cohesion was built so that when finally confronted with the idealized Faustus, after years of waiting, Augustine was able to face up to the disillusionment engendered by the failure of Faustus to live up to his expected ideal. Manichaeism had done its job, and Augustine was now ready to move on. Ambrose filled the void left by Faustus. Augustine portrays Ambrose in idealized terms as "exceptionally learned," "honored by people of importance," and, most important, commanding the respect and devotion of Monica (6.1–3). Further, intimating that a form of transference occurred, Augustine goes on to say, "That man of God welcomed me as a father. . . . I began to love him at first not as a teacher of the truth . . . but simply as a man who was kind and generous to me" (5.13). Ambrose served as a kind of fatherly sponsor for rekindling Augustine's interest in Christianity, not a Christianity as understood by a Manichaean but one imbued with philosophical sophistication. It is significant that Ambrose, among others, used Neoplatonic ideas in his sermons. As Brown notes, "it is possible to trace literal borrowings from Plotinus in the bishop's sermons."[41] This suggests that the impact of texts ("the books of the Platonists" and the writings of Saint Paul) were heightened precisely because they were mediated by idealized significant others. Augustine's enormous capacity for inner reflection added to this mix. Brown writes, "as with many immensely fertile thinkers, it is difficult to imagine Augustine as a reader. Yet, what happened at this crucial time, and in the years that follow, was a spell of long and patient reading, apparently aided by some discussions."[42] Such ideas were, as is evident, "thoroughly absorbed, 'digested' and transformed by Augustine."[43]

The therapeutic leverage mediated through the figure of Ambrose and others, alongside the transformative effect of ideas, pivotal visions, and "soul searching," engaged not only the conceptual dimension of Augustine's God's representation but the developmentally based image aspects (both paternal and maternal) as well. It gave him the requisite ego strength and self-cohesion necessary to withstand what was not only a Pandora's box of unearthed unconscious content but the ability to work through and theorize about it. What Augustine saw was the navel and whirlpool of the unconscious—an opaque darkness he spent the rest of his life trying to pierce, unravel, and integrate.

Toward Integration—Classic, Adaptive, and Transformational

How, then, are we to reconcile the earlier psychoanalytic studies with the present emphasis on the depth and reality of Augustine's introspective insights? What we have in the *Confessions* is the reality of an ancient text that we must strive to understand in its textual, theological, sociohistorical, and literary contexts. I have stressed throughout this study that any psychoanalytic probe needs to engage such perspectives to make the best educated guess about the trajectory and nature of Augustine's narrative. In so doing, this study goes beyond previous ones by reading Augustine as a mystic, offering a textual reconstruction of Augustine's mystical theology, and accounting for the possibility of his Christian visions through the theories of the mystics of psychoanalysis and the insights of cognitive neuroscience, in conjunction with a Winnicottian evolving God representation.

With respect to familiar designations in the psychoanalytic study of religion, such an analysis can be said to be adaptive-transformational. At the same time, owing to the generality of the metanarrative I am proposing, it would not be incorrect to say that the presentation could be considered programmatic. In other words, while allowing for the possibility of the More of vision, the working frame I am developing is, theoretically at least, inclusive enough to incorporate even the earlier, classic reductive studies. In part this is so because psychoanalytic method insists that any form of ultimate concern carries with it developmental and cultural baggage. Religious symbols, teachings, and narratives may point to a divine ground and participate in them, as Paul Tillich would say, but they also invariably reflect the all too human interests found in the imaginative products of individuals and cultures. Augustine's interest in the inner world is replete with suggestive material of just such a kind. The matter is how to justify incorporating even the most reductive of psychological studies.

A significant hurdle in integrating some psychoanalytic studies (and by way of returning to a thread of argument left unfinished at the end of chapter 1) is posed by those who seek to base their interpretative forays on what they see as clear instances of the "historical" Augustine in the text. They point out that Augustine does state (in 10.3) that "I am not lying about myself in my confessions." And so, to take the example of Augustine's relation to Monica, the argument might proceed something like this: he admits that his relation to Monica exhibited a "too carnal affection" (9.13), and that her unnecessary weeping fits and lamentations were due to the "heritage of Eve" and of "an affection that was too much of the flesh" (5.8). We have some indication, then, that Monica was more invasive than the typical mother, or, as Augustine puts it, "she loved having me with her, as all mothers do, only she more than most" (5.8). But here we need not rely simply on

Augustine. Monica's anxiety was evident to others in his culture. In *Confessions* 3.12, Augustine relates that a local Christian bishop, when asked by Monica to wean the adolescent Aurelius from the Manichaeans, advised her to desist and let him be, for he had concluded that Augustine was too young, impetuous, and full of self-conceit to be taught. He advised Monica to take himself as an example: he himself had been attracted to the Manichaeans as a youth but over time came to see that they were in error. He reasoned that the best thing for Monica to do was to give her adolescent son some space, for there would come a time later when he would be more amenable to being taught in ways that would be ego-syntonic. (Augustine the bishop, reflecting on his youth, notes that he came to understand that the approach advocated by his local bishop was "very sensible.") Monica, however, "refused to be satisfied" and kept on "begging" and "weeping many tears." In the end, the bishop became "annoyed," stayed his course, and sent her away, saying it would be impossible for the son of such tears to perish. One cannot help but contrast the sober, mature response of the bishop with what can justifiably be referred to as the immature, possibly hysterical, behavior of an overweening mother.

Yet while it is apparent that the actuality of the ways in which the bishop and Monica behaved are not in question, and there is no rhetorical overlay that would preclude accepting the passages cited here as close to accurate depictions of the event, it is questionable whether this scene rises to the level of a developmental "photograph" of the historical Augustine. Indeed, even a cursory survey of extant studies reveals little agreement on the developmental vicissitudes of his life and their impact on his thought. While the text is suggestive enough to provoke a variety of interesting, competing, and sometimes compelling narratives, it is more reasonable to conclude that what extant psychological studies offer are not photographs but imaginative portraits of Augustine. And even though, as I argue in this study, the developmental and unconscious determinants of Augustine's life and thought are unknowable, some portraits are better than others.

One could add a caveat to this conclusion. If one abandons the need to get to the "historical" Augustine, concentrating instead on the nature and value of reception history—what they are and what they are designed to do—then one can considerably expand the argument to justify even the most reductionistic of studies. After all, reception histories hardly recapitulate authorial intent, for they are characterized by the notion that any classic text transcends its author, if only because the great works are read and reworked by subsequent generations. Augustine himself illustrates this thesis by creatively misreading Saint Paul's notion of the divided will and ascent to Paradise in the biblical texts of Romans and 2 Corinthians, respectively.

Put in psychological terms, reception histories afford individuals and cultures an opportunity to individuate. Creative misreadings, in this psychological sense, means that a text like the *Confessions* will invariably be read in a way that invites projection and reflects culturally valorized forms of introspection. Capps and Dittes suggest this when they state that any contemporary reader "tries to see himself or herself in the story, and so, of course, tries fitting to Augustine theories and interpretations—whether Oedipal, narcissistic, or more subtle—that are in some sense, self-portraits."[44] Indeed, Augustine's narrative reveals notions that, from a twenty-first-century perspective, seem so dated as to invite sharp, polemical responses. Capps chastises Augustine for glossing over the implications of his childhood school beatings, while John Updike weaves a short story about his concubine in which it is she, not Augustine, who is the true saint.[45] Again, while it may be difficult to ascertain the precise relation between Augustine's own unresolved conflicts and his theological teachings, we do know, as a result of the development of theory, a great deal about the psychosocial ramifications of such doctrines with respect to contemporary culture. Perhaps one could, in Augustine's defense, say that he could not have known about what might be called the unintended consequences of his more questionable theological doctrines. At the same time, we simply know more than Augustine did. Psychobiographical analyses of text, regardless of the exact nature of Augustine's conflicts, are necessary antidotes that reflect the concerns of individuals and cultures in their efforts to move forward and correct the excesses of both the intended and unintended consequences of a great mind.

While this study, then, is willing to valorize and integrate previous studies along such lines, it still holds that the analysis I advance is an improvement because it brings to the fore what earlier studies have missed or failed to adequately appreciate: that Augustine was a mystic. While this fact in itself does not necessarily devalue previous psychoanalytic studies, it does shift the debate by insisting that Augustine be read first and foremost as a mystic; that his therapeia be taken as a legitimate effort to formulate a working soteriology based on, among other things, his visions; and that his effort at therapeia, sharing as it does the psychoanalytic goal of unearthing unconscious content, be open to clinically based disciplines with more precise knowledge than what was available to Augustine.

CONCLUSION

The discussion to this point has been directed toward establishing a new chapter in the ongoing psychoanalytic reception history of Augustine's *Confessions*. In laying out the argument, I have had occasion to touch on multiple issues germane to the broader academic study of mysticism, the place of psychoanalysis in it, and what seems to be the widespread emergence of a psychologically informed culture invested in mysticism and spirituality. It is this latter, wider and socially relevant fact that, in this concluding chapter, I take up in greater depth. The discussion proceeds by way of something assumed throughout this book, namely, that there is a force in contemporary culture that is driving psychoanalysis, against Freud's wishes, to a greater appreciation of the wisdom to be garnered from mystical texts, figures, and practices.

It should be said at the outset that the complex origins and interactions of the multiple cultural strands and eddies that have collaborated in the rise of a psychologically informed modern spirituality are well beyond the purview of the present study. My aim, decidedly more modest, is to refine selected lines of argument concerning psychoanalysis and Augustine entertained in previous chapters in light of this ascendant cultural milieu. Although this approach has implications that go well beyond the material discussed in these pages, the attempt should at least reveal the general contours of that culture and encourage a greater appreciation of the kinds of issues, problems, and debates confronting both psychoanalysis and the study of the mystical. In other words, as befitting concluding remarks, I will not only hone the various analyses entertained and conclusions offered thus far but also underscore those issues in need of future exploration.

To accomplish these aims I will, first and briefly, contextualize the present study in a more detailed, substantive manner with respect to what I have called the psychology-and-religion movement.[1] I will then elaborate on relevant elements of the analysis of the previous chapters by applying them to selected aspects of three of this movement's dialogical enterprises: the psychology-theology dialogue, the emergence of a modern psychospirituality, and the psychology-comparativist dialogue. Since all three of these dialogues have contributed to the emergence of a psychoanalytically informed spirituality, they link the case-history approach to the spiritual concerns of the wider cultural milieu. The organizational strategy proceeds by grouping the various threads of previous discussions, now rendered along more sociological lines, into three interrelated vignettes, each of which revisits and adds considerable sophistication to the analysis of cultural issues. Like each chapter of the book, each section builds on the analysis and conclusions of the previous one. Although the analysis will be—indeed, must be—of a sweeping, sprawling nature, each section clearly indicates how a more sociological focus serves to link the case study of Augustine to wider cultural concerns about mysticism, spirituality, and psychoanalysis. The hope is that these three linked vignettes, which amount to historical and conceptual snapshots, will help begin the process of developing a portrait of a psychologically informed modern spirituality and the place of psychoanalysis within it.

To briefly summarize the argument to come, the first vignette ("Psychoanalysis, Inner-Worldly Mysticism, and Augustine") focuses on what I have called the dialogue between psychology and theology. By addressing one particular slice of that dialogue, namely, the ebb and flow of the psychoanalytic reception history of the *Confessions,* it asks why it is that only recently do we find the turn in that history (most fully evinced by this study) toward the mystical. The explanation proceeds by way of championing that methodological perspective that has been dubbed the "sociology of psychological knowledge" by noting the influence of the rise of the spiritual but not religious movement and by playing on the distinction between Weber's inner-worldly ascetic and his inner-worldly mystic.[2]

The second vignette ("Mystical Theologies, Modern Spiritualities") delves more deeply into that emerging cultural milieu by focusing on the complicity not only of psychoanalysis but also of those psychological models that animate the psychology-and-religion movement itself. Psychoanalysis, however unwittingly, has not only influenced the rise of the spiritual but not religious trend but has in turn been influenced by it. As I show, this emerging social base fits hand-in-glove with that project in the broader psychology-and-religion movement that I refer to as psychospirituality. Methodologically, I focus on the articulation of a psychosocial theory of mourning and its impact on the emerging theories of the originative psychologists and of psychospirituality in general. I hope to show that the emergence of a psychologically informed modern spirituality is a "mourned" product of more traditional forms of churched mysticism, such as Augustine's mystical theology. Revisiting the analysis offered in chapters 3 and 4, I propose that Augustine's understanding of mysticism as mystical theology and our analysis of it may not entirely jibe with either traditional theological, churched accounts of Augustine or that championed by a simple form of psychospirituality. In other words, although a major aim of this more sociologically oriented chapter is to show how a social base drives diverse projects in the psychology-and-religion movement toward the mystical, this does not mean that Augustine's mystical theology should be read as just another instance of psychospirituality. Clearly, a growing cultural interest in things mystical can coexist with diverse positions on how it ought to be addressed by psychoanalysis. As I have argued, the encounter between psychoanalysis and mysticism, whether in scholarship or in the clinic, should take the form of a transformational, constructivist dialogue while avoiding the generic, amorphous perennialism that characterizes much of the religio-ethical base of psychospirituality.

Finally, the third section ("The Academy, the Clinic and Comparative Contributions") takes up the psychology-comparativist dialogue to show how psychoanalysis has been influenced by the cultural move toward a psychologically informed inner-worldly mysticism. Here the test cases are twofold. First, I offer brief psychobiographical portraits of two of the psychoanalytic mystics discussed earlier, Sudhir Kakar and Jeffrey Kripal, to show how their scholarship evinces a mourning process that dovetails with the arguments of the previous two sections. I then look at the dialogue between psychoanalysis and Buddhism.

This dialogue, which is nearly a century old, has been well documented and offers a wealth of information that can be used for a variety of agendas. For the purposes of this book, it provides a supplement to the foregoing analysis on two major fronts. First, it allows us to chart the evolution of new psychoanalytic theoretical models that seek to synthesize psychoanalytic notions of development, self, and insight with their Buddhist counterparts. The psychoanalytic encounter with Buddhism parallels the history of psychological studies of Augustine, beginning with reductionism, moving on to adaptive views, and transitioning more recently to transformational models. The encounter with Buddhism also offers a comparative contrast to both Augustine's mystical theology and unchurched psychospirituality, buttressing this book's thesis that a nonreductive constructivism that admits of real differences among traditions, combined with transformational ways of thinking, makes psychoanalysis a bona fide partner in the study of mysticism.

Mapping Psychology Meeting Religion: Of, As, and "in Dialogue With"

Throughout this book I have referred to the psychology-and-religion movement in contrast to the more traditional psychology of religion. The latter as usually practiced assumes a one-way relationship between psychology and religion, with psychological models providing the lens through which the practitioner deciphers the meaning of religious ideation and practice. Historically speaking, the term came to be defined and used in the originative period of the field (1880 to World War II), during which such seminal figures as Freud, Jung, and James introduced their different theories of the mind and culture. It is unfortunate that the stress on these originators has all too often helped obscure the contributions of other, lesser-known figures, such as R. M. Bucke, Théodore Flournoy, Wilhelm Wundt, G. Stanley Hall and his Clark school, James Leuba, Girgensohn and the Dorpat school, Joseph Maréchal, Frederic Myers, James Pratt, George Coe, and Georges Berguer. Certainly there was more than one international conference on psychology and religion at which many of these figures met and influenced one another, perhaps best illustrated by the famous 1909 photograph at Clark University of Hall, James, Jung, Freud, and more than thirty-five others standing together. Many diverse psychological approaches to religion, ranging from depth psychology and experimental analyses to pragmatic evaluations and comparative approaches, emerged during this era, some of which subsequently lapsed into obscurity.

The period after World War II ushered in a panoply of new models, including behaviorism, neurocognition, ego psychology, and object-relations theory, as well as humanistic, phenomenological, and existential approaches. These postwar developments came to be identified with names that rival those of the nineteenth-century founders, especially Erik Erikson, Gordon Allport, Victor Frankl, B. F. Skinner, and Abraham Maslow. The period from 1970 to the present constitutes a third phase of theorizing and includes evolutionary psychology, transpersonal psychology, attribution theory, attachment theory, intersubjectivity, and poststructural psychology. At the same time, a number of contemporary issues, such as race, feminism, spirituality, and alternative sexualities, came to the fore.

This diverse and exuberant theorizing is best categorized as the "psychology-and-religion movement." The "and" indicates that neither psychology nor religion is the dominant partner. Rather, "and" imposes neutrality: it recognizes that the participants who have entered the field often have diverse sympathies vis-à-vis religion and promote different and competing intellectual agendas. Moreover, it recognizes that such diversity has, throughout the history of the field, eventuated in multiple dialogical projects and enterprises. Thus, the use of "and" is essentially inclusive and interdisciplinary. Moreover, the new designation includes not only the psychology of religion, with all that entails, but a number of other composites as well. These include what I have called the psychology and theology dialogue, the psychology-comparativist dialogue, psychospirituality (what is sometimes referred to as "psychology *as* religion"), and such interdisciplinary hybrids as psychoanalytic anthropology and psychoanalytic sociology.

Although there is room to narrate the history and describe the various enterprises in alternative and justifiable ways,[3] the concept of psychology *and* religion not only is defensible, it furthers our understanding of the encounter between psychoanalysis and mysticism. Thus, it should be evident that most extant psychobiographical studies of Augustine, including this one, combine elements of a straightforward psychology *of* religion approach with insights from the psychology-theology dialogue. In addition, I have found it useful to borrow resources from the psychology-comparativist dialogue, from psychoanalytic anthropology, and, of course, from psychospirituality.

The task now is to use this mapping of the field to link the present study to wider cultural and spiritual concerns, a task that begins with the dialogue between psychology and theology.

Psychoanalysis, Inner-Worldly Mysticism, and Augustine

Most of the previous psychoanalytic studies of the *Confessions* fall under the rubrics of the psychology *of* religion and the psychology-theology dialogue, sometimes called practical theology. Indeed, there is general consensus that the dialogue between Christian theology and academic psychology played a major role in the initial, originative period (1880–1944) of the movement. Even a cursory survey reveals that a majority of researchers were from Christian backgrounds and that some attempted to integrate the professional identities of pastor and scholar, evinced so well in the cases of Georges Berguer and E. S. Ames. As David Wulff notes, many of these figures were swept up in the Progressive movement and the social gospel movement, the latter a post–Civil War, Protestant intellectual movement that sought to address the social problems associated with industrialization through religious teachings, and their interest in drawing relations between psychology and Christian theology was especially strong.[4] Pastoral psychology can trace its origins to this period as well, as exemplified in the work of Oskar Pfister, a Swiss pastor who was a lay analyst and correspondent of Freud, and the American Anton Boisen, a minister (afflicted with schizophrenia) who spearheaded the American hospital chaplaincy movement and clinical pastoral education. What is of specific interest for us now is just how deep the interest in mysticism was during this time. Any number of studies by William James, Henri Delacroix, Frederic Myers, and many others document this point.[5] The Catholic psychologist Joseph Maréchal is particularly notable not only for his deeply sympathetic studies of mysticism but also for his explicit engagement with Augustine's visions. His analysis is part of the long debate in Catholic circles, chronicled by André Mandouze, concerning the exact nature of Augustine's visions.[6] In light of this burgeoning interest in mysticism and the occult, it is all the more notable that psychoanalysis was a latecomer to the party. Its evaluations of mysticism were mostly pejorative in the earliest, first period and adaptive during the second. This is in part the result of the emotional pull of the received view of Freud's analysis of the oceanic feeling, a view I endeavored to decompose and reconstruct in chapters 2 and 3. Nevertheless, it is singularly unfortunate that this view is reflected in some of the most influential psychoanalytic studies of Augustine, most notably in Dittes's use of "Mom-ism" to designate Augustine's visions. Moreover, one searches in vain in this body of literature for any sustained inquiry into

Augustine's take on Plotinian and Christian teachings on mysticism, or, for that matter, any reference to the substantial debates on Augustine's mysticism as referenced by Mandouze and Maréchal. This omission confirms how unessential Augustine's ascents were for previous scholars who took up the psychoanalytic reception history of the *Confessions*. This prompts the search for additional and underlying reasons why most previous psychoanalytic studies considered Augustine's mysticism to be a secondary, if not unessential, element in the narrative of the *Confessions*.

The line of explanation I follow here investigates the contribution of social bases to the variability of psychoanalytic reception histories. It proceeds by looking at the sociological contribution to the ebb and flow of theorizing within the psychology-and-religion movement—what has been dubbed the "sociology of psychological knowledge."[7] The question here is basic: what social conditions have determined the selection of models and the nature of analyses found in extant psychoanalytic studies of Augustine?

I begin to address this question by noting the gradual influence of the psychology-theology dialogue during the course of the twentieth century, particularly in the United States. If the first period saw a strong interaction between psychology and Christian theology, then it was the second, postwar period that witnessed the true maturation and cultural hegemony of the psychology-theology dialogue. In fact, despite the presence of other enterprises and dialogical projects, it would not be an overstatement to say that the psychology-theology dialogue became the dominant intellectual enterprise in the field. Although there were comparativist (for example, Mircea Eliade), Jewish (Martin Buber), and Buddhist (D. T. Suzuki) contributors to this dialogue, the cultural soil of the United States was more welcoming to Protestantism and Protestant intellectuals. Noted Protestant theologians such as Paul Tillich and the Niebuhr brothers set the parameters of the debate, which was taken up by numerous pastoral psychologists, clinicians, and academics with links to Protestantism, among them Albert Outler, Seward Hiltner, and Erik Erikson, and most of the debate took place within the dominant social institutions of the seminary, church, university, and clinic. Psychological analyses of religion had undercut religious claims to transcendence, casting suspicion on the conceptual categories of theological discourse. In their efforts to revitalize faith after the horrors of the world war, such religious philosophers and theologians knew that the deconstructive analyses psychological models offered could be beneficial to rearticulating religious subjectivity. Indeed, a survey of the relevant literature shows that, in general, the dominant intellectual discourse concerned investigating the relations between and among developmental determinants, existential issues (freedom, choice, and responsibility), and theological issues (faith, sin, morality, and redemption).[8]

A specifically Weberian line of analysis can be utilized to unearth some of the deeper cultural reasons behind the apparent cultural links among psychoanalysis, Protestantism, and previous psychoanalytic studies of Augustine. For example, the sociologist Philip Rieff traced what he thought was a discernible sociohistorical affinity linking Calvin with Freud. Weber cast the cultural world built by Catholicism as magical and enchanted, populated by a host of saintly intermediaries to God. The latter, alongside the church and confessional, gave the believer a psychological release from guilt and anxiety over salvation. In Weber's account, it was the emergence of the Protestant tradition and its attendant social type, the inner-worldly ascetic, that sheared the world of such magical releases.[9] Faced with the twin theological doctrines of predestination and a repudiation of iconography as a path to salvation, the Protestant became more prone to anxiety, feelings of guilt, and neurosis than his fellow Catholic. The widespread appeal of Freud in part owed to this cultural atmosphere, now internalized developmentally as part of the cultural superego of the Protestant, in conjunction with the ability of classical psychoanalysis, whose theory and practice focused on the *Über-Ich,* guilt, and anxiety, to address the psychological world of the inner-worldly ascetic. In other words, and speaking psychosocially, classical Freudian psychoanalysis fits hand-in-glove with inner-worldly asceticism.[10]

This provides the social context for most extant psychoanalytic studies of Augustine, which start with the so-called basement theology founded by Dittes and Capps at Yale Divinity School in the 1960s. Insofar as psychoanalysis addresses Protestant anxiety and guilt, it is understandable that its analyses focus not on the centrality of the *visio Dei* but on episodes such as Augustine's boyhood stealing of pears, the bath episode, the garden conversion scene, Augustine's views on original sin, his relation to his son Adeotatus, oedipal and preoedipal constructs, sexuality, fragmentation, and so on. Although it is possible to counter any generalization by pointing to contradictory evidence, such criticism is applicable to any system that champions the sociological tradition of social types.[11]

This is so because the weakness of such methodological strategies is their overly "meta" character: they are by nature general and, because they favor broad brush strokes, they tend to omit the particular. Nevertheless, such portrayals can be convincing because they explain why an entire segment of the psychoanalytic reception history of the *Confessions* has ignored, misrepresented, or misunderstood not only Augustine's mystical theology but also what I have called the hidden history of psychoanalytic theorizing about mysticism. Moreover, this line of methodological reasoning is far from absent in the psychoanalytic literature. This same general sociohistorical analysis animates the thesis of Stuart Hughes's classic work *The Sea Change,* which identifies a cultural fit between the rise of the "executive ego," conveyed in the works of Hartmann and Erikson, and the growing technological sophistication of capitalistic America. It also informs the work of Heinz Kohut and Christopher Lasch, both of whom held that the emerging cultural conditions of the postwar period increased the fragmentation of the family and contributed to the growth of narcissistic personality disorders, thus creating a need for new theories of the psyche that emphasized the narcissistic element.[12]

While there has been an interest in things mystical from the beginning of the psychology-and-religion movement, the question is why the transformational school and the mystics of psychoanalysis have emerged primarily in the most recent, third period. To return to Weber, if the formation and reception of Freud's theories were culturally bound to the rise of the inner-worldly ascetic, then, as both Weber and especially his colleague Ernst Troeltsch observed, social conditions during the twentieth century presaged the rise of a new ideal type, the "inner-worldly mystic." While Weber had little to say about the latter, recent sociological studies have made clear the contemporary pervasiveness of inner-worldly mysticism.[13] The sociologist Roland Robertson, for example, takes his cue from Troeltsch's observation that a modern, noninstitutional, individualistic form of mysticism was emerging. Drawing on Weber's concept of the inner-worldly mystic, Robertson expands on this ideal type by linking it to the rise of individualism, pluralism, rationalization, and the scientific-bureaucratic ethos. He then goes on to examine various modern introspective techniques for the realization and actualization of the self as found in the transpersonal and human potential movements.[14] In analyzing this new form of self-cultivation Robertson notes that it is, in fact, socially engaged, being a modern form of social adaptation that seeks to synthesize that ethos that champions an orientation toward work in the world and societal involvement, on the one hand, and the inner injunction to seek wholeness, self-realization, and self-perfection on the other. The modern mystic is a psychologically informed individual seeking self-fulfillment in a capitalistic, bureaucratic society. Thus, in a very real sense, there is a cultural fit among inner-worldly mysticism, modern spirituality, and psychoanalytic theories that view the mystical in a positive light. This is precisely the thesis stated in the introduction to this book: a positive shift in the psychoanalytic treatment of mysticism reflects the cultural ascendancy of the spiritual but not religious movement and the inner-worldly mystic. Just as previous studies spoke to a social base that "read" the *Confessions* through the lens of Oedipus and pre-Oedipus, so there is a new social base with different existential concerns that reads Augustine's vision as a roadmap to mystical wholeness. Indeed, for many who have been influenced by the rise of modern spirituality, a transformational psychoanalytic approach to the *Confessions* illuminates that work in ways that previous studies have not done and cannot do.

Mystical Theologies, Modern Spiritualities

Insofar as the present study was motivated by an interest in the rise of inner-worldly mysticism and the spiritual but not religious trend, it behooves us to look more carefully at the relation between that social soil and psychology, particularly that enterprise in the psychology-and-religion movement I have called psychospirituality. Earlier I noted that the first empirical studies found the spiritual but not religious persuasion to have the support of just over 20 percent of the U.S. population, while more recent studies have concluded that more than 70 percent of eighteen- to twenty-nine-year-olds are so inclined.[15] In previous chapters I articulated the contours of the spiritual but not religious line of thinking, referring to the research of Mary McDonald, Leigh Schmidt, Michel de Certeau, Robert Fuller, and many others.[16] This form of mysticism, as I noted in previous chapters, is to be distinguished from Augustine's own take on the matter, his mystical theology.

In seeking to contribute to the work of the aforementioned theorists by examining just one important cultural strand in the rise and development of modern spirituality, namely, the creation and dissemination of psychological models, I must admit that the analysis is necessarily limited. This is so because the rise of such a movement involves multiple cultural strands interacting in a manner captured by Weber's famous term, "elective affinity." In the following discussion I look closely at two interrelated factors. The first is the psychosocial dynamics involved in the formulations of those originative psychologists responsible for the theoretical development of psychospirituality; the second is the means by which such formulations broadened to command the allegiance of, as Weber would have it, "whole groups" of people.[17] This is crucial, for many in contemporary culture use such formulations for the purpose of organizing, monitoring, and expressing the need for wholeness, numinous experiences, and individuation. Such systems offer themselves as a modern, unchurched, nontraditional way of mapping one's religious proclivities. At the end of the analysis I return to Augustine, not only to clarify anew the definitional debates surrounding the use of the term mysticism but to sharpen the difference between modern spirituality and mystical theology. I also attempt to show how the transformational approach championed here is to be distinguished from a simple understanding of psychospirituality.

The key to understanding the emergence of psychospirituality lies in what Peter Homans, following Weber, dubs a "double ideal type," which he characterizes as "the tension between a common culture and analytic access."[18] Analytic access, by which he means the kind of introspective activity found in depth psychology, is in tension with what Talcott Parsons refers to as a "common culture," for, sociologically speaking, analytic access always takes place at the margins of culture. The double-ideal type thus presupposes an inclusive concept of mourning, one that is defined with respect to the psychological concept of disillusionment or de-idealization, involves both the cognitive and affective dimensions of the psyche, and extends what is mourned to such social and cultural "objects" as values, ideals, and symbols. In an ideal-typical sense, the process is envisioned as starting when the power of a religious worldview or common culture to command allegiance wanes and symbols "die" (a process of disenchantment, in Weber's language). What was previously idealized, and hence believed or given allegiance to, becomes de-idealized. That is, what had previously been expressed externally through religious ideation becomes, to various degrees depending on the person, an introspective engagement with unconscious contents. Moreover, this loss leads to mourning, a regressive process that loosens unconscious contents, including in some cases unchurched mystical experiences. The dramatic upsurge of the unconscious may result in breakdown, despair, or cynicism. However, it also provides an opportunity for individuation, or a growing out of the social womb and an integration of previously unmonitored unconscious contents—a process that can result in a response to the loss of religion that takes the form of creating new ideals and symbols. Among the latter, at least with respect to the originating psychologists, is the formation of psychospirituality. And, as evinced by the latter, such ideas usually display some form of connection with the religious past. While de-idealized and in some sense rejected, religion is never wholly left behind but rather repudiated and assimilated in varying degrees and proportions. In a very real sense, religion lives on in psychological formulations.

The paradigmatic case here, as Homans notes, is that of Jung. The formation of his theory in part depended on secularization, the de-idealization of religious ideation, and the subsequent theorization of unconscious processes previously expressed through and monitored by public religious narratives. Thus it is that Jung was initially drawn to the Protestant faith of his father. However, secularization and subsequent de-idealization soon entered the scene. Jung attributed his waning faith to a father who, despite being a pastor, was influenced by a secular culture and ambivalent about Christian doctrines, and communicated as much to his son (Marthe Robert's "vague father"[19]). This disillusionment was furthered by significant experiences (recorded in his *Memories, Dreams, Reflections*) of disappointment with religion, notably his cathedral fantasy and his reaction to Communion. Jung's subsequent self-fragmentation and encounter with archetypical material led to a series of reflections that became the primary material for his budding theory. Jung literally created, as he himself admitted, a public psychological theory out of his own private experiences. In his view, what had been historically expressed and contained in religious symbols and narratives was to be rightly understood as located in the psychological processes of the collective unconscious and its archetypical modes of expression. With respect to Jung's works, then, it is possible to draw a direct correlation between Jung's personal "confrontation with the unconscious" (in chapter 6 of *Memories, Dreams, Reflections* and in his *Red Book*) and his theorizing about them (most evident in part 2 of his *Two Essays on Analytical Psychology*). Institutional religion was repudiated but lived on in the psychospirituality of Jung.

A similar progression can be identified in the case of Romain Rolland, a figure who contributed greatly to the cultural dissemination of the term "the oceanic feeling." Indeed, one could say that Freud's debate with Rolland is nothing less than the locus classicus of the psychoanalytic entry into modern spirituality. Michel de Certeau intimates as much when he marks that debate as a paradigmatic example of the shift to an unchurched spirituality.[20] Socialized into Catholicism as a young child, Rolland became disillusioned with institutional religion when his family moved from the countryside of Clamecy to Paris. While a student at the École Normale Supériere he met with a culture that showed the influence of secularization, and he formally renounced his ties to organized Catholicism. Afterward, still an adolescent, he was privy to a series of mystical experiences. In describing them he recalls how he "was possessed by Nature like a violated virgin. For a moment my soul left me to melt into the luminous mass of the Breithorn. . . . Yes, extravagant as it may sound, for some moments I *was* the Breithorn."[21] These experiences formed the existential basis for a philosophical statement he termed the *Credo quia verum*. The latter indicates a repudiation of a specifically Christian ideology. The very title ("I believe because it is true"), which gives preference to seeing over believing, mystical experience over doctrine, seems directed against the more familiar claim attributed to Tertullian, *Credo quia absurdum* ("I believe because it is absurd"). In fact, the figure that animates Rolland's *Credo* is not Christ but Spinoza. Forty years later, Rolland observed that Spinoza "still remains sacred to me, like the Holy Scriptures for those who believe in them; I never touch those volumes except with reverence."[22] For Rolland, Spinoza thus served to mediate a conception of God that resonated with the reality Rolland encountered in his mystical experiences. "One page [of Spinoza's *Ethics*]," writes Rolland, was enough to strike "sparks of fire." And what did he find? That God and nature are one. In sum, what Rolland advocates in the *Credo* is an unchurched, nature-based mysticism.

It was this unchurched mysticism that became the basis for Rolland's request to Freud to analyze mysticism. In his biographies of Ramakrishna and Vivekananda, Rolland expresses confidence that the "modern psycho-physiologist, armed with all the latest instruments of the new sciences of the soul," would be able to "attain to a full knowledge" of the workings of the mystical subconscious.[23] Rolland hoped Freud would join him in this cultural agenda, which consisted in nothing less than what he referred to in his biographies of the Hindu saints as a "universalistic science-religion" and "mystical psycho-analysis." As Rolland wrote to Freud, the oceanic feeling is "completely independent of all dogma, all credo, all Church organization. . . . [It is] the true source of religious energy which has been collected, canalized and dried up by Churches to the extent that one could say it is inside the Churches that one finds the least true religious feeling."[24] This "rationalistic religion" would be that "religion of the future" on which "the salvation of Europe depends."[25] This alarmed Freud, who, as Certeau notes, could only be reminded of another advocate of a religious psychology who played an important role in his life, Carl Jung.

This theory of mourning, then, provides psychosocial depth to the textual and historical analyses found in Schmidt and Certeau: the psychological forms of modern spirituality are the de-idealized and mourned cultural products of classic, traditional mysticism. What is further interesting in both Rolland and Jung is how they came to join the definitional debates surrounding mysticism. Rolland was a perennialist. For him, the fundamental source of religion was dynamic in character, a free and vital becoming that, given the proper individual and social conditions, "spontaneously" manifested itself and eventually solidified into discernible religious forms. As Rolland put it, "mysticism is always and everywhere the same."[26] Yet this view was clearly based on his own mystical experiences. In a letter to an Indian friend, D. K. Roy, Rolland related how he had discovered, in the works of Sri Aurobindo, "just what I myself had found, unaided, at the age of twenty, when I wrote the same thing in my Credo Quia Verum."[27] It was the mystical experiences of his youth, he went on to say, that brought him "singularly near to the spirit of India when I later came to know it."[28]

Jung, on the other hand, may also be classified as a perennialist, although his entry into the debates is a true variant on that advocated by Rolland. Jung turned to Rudolph Otto, proclaiming that religion "is a careful and scrupulous observation of the 'numinosum' . . . by the term 'religion' I do not mean a creed. . . . Creeds are codified and dogmatized forms of original religious experience."[29] Of course, for Jung the experience of the numinosum came to mean the emergence of strong archetypical material. His definition of religion and mysticism, like that of Rolland, fit quite nicely with his own personal experience.

To take this further, the definitions of religion and mysticism found in many of the psychological theorists linked to psychospirituality cannot fail to pique interest. Generally speaking, the proponents of psychospirituality insist there are germs of wisdom hidden in the deeper, mystical elements of traditional religion, germs that can be separated from the religious soil and planted anew for a disillusioned populace seeking wholeness. For example, the Canadian psychologist R. M. Bucke, one of

James's correspondents, broke with institutional Christianity as a youth. Then, at the age of thirty-six, he had a mystical experience, which he referred to as an instance of "cosmic consciousness." After a pleasant evening with friends reading poetry he found himself on the ride home in a state of quiet, passive enjoyment. Being suddenly surrounded by a flame-colored cloud, he had an "intellectual illumination," a drop of "Brahmic Bliss," through which he came not simply to *believe* but to *know* that "the Cosmos is not dead matter but a living Presence, that the soul of man is immortal . . . that the foundation principle of the world is what we call love and that the happiness of every one is in the long run absolutely certain."[30] The latter became the basis for a new understanding of religion, culture, and history. Cosmic consciousness became the "common core" on which a mystical perennialism was established. And, like James, Bucke listed a variety of universal "marks" or characteristics that he thought constituted a genuine instance of cosmic consciousness, including intellectual illumination, moral elevation, a sense of immortality, and loss of the fear of death.[31] Cosmic consciousness was to be distinguished from the simple (perceptual, receptual) consciousness of animals and the reflective, conceptual self-consciousness of humans.[32] It entailed a move from states of fear and hate to love and faith—a move rooted in the evolution of the nervous system. Developmentally, Bucke claimed that a strong and athletic mother, a father of superior physical and spiritual powers, parents with diverse temperaments, a perfect blending of diverse parental characteristics in the child, and a particular life stage (mid-thirties) were determinative factors favoring the move to cosmic consciousness. Bucke held that cosmic consciousness evolved over time such that "men with the faculty in question are becoming more and more common" and that "our descendants will sooner or later reach, as a race, the condition of cosmic consciousness."[33] For Bucke, there is an essential unity of the world's religions, obscured by the limitations of language, the diversity of cultures, problems in translation, tradition, and other barriers. Cosmic consciousness places the individual "on a new plane of existence," elevates his moral and intellectual stature, and renders him "a member of a new species."[34] It is this "new race" that is "in the act of being born from us" and that will, in the "near future," inhabit the earth.[35] Then, becoming more specific, he called attention to the "three revolutions" now facing mankind: (1) the establishment of "aerial navigation" and its sociomaterial consequences, (2) the abolition of private property and the move to a socialist economy, and (3) the religio-psychical revolution, as detailed in his book. These three would, according to Bucke, lead to "a new heaven and a new earth." The result would be nothing less than unchurched mystical man in a socialist state.

To take another famous case, Abraham Maslow posited above and beyond physiological safety, belongingness, and self-esteem needs that of self-actualization. It is the well-developed self-actualizer who ends up having "peak-experiences." Peak experiences here are synonymous with mystical experiences and can be defined with respect to a laundry list of characteristics: unity, transcendence of space and time, awe, wonder, loss of fear, and the like. More important, Maslow saw peak experiences as that common core around which all religions are built: "to the extent that all mystical or peak-experiences are the same in their essence and have always been the same, all religions are the same in their essence and always have been the same."[36] He goes on to distinguish between two religious social types, the "mystics" (those granted peak experiences) and the "legalists" (the non-peaker church bureaucrat). The latter tries through the accoutrements of church tradition and theology to communicate the original insight of the mystic, an effort Maslow thought was all too often in vain. Indeed, for Maslow, "all the paraphernalia of organized religions . . . are to the 'peaker' secondary, peripheral, and of doubtful value . . . each peaker discovers, develops, and retains his own religion."[37] It is psychology that has divested religion of its supernatural character and put mysticism in its rightful place as an object of scientific study. Of course, it was Maslow who went on to institute transpersonal psychology, that branch of psychology concerned with the scientific study of "unitive consciousness, peak experiences, B values, ecstasy, wonder," and so on.[38] While the theorists and agendas that are covered under the banner of transpersonal psychology are numerous and varied, they tend to valorize immediate, firsthand, unchurched mystical experience.[39]

One even finds this trend manifested in those pivotal researchers who champion brain science. Some researchers have taken their personal unchurched experiences, run them through the lens of various neurocognitive theories, and offered them to the public as a way of expressing their religious proclivities. This is particularly clear in the case of the psychologist and near-death experience researcher Kenneth Ring's notion of "*Homo noeticus.*" The latter, based on Ring's own near-death experience, is an "emerging form of humanity" that seeks a "culture founded in higher consciousness, a culture whose institutions are based on love and wisdom, a culture that fulfills the perennial philosophy."[40]

Jill Bolte Taylor, a brain scientist who writes eloquently about a stroke she suffered, recasts religious ideation and the value of multiple spiritual techniques in terms of right brain functioning, proclaiming, "I find that my right hemisphere consciousness is eager for us to take that next giant leap for mankind and *step to the right* so we can evolve this planet into the peaceful and loving place we yearn for it to be."[41] Taylor's admonition echoes others' at the intersection of religion and brain science, especially those of Robert Ornstein, author of *The Psychology of Consciousness,* who saw mysticism as the manifestation of right hemispheric functioning, a resource for cultural advance, and the meeting place of all religions.[42]

The above examples illustrate that the psychological proponents of modern spirituality, in holding to a religio-mystical conception of the mind, ensured the persistence of religion even in the event of the waning of its more familiar traditional, institutional forms. And lest one think psychoanalysis has been left behind, one need only recall how subsequent generations of psychoanalysts have seen fit to expand Freud's initial forays in a bona fide mystical direction. As we have seen, Lacan's valorization of the Real and *jouissance* can be taken as headed in this direction. So too can one cite in this regard Bion's concept of "O," the encounter with which becomes for him the goal and aim of the farther reaches of the psychoanalytic process. Bion refers to it as "the absolute truth, the godhead, the infinite, the thing-in-itself," further noting that "psychoanalysis itself is just a stripe on the coat of the tiger. Ultimately it may meet the Tiger—The Thing Itself—O."[43] And it bears repeating that Heinz Kohut is paradigmatic in this regard insofar as he explicitly called for "an as yet uncreated system of mystical rationality which could take the place of the religions of the past"[44]—one that, as we have seen, finds its ideal in the person of Dag Hammarskjöld, who described his contentless mysticism in the following words: "Faith is a state of mind and of the soul . . . the language of religion is (only) a set of formulas which register a basic religious experience."[45]

If we turn now from psychological formulation to psychological practice, we cannot fail to notice that the paradigmatic psychological social space—the psychoanalytic session—was instrumental in bridging the gap between the creative product of originative theorists and their widespread cultural acceptance. To illustrate this starkly, at one end of the mourning spectrum lies (in an ideal-typical sense) any fundamentalist religious place of ritualistic learning (such as Whahabi madrassas) where scripture, understood as eternal, unchangeable, and revealed, is summoned for memorization. There is little, if any, room for de-idealization or mourning here. On the contrary, what is valorized is the internalization of an ethos and a truth that cannot, under any circumstances, be de-idealized. To do so would be to risk communal ostracization, excommunication, or violence.

In contrast, psychoanalytic social spaces are potentially revolutionary—a fact that has been as true for how we think about gender and sexuality as it has been for how we think about religion. For example, with respect to the former, it is clear that the cultural legitimacy of the clinic has promoted a greater tolerance for sexual fantasies as well as sexual aims aside from those of heterosexual monogamy (which Freud critiqued as one facet of the religious cultural superego that fermented *Unbehagen*). And while feminists have long noted that Freud was a misogynist who essentialized women, one can, in separating Freud's creation of a socially legitimated ritual space from his theoretical edifice, also view the liminality of the clinic as that social space where women have been afforded an opportunity to explore their inner space and theorize about it. In psychoanalysis the data of the clinical space have been the source of theory and, insofar as theory is falsifiable, take precedence over it. Indeed, some have discerned "a feminist revolution" in psychoanalytic theory, evidenced, for example, by the ascendancy of object-relations theory. From this perspective, the cultural trend toward gender equality and the legitimation of alternative sexual orientations owe something to the liminal space of the clinic.

Psychoanalysis has also contributed to the formation of modern spirituality through the dissection of culturally normative forms of religion, and it did so in two ways. The first contribution concerns the well-known psychoanalytic distrust of institutional religion. Freud defined religion quite narrowly in terms of what he called the common man's religion, which he saw as declining through the process of secularization. This definition undermined the relevance of any and all more sophisticated philosophical or theological formulations. In *The Future of an Illusion* he defiantly chastised those "philosophers" who tried to "stretch the meaning of words" to the point that words like "God" and "religious" ceased to bear any resemblance to the Being worshipped by the common man.[46] This tallied well, as do all such definitions when dealing with originative theorists, with his view, articulated most succinctly in the *Psychopathology of Everyday Life,* that the ideation of religion is "nothing but psychology projected into the external world . . . *supernatural reality* . . . is destined to be changed back once more by science into the *psychology of the unconscious*."[47] The distrust of modern spirituality vis-à-vis institutional religion, then, owes no small debt to Freud, for he was instrumental in developing that "hermeneutic of suspicion" in which the narratives of religious traditions are understood as disguised expressions of deeper, latent unconscious proclivities. In the clinical space this has become very evident: religious beliefs, motives and expressions are traced to their developmental and very human origins, a fact that has led an increasing number of people to think that what is really transpiring in institutional forms of religious narratives reflects less the directive of a holy ontological source than it does that of gendered, class, and cultural interests. What has been mourned, then, is the ethos and worldview of traditional religion as mediated through the auspices of its normative institutional forms. In this negative sense, psychoanalysis has contributed to the rise of a modern, unchurched spirituality.

This line of argument is given sociological depth in Rieff's notion of negative communities.[48] For Rieff, what "came before" were communities, which he characterized as "positive." The defining characteristic of such communities is an elaboration of a cultural symbolic in which controls and restraints on behavior outweigh permissions and an ethic in which the group takes precedence over the individual. In such communities there exists a "language of faith," deemed authoritative, that undergirds a cultural superego that is both idealized and internalized and that serves to keep the "lower," socially disruptive instinctual forces (sex and aggression) in check through repression and guilt. Represented institutionally by the "church" and the "party," positive communities reintegrate the anomic/neurotic through what Rieff called "commitment therapies." The latter are those therapies, typical of all forms of religious healing, that enable the afflicted to encounter their unconscious in what Kohut termed an "experience-distant" manner. This is so for the language of sin and redemption, and the multiple symbols, myths, and narratives that invariably accompany the healing ritual are seen, at least from a psychodynamic perspective, as cultural dreams, being disguised projections of the unconscious. This religious language, mediated through rituals and the commanding, idealized figure of a religious functionary, serves to edify and release aggressive and sexual tensions, further allowing for the reenactment of the internalization of the cultural superego. In short, "commitment therapies" are "suggestive-supportive" in nature, being in the service of the reigning cultural symbolic.[49]

Negative communities, on the other hand, are of recent historical vintage and find their origin in a modern cadre of the cultural elite, one championing a psychological and therapeutic mode of self-relating. This new mode of therapy is not so much suggestive-supportive as it is "analytic" and "uncovering." In the case of Freud and his psychoanalytic followers, the point is to engage the unconscious directly ("where id was, there ego shall be"), thus widening the ego and a sense of one's unique individuality. Indeed, cultural forms such as religion and politics are rendered suspect, being understood as symbolic manifestations of the contents of the unconscious. An "analytic attitude" of observation, detachment, and tolerance of psychical discontents replaces the language of faith and the command to repress. The result is "deconversion" in the sociological sense: the collapse of the cultural superego, the replacement of the normative institutions of church and party with the "hospital" and the "theater," the valorization of the individual over the group, and the emergence of a therapeutic character type, namely, "psychological man."[50] Insofar as the concept of negative communities is designed to show the shift from the social hegemony of religion, the group, and "therapies of commitment" to the rise of the individual and analytic access, it gives psychosocial depth to the corresponding shift away from tradition-based mysticism that we have discussed, starting with Certeau.

Even though the above still characterizes the majority of those who hew to a Freudian approach to religion, there is a second sense, quite contrary to the first, in which the psychoanalytic ritual has functioned as an agent of change commensurate with the rise of modern spirituality. Turning the psychoanalytic eye back on itself through an anthropological lens, one can see it as a secularized Western ritual offering secular versions of phenomena usually associated with trance states and ritual: contorted physical manners and expressions, severe and at times abnormal emotional vocalizations, claims of unusual knowledge, gender confusion, and antisocial ideation, impulses, and behavior. The institutionalization of psychoanalysis under the rubric of medicine ensured its conformity with the norms of secular society, but when linked to religious retreats and ascetic practices, contemporary psychoanalytic sessions are marked by the occasional influx of mental phenomena that go beyond the borders of accepted standards of normality. It is this clinical data that led both Freud and Kohut to agree on the reality of thought transference and led the "psychoanalytic mystics" to theorize about a spiritual dimension to the personality. Moreover, if the clinic is one social space in which such altered states may be found, it is clear that linked such spaces, such as the monastery and retreat center, in conjunction with alternative forms of introspective practices, generate other, related psychological states and modes of knowledge. It is precisely the growing number of both analysts and analysands who have experimented with a variety of such social spaces and introspective techniques, as befitting the cultural ascendancy of a "psychoanalytic spirituality," that has helped drive new post-Freudian formulations on the mystical.[51] In other words, psychoanalysis has also contributed in a positive sense to the rise of unchurched, nontraditional modern spirituality—and it, too, can see germs of wisdom in the formulations of religious mystics.

The final matter of this section is to bring the above discussion to bear on our previous analyses, in chapters 3 and 4, of Augustine's mystical theology. It should be clear that this work has not advocated an unqualified use of the theories of psychospirituality. The discussion thus far has shown how the latter, as one of several projects or enterprises within the broader scope of what I have called the psychology-and-religion movement, owes its origins, development, and cultural ascendancy in part to shifts in the larger culture. And as one of the many strands that have contributed to and been influenced by the rise of modern spirituality, it often partakes of modern spirituality's unchurched character. With respect to debates about mysticism within the academy, not only do many of these psychologies evince a naive perennialism but their "common cores" are really quite different. Going by the descriptions in the text (which is all we have), Rolland's oceanic feeling is not equivalent to Bucke's cosmic consciousness, Jung's Self archetype, Bion's O, or Maslow's peak experience. And none is equivalent to Augustine's intellectual visions. In sum, such psychologies can be said to evince unchurched, modern, psychological *varieties* of perennialism.

Such psychologies have engaged in what I have called dialogical projects, typified by the psychology-comparativist dialogue and that between psychology and theology, but such attempts are all too often a more subtle form of reductionism in which traditional expressions of mysticism are equated with peak experiences, archetypes, and so on. One need only look at Jung's famous and contested conversation with the Zen adept Shin'ichi Hisamatsu or Anne Hawkins's Jungian analysis of Augustine's ascent at Ostia (where in both cases archetypes rule the day) to see the kinds of difficulties involved in such a simple application of psychospirituality.[52] Although my analysis of Augustine partakes of the ethos of the psychology-theology dialogue, I have maintained a dialogical transformational approach, one that advocates a constructivist stance while accepting that mystical states and experiences may be different in degree, and perhaps in kind, despite their family resemblance. Also, in our interpretation of "dialogue," psychoanalysts are seated at the same table as textologists, theologians, literary critics, historians, and philosophers. But this sort of dialogue presumes those psychoanalytic and psychological formulations that accept the possibility of Augustine's claims without imposing any specific mystical content. It would be as reductionistic to interpret Augustine's mystical ascents as instances of the numinous emergence of the Self archetype, peak experiences, or as moments of cosmic consciousness as it would be to interpret them as regressions to the unity of primary narcissism. Again, when I say "grounds" or "possibility," it does not imply that any claim to an *ontos* "is" or "is not." On the contrary, I have pointed to the constructivist appeal to Kant. But again, this is not to deny that such an *ontos* is not real, only that there has yet to be convincing philosophical grounds for establishing it. It is these considerations that led us, in chapter 3, to use the Lacanian notion of the Real, an expanded view of Eros, and psychoanalytic theorizing about deep, unused, and often undeveloped mystical capacities "in dialogue with" Augustine's specifically theological formulations. Further, while the exact identity and nature of the *More* is left unchallenged, what one can say is that for all intents and practical, everyday existential purposes the *meaning* of mystical noesis is invariably bound up with (in the case of Augustine) his therapeia and "mystical theology," which I considered as an instance of an evolving God-representation and transitional modes of experiencing, the latter further characterized as the developmental infrastructure of constructivism. Since individual and cultural baggage are often brought along for the ride on such a faith journey, I have argued that a full spectrum of psychoanalytic models is admissible in, for example, looking at the role played by sexuality or archaic narcissistic structures in mystical formulations. Indeed, I have stressed how such critical analyses can deconstruct the more psychologically defeating aspects of Augustine's theological formulations.

Theologians may well applaud taking seriously varying definitions of the mystical and the need to set any mystic in the context of their culture, written corpus, and tradition. And those who are wedded to the metaphysical might find solace in Katz's view that constructivism does not undermine the possibility that mystics access the More (only that no convincing epistemology has yet to provide the grounds for it). The epistemological implications of transitional modes of experiencing could be made to tally with this insofar as, contra Freud, Winnicott's notion of reality is that of an *x* that is ever receding and never fully discerned. Indeed, and again speaking to the theologian, one could go further to speak of a "metaphysical horizon" to transitional forms of mystical experiencing. That being said, if a dialogical transformational approach is not to be understood as just another instance of psychospirituality, then one must also say that it is not another instance of mystical theology. On the contrary, even if one were to accept a "metaphysical horizon" of any proclaimed *ontos* it would, by virtue of it status as transitional, render it closer to an art form than to a monolithic truth. The psychosocial advantage of such a rendering is that it undermines the psychological totalitarianism of dogmatic intransigence and the kinds of sociocultural abuse that have been historically linked to ontological difference. The focus on the individuating human imagination and transitional experiencing keeps any proclaimed *ontos* from becoming a very hard reality—intransigent models of and for the world, as Geertz tells us. In this sense, transitional modes of being, the social sciences in general, postmodern deconstructive analyses, and even some theological formulations (such as Tillich's Protestant Principle) all provide a needed antidote, namely, the proposition that any cosmological scheme is also a human creation that brings with it some very human baggage, both developmental and cultural.

The mourning thesis also allows us to present Augustine's mystical therapeia as just another instance of mourning and theory building in which private experience (his particular visions) becomes part of public theory (his mystical theology). Augustine de-idealized the Christianity into which he was socialized as a boy because of its perceived lack of sophistication. Then, with the failure of Faustus, he went on to de-idealize Manichaeism. Augustine was once again open to being taught, and with the help of Ambrose and philosophical and religious texts, he undertook significant inner reflection, which led to seminal insights that creatively used the resources of his culture in fashioning the framework for a mystical therapeia—one that engaged elements of the inner world in a way that classifies him, from the perspective of depth psychology, as an "intuitive psychologist." In so doing, the underlying psychosocial dynamics of Augustine's process of mourning and creative response were similar to those of Rolland, Jung, and others. In all these cases we have private experience and individual reflection in dialogue with extant cultural texts and narratives, a dialogue that ultimately manifests as a public theory or, in Augustine's case, as mystical theology.

Of course, this is not the way Augustine presents his work. He attempted to establish an ontological truth as well as map a universally valid faith trajectory. In this he is not wholly unlike Freud, who universalized and (in borrowing a religious term) "ontologized" Oedipus in *Totem and Taboo* so that it became the phylogenetic basis for all individual fantasies as well as all cultural, historical, and religious expressions. It was only through the initial efforts of anthropologists and psychoanalysts that we can now safely say that Freud was a psychologically gifted ethnographer of his culture and that Oedipus remains a universal possibility but not a universal actuality. Similarly, Augustine merged his personal narrative with his interpretation of scripture, thus "ontologizing" his "developmental scheme" and presenting it as a universal pattern to be used by all in their quest for salvation. Surely there are many who have found and will continue to find that the *Confessions* speaks directly to them. However, as with Freud, such a narrative is hardly universal. It is a universal possibility, yes, but hardly a universal actuality. It remains relevant to and actualized for certain groups of people in certain climes and eras whose developmental trajectories are condensed with and ordered by a particular sociocultural surround.

The Academy, the Clinic, and Comparative Contributions

Among other things, the above indicates that while the enterprise known as psychospirituality and that project known as the dialogue between psychology and theology are not mutually exclusive, often sharing mutual interests and methodologies, they nevertheless warrant being seen as distinct entities within the broader scope of the psychology-and-religion movement. The same can be said for another project animating the latter, a project I have called the psychology-comparativist dialogue.

Like the dialogue between psychology and theology and the emergence of psychospirituality, this dialogue goes back to the originative period of the psychology-and-religion movement. While the reasons for this are complex and beyond the scope of the present book to catalogue fully, it is possible to point to the interaction of several related factors that can be conveniently denoted by Raymond Schwab's term, an "oriental renaissance."[53] The latter cultural shift helped secure the presence of Eastern religious practices and institutions through multiple social channels:

the formation of academic positions in oriental studies and comparative religion at leading universities (such as those held by Max Müller, Hermann Oldenberg, and Sylvian Levi), the establishment of a new generation of intellectuals and lay sympathizers (Emerson, Henry Steel Olcott, Madame Blavatsky and the theosophy movement), a migration of Asians into Western countries, and the missionary activity of Buddhists and Hindus (here we may note Vivekananda, Anagarika Dharmapala, Soyen Saku, and Yogananda). That this cultural shift had an impact on the psychological analysis of religion is beyond dispute. Well-known examples can be found in the work of Carl Jung, J. B. Pratt (who studied under James), James Leuba, Kristian and Harald Schjelderup, and the Asian contributions of, among others, Girindrasekhar Bose and Heisaku Kosawa.[54] Indeed, Rolland's request to Freud to analyze the oceanic feeling in no small measure owed to his research on, and eventual biographies of, Ramakrishna and Vivekananda.[55]

With respect to the postwar period, one sees an exponential rise in the level of psychological interest in and interaction with Eastern religious ideas and practices. The "countercultural" movements of the late 1950s and 1960s, combined with the rapid dissemination of Eastern introspective practices, led to multiple psychological investigations on a variety of subjects pertinent to mysticism. This firm social base has carried into the present, leading to a third period of the flowering of the psychology-comparativist dialogue, best evinced in continued experimental and neurocognitive studies of mysticism, the development of a host of retreat centers (such as Esalen) and therapeutic attempts to assimilate Eastern practices (such as Jon Kabat Zinn's mindfulness-based stress reduction at the University of Massachusetts Medical Center), and the continued proliferation of attempts by psychospiritualists to engage Buddhism and Hinduism.

Again, the exact nature and full analysis of the shifting contours of this dialogue, much less the profound and interesting series of questions and issues such an analysis would raise, are well beyond the reach of this discussion. Nevertheless, at least some part of the dialogue must be addressed if we are to expand our analysis of Augustine to engage the wider cultural background of a psychologically informed modern spirituality. Limiting the discussion to the issues and debates entertained earlier in this work, I turn first to Hinduism. Since the early days of Freud's dialogue with Girindrasekhar Bose, a number of psychoanalysts, comparativists, and psychoanalytically informed anthropologists—from

Carstairs and Devereux through Kurtz, Caldwell, and Roland, to the most recent attempt by Obeyesekere, with his notion of a "dream-ego"—have expanded our notions of Indian developmental lines while in some cases also reaffirming the intuitive validity of mystical modes of knowing.[56] However, in keeping with the narrative line and argument developed in this book, I will limit the scrutiny to a reframing of two of the "psychoanalytic mystics" we have already seen: Sudhir Kakar and Jeffrey Kripal. The aim of the analysis is to show how the transformational psychoanalytic theorizing of the third period of the psychology-and-religion movement has been influenced by the kinds of social shifts discussed in the previous two sections. This will be shown through psychobiographical portraits of the two thinkers in question. Turning then to specifically psychoanalytic engagements with Buddhism, I adopt a different strategy and look at representative studies from all three periods. From a sociological perspective, this approach allows a more nuanced (but hardly exhaustive) examination of the relation between psychoanalysis and the complex cultural eddies that have served to fertilize the spiritual but not religious movement. From a comparative perspective this will allow us, on the one hand, to document that the history of models employed (classic, adaptive, transformational) mirror those we have employed in the case of Augustine and, on the other, how the kinds of "mystical experiences" under consideration offer a counterpoint to the intellectual visions of Augustine, thereby serving to further chisel a dialogical transformational approach and the broader psychoanalytic study of comparative mysticism.

Starting, then, with the cases of Kakar and Kripal, I have noted that the methodological strategies each has utilized reveal how both are intellectually committed to psychoanalysis yet also to the wisdom contained in mysticism. Understood in light of the methodological focus of the present chapter, their respective analyses evoke further interest. This is so for both offer throughout their works autobiographical reflections—reflections which support the arguments of the previous two sections concerning the importance of mourning and the rise of the spiritual but not religious movement.

The case of Jeffrey Kripal is of particular relevance in that the transformational approach he utilized in his psychobiography of Ramakrishna (who can, though with a wink, be characterized as Augustine's counterpart in Hinduism) railed against a history of psychoanalytic pathologizing.[57] Kripal tells us that he was born into a Catholic family and attended a Catholic seminary with the desire to explore the possibility of a monastic vocation. At the seminary, in reading the works of Saint Teresa of Avila and Saint John of the Cross and in praying with the Song of Songs, he became interested in the relation of sexuality and mysticism. But he was troubled by the reality of celibacy when set against the homoerotic language of bridal mysticism. Additionally, in taking the mystical injunction toward things ascetic seriously, Kripal lost over one hundred pounds and gained a diagnosis of anorexia. These conflicts led him into therapy with a professionally trained priest at the seminary. Through therapy he understood the dynamics of a rather pronounced oedipal conflict and learned how fasting and sexuality were equated in his unconscious. Gaining much of his weight back during this process, Kripal could admit that "Freud, compassionately and deftly mediated through the structures of an enlightened Catholicism, literally saved my life."[58]

Therapy bore fruit in other, more defining ways. As an adolescent, Kripal had been tormented by a fantasy "very much as Jung's fantasy of God shitting on a Cathedral used to torment him."[59] The content of the fantasy consisted of "a naked ithyphallic Jesus on the cross with myself and the Virgin Mary standing beneath him."[60] This fantasy was similarly understood to be structured around oedipal themes (the phallus rose up in the Virgin Mother's presence) and related to his later asceticism: "I was about to 'crucify' my sexuality for its unresolved oedipal dimensions."[61] However, the imagery of other dreams, myths, and visions that erupted during and after the course of analysis made Kripal pause to reconsider the adequacy of a reductionist psychoanalytic hermeneutic:

> Freud was undoubtedly right, but he was also limited, for something other than an Oedipus complex was being revealed in my nights. This "something more" soon crystallized itself, not surprisingly, in another dream. . . . The dream involved three presences: myself, a young, attractive maiden dressed in the manner of a Greek or Roman woman, and a winged unicorn whose literally burning body appeared like brilliant black lightning. The maiden said nothing but simply smiled and led me to the edge of what looked like a very deep, very turbulent black sea. Just below the waters burned the fires of a terrifying beautiful winged horse with a single horn coming out of its head. Neither the horn nor the wings were fully grown. The Fire fascinated me—dangerous, dark, and yet filled with light. I instinctively knew that it was my task to get this mysterious being out of the

water, and so I entered the waves and tried to pull him up, but to no avail. The scene then shifted and I saw myself as a youth riding naked on the now fully winged and fully horned being into the sky.[62]

Kripal understands that the above could be conceived of in oedipal terms (for example, "the small horned unicorn can be read as a self-representation of the little boy and his feelings of sexual inadequacy before the Mother"[63]). But this "myth-dream" or "dream-vision" (which he later called the "vajrasva vision") was far too numinous and mythological to be wholly subsumed under Freudian categories. So Kripal, in typical Jungian fashion, searched books in the history of art and religious myths to find similar structural content. He came to realize that the dream was "structured around a profound *coincidentia oppositorium* that would engage me for years to come, that between the mystical and the sexual, or what I would later call the erotic . . . if this was sex, it was God's sex."[64]

The problem presented to him by this vision, alongside his heterosexual orientation and his "ontological crisis," eventually barred him from seeking religious fulfillment in the Catholic Church. Kripal admits he could not find the solutions to the existential and intellectual problems he was seeking in the resources offered by Christianity. As Kripal puts it, this quandary "exploded my Catholic world."[65] Becoming intrigued by the analytic dynamic promoted in academia, the depth hermeneutic of psychoanalysis (the latter functioning as "a modern or post-modern mystical path"[66]), and in following the advice of his monastic spiritual director to become his own spiritual director, Kripal enrolled as a doctoral student at the University of Chicago Divinity School in the history of religions, there to be directed by the heirs of Mircea Eliade. It was also there that he found, in the texts of Hinduism, legends and myths that bore "an almost uncanny resemblance to the truths of my myth-dream," as well as a mystical path "in which a heterosexual male could remain a heterosexual male and approach the divine in an explicitly erotic fashion."[67] Embarking on a study of Ramakrishna (later to become *Kali's Child*), Kripal was disappointed to find that here too was a mystic whose spiritual path was homoerotic in nature. At first he was inclined to interpret Ramakrishna along the lines of previous studies that had championed classic reductive psychoanalytic models: "I would have been quite happy with such reductionisms and would have painted the saint as hopelessly neurotic."[68] But then, once again, a vision intervened. In

Calcutta, in the midst of research for his dissertation, Kripal entered into a waking dream state "much like the mystico-erotic states I was then uncovering in the Bengali texts."[69] It was this experience, which he refers to as "that night" and which to him was so reminiscent of the experiences of Ramakrishna, that changed his hermeneutical strategy. It made him "very wary of methods that would reduce Ramakrishna's own mystico-erotic experiences to the 'nothing buts' and clinical jargon of classical psychoanalysis."[70] Alongside textual analysis, psychoanalysis, and the methodologies found in comparative mysticism, the experience became part of his hermeneutical strategy. Detached from a faith commitment to a religious tradition, he utilized the tools of academia (as we saw in the summary of his thesis in chapter 3) to extend psychoanalytic metapsychology with recourse to one of the "mystics" of psychoanalysis, Lacan, and a new formulation of "the erotic," using Obeyesekere and Ricoeur to arrive at a satisfying intellectual and personal solution. It is perhaps not so surprising to learn that he subsequently came to promote a "mystical humanism" and embarked on a study of the Esalen Institute and the "religion of no religion."[71]

Like Kripal, Sudhir Kakar, a practicing Indian analyst who trained under Erik Erikson, has railed against the psychoanalytic pathologizing of not just the figure of Ramakrishna (though him as well) but of all things Indian and mystical. And again like Kripal, he offers multiple autobiographical reflections, which reveal a form of mourning that links his Indian identity with his Western training and methodological preferences. For example, he tells us he grew up in India socialized into the lore and mores of Hindu culture. On the one hand, he speaks of his clinical training in Europe and America as a "self-chosen exile" during which he underwent a process of disillusionment about his native land (what he refers to as a "violent rejection").[72] Yet he also refers to the recurrence of a "passionate extolling" and "deep and persistent undercurrent of nostalgia, almost sensual in character, for the insights, smells, tastes, sounds" of India.[73] The latter was manifested in the nostalgic pull of Ayurvedic medicine, his use of a tongue scraper, his "reluctance to eat radishes and guavas at night," and his superstition that the twig from the neem tree "does infinitely more than just clean the teeth."[74] He thus remarks that his main psychological and professional conflict manifested as a personal "battleground"—one where he tried to bring together "the Indian 'background' and the Western 'foreground' onto a single canvas."[75] Indeed, in his first breakthrough work, *The Inner World,* he confesses that what the reader will find there is not simply a work of scholarship but one that "is also related to personal needs . . . a return to and into a personal past, a reconnaissance of my own origins,"[76] and that the insights gleaned during the course of his research had "a therapeutic effect insofar as they have clarified and engaged the deeply Indian parts of myself."[77] In particular, Kakar reveals that he came to locate himself in that cadre of persons belonging to the tradition of the "Indian intellectual," characterized as "an intellectual tradition more than a hundred years old, starting with Ram Mohan Roy (1774–1833), a tradition devoted to the vicissitudes of Indian identity in modern times."[78] With great passion Kakar shares with us his deep identification with Nehru, another member of this tradition, who made it part of his life task to capture not simply the geographical, physical, and diverse cultural strands of India but also that "peculiar spirit" and "identity" that mark India as unique.[79]

This personal background became instrumental in determining Kakar's stress on a truly interdisciplinary nonreductive psychoanalytic orientation. Indeed, the pervading postmodern theme of his work lies in denying the (culturally mandated) discovery of an absolute truth, walking the fine line between psychological universalism and cultural relativism, and respecting different (and equal) visions of reality, mental health, gender identity, and selfhood. This is, as we have seen, particularly true of his stance on mysticism and his use of what he calls the "mystics" of psychoanalysis. In this regard, Kakar is unrelentingly critical of those psychoanalysts who pathologize mysticism. Citing the need for new paradigms in the psychoanalytic study of mysticism, Kakar casts a disparaging eye on representative studies in the field, which he thinks are still taken for granted as the norm by too many psychoanalysts and psychoanalytically inclined researchers. In building his case, Kakar asks us to "consider, for instance, the following remarks made by an eminent analyst":

> I am afraid that the Hindu striving toward Nirvana may well be related to the terrible failures and cruelties of this culture (as the appalling prevalence of abysmal poverty, the infantile death rate, the infamous caste system, with its ugly notion of the "untouchable," the dismal failure to control over population) and the dangers of escapism implicit in a too unworldly approach to life. The unhappy results are of a magnitude which cannot be overlooked; I am afraid that reality testing may well have fallen by the wayside in the striving toward "moksha."[80]

Kakar sees in the latter the orientalist and colonialist tendencies of some working within psychoanalysis. Such efforts, he thinks, are "neither careful enough nor sensitive enough to its subject matter," resulting in the "banal oversimplification of human motives and debunking of human endeavors."[81] Such work, continues Kakar, is of "special interest to an Indian psychoanalyst" for it is the "refusal of psychoanalysis to engage themselves with the mystical model of man and their predilection to dismiss it perfunctorily" that is but "another example of Western parochialism in the human sciences."[82] Thus for Kakar, Vedanta philosophy does indeed harbor a transformation of narcissistic structures that jibes with the directionality of Kohut's psychoreligious goal of "cosmic narcissism" and Winnicott's goal of a subjectivity imbued with the delight of creative apperception.[83] Buddha's proclamation of dukkha does not mean he is "depressed but in perfect attunement with the reality principle."[84] At the same time, Kakar does go on to say that even so, it would be a mistake not to embrace the potentially liberating insights psychoanalysis offers: "the freedom from imaginary terrors, unnecessary hypocrisies and enslaving ideologies."[85] The point is that mystical models have elements of both buried wisdom and ideological blindness. In making these observations, then, Kakar evinces a process of mourning that can be linked to that sector of a social base that has been affected by expanding pluralism, the introduction of and experimentation with mystical philosophy, and the attempt to integrate psychoanalytic models of the mind with the mystical.

If the psychobiographical analyses of Kakar and Kripal have enriched the present discussion, it is also the case that the argument put forth in this chapter can be buttressed in a different way, by looking closely at the history of another facet of the psychology-comparativist dialogue, the specifically psychoanalytic engagement with Buddhism. This dialogue is particularly informative, for the successive history of models employed mirrors those I introduced in the case of Augustine. Moreover, an examination of the precise nature of the cultural eddies that have produced such models can only add sophistication to the sociological analysis of the previous two sections. Finally, such an overview will afford a comparative contrast to both mystical theologies and psychospiritualities, reinforcing once again the complexity of terms like mysticism and spirituality, as well as the various definitional and hermeneutic strategies involved in studying such linked terms. It is my view that a nonreductive constructivist and dialogical transformational approach, which admits of real differences among traditions, is the most suitable way that psychoanalysis can be hailed as a bona fide partner in the interdisciplinary study of mysticism.

In beginning, it is important to observe that there is no evidence to suggest that Freud had anything more than a passing interest in and cursory knowledge of Buddhism. He wrote almost nothing that directly engaged Buddhist thought and practice, except for a brief reference in *Civilization and Its Discontents,* where he equates Thanatos with the nirvana principle. Yet the pejorative treatment that most think Freud accorded to the oceanic feeling is reflected in psychoanalytic interpretations of Buddhism during the originative period (1880–1930) of the psychology-and-religion movement.[86] Paradigmatic in this regard is a seminal essay by Franz Alexander that was delivered first as a lecture on September 25, 1922, at the 7th Congress of the International Psychoanalytic Association in Berlin, and later published in the German psychoanalytic journal *Imago.* Finally, it was published in English translation in 1931 in *The Psychoanalytic Review* under the title, "Buddhistic Training as an Artificial Catatonia (The Biological Meaning of Psychic Occurrences)." As the title indicates, it is here that we find, well before Freud's interpretation of the oceanic feeling, a true psychoanalytic pathologizing of Buddhism. Indeed, speaking historically, it is Alexander's essay, and not Freud's ruminations on Buddhism, that became the locus classicus of the pejorative psychoanalytic stance toward Buddhism. This is a crucial point, for the analysis of what may seem to some to be a relatively obscure figure becomes a necessity if one wishes to champion a transformational approach. In other words, to overturn the ingrained inertia of previous psychoanalytic orientations one must seek out and uproot its historical and conceptual origins.

Alexander began his essay by elaborating on what philosophers would call the mind-body problem. Contrary to the extremes of materialism (which Alexander identified with his contemporary, Vogt) and idealism (which he linked with Berkeley), Alexander held fast to a psychoanalytic rendering of philosophical positions he ascribed to Spinoza and Schopenhauer: a virtual identity between psychic and biological processes. Indeed, he noted that the essay could have been subtitled "The psychic meaning of biological occurrences." For Alexander, Buddhism, like psychoanalysis, was an attempt at the therapeutic alleviation of suffering, and, also like psychoanalysis, it entailed a regressive withdrawal into the self. However, unlike psychoanalysis, Buddhism never sought a reconciliation between instinctual demands and external reality but rather espoused a total break with and abandonment of the external world. For Alexander, Buddhism was a "nihilistic" philosophy that aimed at the alleviation of suffering through a very specific form of salvific knowledge: nirvana and its linked doctrine of reincarnation. Alexander characterized Buddhist meditation as progressing through four stages, each revealing its own level of pathology, ranging from melancholia to catatonia. Nirvana is interpreted as a regression not to primary narcissism but to intrauterine existence: "Nirvana is the condition (i.e., regression to) in the mother's womb."[87] Alexander posits the stage of nirvana could conceivably include the biopsychic knowledge of the conditions of birth, for in the womb one finds conditions ranging from the beginning of embryonic development to a formed fetus. Buddhist mediation, then, is a reverse tracing of the stages of development through multiple pathologies, culminating in the intrauterine knowledge of the process of birth.

For Alexander, Buddhism was a narcissistic-masochistic religion that ran contrary to the aims of the "transference" religion of Christianity, which was based on the father and aimed at regulating the affective relations between people. With respect to psychoanalytic theorizing about Buddhism, Alexander's thesis bears an initial resemblance to Freud's idea, elaborated in one of his later letters to Rolland, that mystical intuition could be valuable for an "embryology of the soul" but was useless for adaptation to the external world. Freud saw in the Christian narrative of the Fall a disguised and distorted version of the "primal deed." So Alexander reasons that in Buddhism we have, through the deeply regressive form of psychic surgery known as meditation, the dimly perceived knowledge of the origin of birth, now cast in the disguised and distorted doctrine of reincarnation.

Alongside this unadulterated pathologizing of Buddhism lies another strand of psychoanalytic reasoning that, in following Freud's more positive evaluations of mystical intuition, emphasizes the more adaptive, therapeutic aspect of Buddhism. This adaptive rendering of Buddhism is paradigmatically exemplified in an essay by the eccentric psychoanalyst Joseph Thompson (1875–1943). Thompson was an American-born analyst who trained at the Washington-Baltimore Psychoanalytic Institute. He was also a naval surgeon raised in Japan by a missionary father. His many years spent in the Far East led him to a deep interest in the relationship between psychoanalysis and Buddhism. It was because of such interest that he published under the pseudo-Chinese version of his name, Joe Tom Sun.[88]

Thompson made his views on psychoanalysis and Buddhism known in a 1924 essay titled "Psychology in Primitive Buddhism." The article is marred by generalizations and a total absence of citations, so we are left wondering what sources informed Thompson's understanding of Buddhism. Yet the essay is important, at least historically, for Thompson presents Buddhism as a culturally distinct therapeutic enterprise that parallels and prefigures the insights of psychoanalysis. Specifically, Thompson thinks that both systems aim at the alleviation of suffering and attainment of wisdom, and both use introspection and insight to attain their goals. Both systems stress the centrality of desire and misguided desire and, in contradistinction to the views of Franz Alexander, both cure through adaptation to external reality. Meditation is akin to free association, and the Buddhist eightfold path is essentially a cure through sublimation. "Nirvana" is not to be explained by "the mechanism of repression, but by the most deliberate conscious sublimation."[89]

The contributions of Alexander and Thompson have real continuities with extant analyses of Augustine's *Confessions* insofar as they are paradigmatic instances of the classic reductive and adaptive/healing lines of interpretation. Similarly, looking back at this period from the perspective of contemporary trends in the academic study of mysticism is instructive, in that some of the critiques one could level at them bear at least a tangential relation to the case of Augustine. For example, with regard to the text, psychoanalytic interpretations of Buddhism were limited by the then state of comparativist studies. The latter, from the perspective of contemporary Buddhology, was marred by incomplete and at times misleading translations, as well as by a neglect of the richness and complexity to be found in the many extant Buddhist schools, practices, and descriptions of meditational insights and states. Alexander, for example, confined himself not only to Theravada Buddhism but more specifically to *jnana* (concentration, calming) forms of meditation, to the exclusion of *vipassana* (insight) forms of mediation. His understanding of Buddhism was based on the rudimentary translations and commentaries of his time, notably those by Friedrich Heiler and Hermann Oldenberg, which lack the sophistication of contemporary Buddhology. In other words, we are getting a very narrow, incomplete, and ultimately misleading view of Buddhist teachings and practices. Additionally, there was no direct encounter with Buddhist practitioners, lamas, or masters, and no evidence that any psychoanalysts of this era ever experimented with meditative techniques, much less knew of their variety. As we shall see, an "insider" dimension, with its existential experience, has become a crucial element of contemporary psychoanalytic studies of Buddhism. Indeed, one can rightly conclude that the kind of knowledge found in psychoanalytic studies was what James would call knowledge "about" and not knowledge "of." Second-hand and confined to the armchair, it lacked an appreciation of thick description. More important, it presumed a psychological universalism that harbored the prejudices of orientalism and Eurocentrism.

It is hard, then, to speak of a true dialogue between psychoanalysis and Buddhism during this era. What we do have are two lines of psychoanalytic interpretations of Buddhism. The first treats Buddhism as pathology, and a direct line can be traced from Alexander to Bernard Lewin's link between ecstasy and mania, then to the present era through the work of Jeffrey Moussaieff Masson. Following Lewin, Masson sees the Buddha as profoundly depressed and nirvana as a manic denial of feelings of unbearable abandonment.[90] The second line, exemplified by Thompson, offers an adaptive, therapeutic view of Buddhism. What we do not have in this period is a third line (which I have called transformational) that sees Buddhist teachings and practices as embodying at least the possibility of a wisdom that goes beyond that of extant psychoanalytic models of the mind and health.

If the earliest period saw the germs of an adaptive reading of Buddhism, then it is fair to say that the postwar era saw its flowering. There are at least three general, interrelated factors that served to promote this flowering. One of these factors was the development in psychoanalytic theory, found in the advances of Neo-Freudians, the resources of ego psychology, and the stirrings of insight into the developmental line of narcissism and object relations. A second development was the dramatic social, political, and cultural changes that occurred in America during the 1950s and 1960s. These decades evinced a liminal quality in their general disillusionment with the social, political, economic, and religious institutions of the time, and there was a widespread rejection of the reigning forms of Christianity, combined with an interest in spiritual experimentation. A third development was the slow psychologization of Asian culture, particularly Japanese. As is well known, Freud was constantly trying to insert psychoanalysis into Western culture through various devices: his cultural works, relationships with those in socially prominent positions, and institutionalization of his therapeutic enterprise. Freud's ambitions went beyond Europe, engaging those who might serve his cause in the East. Most famous in this regard is his correspondence with the Indian psychoanalyst Girindrasekhar Bose. Lesser known, but more relevant for our purposes, is the psychoanalytic engagement with Japan. The early history of Japanese psychiatry was heavily influenced by the German schools, to which many Japanese flocked for graduate study, as well as American schools such as Johns Hopkins University and G. Stanley Hall's Clark University. However, a psychoanalytic monograph was published in Japan as early as 1919, and by 1930 psychoanalysis was being taught at major Japanese universities, the *Tokyo Journal of Psychoanalysis* had started publication, and some of Freud's works had been translated into Japanese. Several figures are prominent in the development of psychoanalysis in Japan, the most important for our purposes being Akihisa Kondo. Kondo went to the United States in the late 1940s to train at the Karen Horney Institute in New York City, where he befriended Horney and Eric Fromm. Kondo became the central link between Fromm and Horney and the most illustrated Buddhist figure of that time, D. T. Suzuki. It was Suzuki's brand of Zen that would change the dialogue between psychoanalysis and Buddhism.[91]

Certainly Suzuki's impact cannot be wholly divorced from what has been called "Buddhist modernism," a development ably catalogued by McMahan, Prebish, and others.[92] However, for our more limited purposes what is noteworthy is that Suzuki's presentation of Zen to a waiting Western world was deliberately psychological. As Robert Scharf notes, it was not the monastic, heavily ritualized and doctrinal Buddhism of previous centuries that Suzuki taught but a form that focused on the immediate experience of satori as the goal of Zen.[93] The road to Suzuki's Zen began in the nineteenth century, when Japan underwent a phase of rapid modernization and Westernization. In the religious sphere this was manifest as a "New Buddhism," one that was nonsectarian, universal, socially engaged, eminently rational, and in tune with science and psychology. Suzuki was heavily influenced by Western figures in the study of religion, notably William James, and this led him to reconstrue Buddhism to accord with the West's emerging focus on the value of mystical experience. A better match for an American culture disillusioned with institutional religion could not be found. The disillusioned liminal Western culture of the 1960s needed a new psychomystical therapeutic regimen—and found it in Suzuki's Zen.[94]

The best-known series of encounters of this era took place between Suzuki, Karen Horney, and Erich Fromm, although many others, among them Harold Kelman, Hebert Fingarette, Kondo, Ed Maupin, and Koji Sato, participated. This movement led to the creation of journals, such as *Psychologia* and the *American Journal of Psychoanalysis,* and the publication of significant books, such as *Zen Buddhism and Psychoanalysis.* Briefly put, the encounter led to new, creative embellishments of psychoanalytic theory and to the view that Buddhism was a bona fide healing system. Hence Horney's conclusion that Zen enabled the capacity to actualize wholeheartedness, defined as the characteristic of being entirely absorbed in one's actions, operating with all of one's faculties while at the same time remaining oblivious to oneself.[95] The wholehearted person is emotionally sincere, authentic, and capable of putting all of his or her energy and attention into the task at hand. Similarly, Fromm agreed with Suzuki that the experience of satori was not a regression to primary narcissism but "the repetition of the preintellectual, immediate grasp of the child, but on a new level, that of the full development of man's reason, objectivity, individuality. While the child's experience, that of immediacy and oneness, lies *before* the experience of alienation and the subject-object split, the enlightenment experience lies after it."[96] And Herbert Fingarette proferred the view that the paradoxical language of Zen, manifested in terms such as "selflessness" and "emptiness," was not indicative of pathology but rather a culturally specific use of therapeutic terms that, when properly translated and placed in the therapeutic context, had exact analogues in the psychoanalytic clinical setting: what was "lost" in Zen was not the self per se but the "transference self," with its attendant forms of anxiety and intrapsychic conflict.[97]

As we look back over this second period, it is clear that advances took place. Representatives of both Buddhism and psychoanalysis were engaging in dialogue, and a better appreciation of the aims and effects of meditation became available and was integrated into the therapeutic encounter. Certainly psychoanalysis was willing to champion an adaptive-therapeutic interpretation of Buddhist texts and practices. Buddhism, in effect, became a culturally variant form of psychoanalysis. From the perspective of Buddhist thought and practice, this may be a more subtle form of reductionism: it pretends to valorize Buddhism, but only as a form of introspection that finds its better half in the more empirically tested and precisely theorized formulations of psychoanalysis. Be that as it may, it is possible to find a correlate in those adaptive studies that framed Augustine's therapeia as prefiguring the insights of psychoanalysis: Augustine was an "intuitive psychologist," so to speak, who had the ego strength and creativity necessary to fashion a real if rudimentary healing system.

It is only in the third, contemporary period that a transformational approach to Buddhism has come to be seriously entertained and theorized. This accords with the narrative in the previous two sections in that such theorizing has been driven by the rise of an expanded social base composed of inner-worldly mystics. It is clear that this social base has crept into the practice of analysts and the therapeutic expectations of analysands. The training analyst Paul Cooper has noted that spiritual practices have influenced multiple dimensions of psychoanalytic therapy (such as theory, technique, training, and supervision), further drawing attention to the important empirical fact that many of his analysands understand psychoanalytic therapy as part of their spiritual growth.[98] Indeed, the training analyst Michael Eigen refers to psychoanalytic therapy as "a pyschospiritual journey," arguing that meditative practices and psychoanalysis are not separate but part of an allied process of growth. Moreover, a number of psychoanalytic theorists, among them Michael Eigen, Jack Engler, Judith Blackstone, Mark Epstein, and Barry Magid, have admitted to having mystical insights that have informed their theoretical leanings.[99] Some of these theorists can be classified as "cultural insiders" of mystical traditions because they have firsthand knowledge of mystical practices or intimate relationships with multiple masters and gurus. Thus, one can say of some within this group that its members wear more than one therapeutic hat: practicing psychoanalysts (who have been analysands), they are also students and teachers of mystical traditions. Their studies acknowledge the validity of mystical states and, consequently, evince attempts to relativize psychoanalytic theory vis-à-vis what they consider to be the wisdom available in mystical traditions. Clearly, we have come a long way from the armchair analysis of Franz Alexander.

Many of these studies, based on clinical data from both therapists and clients, understand that Buddhist practice is not simply therapeutic. It claims to be soteriological as well, and to catalogue experiences and states that may well lie outside the borders of existing psychoanalytic theory. As Epstein more firmly puts it, something in Buddhism "reaches beyond therapy, toward a farther horizon of self-understanding that is not ordinarily accessible through psychotherapy alone."[100] It is this latter point more than any other that demarcates the studies of this era. A paradigmatic case in point is that of Engler, who, reflecting on years of experience as a professor, as Buddhist *vipassana* meditation teacher, and psychoanalytic clinician, became convinced that those psychoanalytically minded interpreters of the Buddhist *anatta* before him had understood only part of the Buddhist meditational process. Buddhism was not, as with the early effort of Franz Alexander, simply a regression to early development and the womb, or, as with the mid-century efforts of Karen Horney and Erich Fromm, simply an Eastern form of psychoanalysis. Invoking the Jamesian More, which in Engler's case is a specifically Theravadin one, he describes the insight of *anatta:*

> Discovering that there is no ontological core to consciousness or self that is independent and enduring and no stable "objects" of perception . . . no "I" or "thing" enduring across the gap between the disappearance of one construction and arising of the next—this is a profound shock. It is experienced as a free fall into a looking-glass world where, as the Mad Hatter tells Alice, "Things are not as they seem!" It so turns our normal sense of self and reality on its head that, as Niels Bohr once remarked about quantum physics . . . if you don't get dizzy thinking about it, you haven't understood it.[101]

For Engler, psychoanalysis and Theravada Buddhism employ different techniques for different aims. Free association, dream interpretation, transference, and so on are all fruitful ways of heightening introspection and deepening the awareness of the discontents of repressed thoughts and feelings. But *vipassana* is designed to heighten attention to the extent that one is able to retrace the representational process whereby a sense of self, world, and other comes to exist. In its most profound sense the practice of *vipassana* leads to the above description of *anatta:* the insight into the absence of an enduring self. If the therapeutic task can be conceived along the lines of mourning, the psychoanalytic encounter with Buddhism now reveals that the latter engages an even deeper level of mourning and working-through: that of the existence of a continuous, stable, enduring self. The consequences of this perspective for psychoanalytic understandings of self and healing are dramatic. Engler makes the radical claim that the construction of a separate, enduring, continuous self is "a compromise formation with defensive aims."[102] In other words, we repress the fact of an unconstructed core to existence. Indeed, Engler is quick to point out that the insight into *anatta* is not necessarily a discovery. From the Theravada Buddhist perspective, the commonsense understanding that an enduring self exists is an illusion. There never was a self to begin with. Epstein concurs in suggesting that we "repress" the insubstantiality of the self.[103]

An important comparative contrast to Engler's Theravadin formulations can be found in the work of the (Tibetan) Buddhist psychologist Judith Blackstone. Engaging formulations of non-self states and their relation to conceptions of self-other found in intersubjective theory, Blackstone argues that the former "goes beyond" the latter. She chooses intersubjective theory because it seeks to undermine the illusory distinctions between therapist and client, cognition and affect. She applauds the notion that the therapeutic project is always mutual, involving the interface of reciprocal interacting subjectivities, with the aim of gaining a more flexible and functional organization of personality. However, contra intersubjective theory, Blackstone claims that there is a self-existing nondual ground that is the basis of all subjectivities and that can be experienced in meditation. It is the experience not of the contents of consciousness but of consciousness itself: an unmodified dimension of subjectivity beyond the self-representations addressed by psychoanalysis. This deep field of nondual consciousness slowly becomes more apparent as we untangle the obstacles that keep it from manifesting itself. Psychoanalysis, then, is now construed in light of this larger existential project insofar as it helps this process along—it illumines unconsciously held patterns of behavior and helps us develop more flexible organizations of self. As we do this, the more essential nondual field of consciousness begins to emerge naturally. So while the intersubjective goal of an "expanded repertoire of organizing principles" is not enough, being "far from the spontaneity, openness, and directedness of experience that occurs with nondual realizations," psychoanalysis can be reconfigured to aid in the task of bringing to awareness the "obscurations" that impede the manifestation of nondual consciousness.[104]

Recognizing that not all Buddhist forms of mediation necessarily lead to the same insight, Blackstone explicitly takes on the Theravada tradition invoked by Engler and Epstein, arguing that they present what Tibetan Buddhist Rinpoche Tsultrim Gyamtso calls a Rangtong understanding of self. In the Rangtong view, says Blackstone, the "eye" of the observing self cannot find a way to "turn around" and "know" itself. In the Rangtong view, all that one can "see" are fragments of emotions, sensations, thoughts, and volitional urges. This is the view, says Blackstone, to be found in Mark Epstein's proclamation of "thoughts without a Thinker" and in Engler's description of *anatta.* In the Shentong view, on the other hand, the "eye" can see itself. The Shentong view is expressed by the Tibetan notion of the "clear light" of consciousness: a "knowing" that is completely unimaginable and nonconceptual, luminous and blissful, self-knowing and self-aware, naturally shining forth as conceptual and emotional obstructions are dissolved.[105]

These diverse views of mysticism, represented by different traditions, are now making their way into the dialogue between psychoanalysis and religion. This indicates that psychoanalysis is becoming increasingly receptive to the possibility of a More beyond existing psychoanalytic categories, to the possibility that there exists a "trans" beyond the "pre" of Oedipus. The mapping of such insights and states will necessitate the collaboration of psychological and psychoanalytic clinicians and researchers with scholars in religious studies and practitioners of diverse introspective disciplines. No doubt this endeavor will be at least as long, arduous, and complex as has been the investigation of neuroses. It suggests the need for a dialogical, transformational, constructivist approach to mysticism.

Buddhism and Mystical Process

Taking Engler's work once again as a starting point, he proposes that psychoanalysis and Buddhism map discrete states of a single developmental sequence, the former describing the lower stages of what he calls "conventional" development, the latter the more subtle, spiritual stages of what he calls "contemplative" development.[106] The two healing systems have different aims: psychoanalysis (and here Engler follows Kohut) attempts to grow a cohesive self, whereas Buddhism aims at the more difficult insight that there is, in fact, no enduring self. Only when a cohesive enough self has developed can one engage in meditational exercises (*vipassana*) designed to gain insight into the reality that there is no enduring self. But the experience of *anatta,* being episodic, is not the ultimate aim. The latter, in the world of Theravada Buddhism, is the "extinguishing" of all "defilements"—a "process" aim put psychologically by the Theravada monk and scholar Wapola Rahula as follows:

> He who has realized the Truth, Nirvana, is the happiest being in the world. He is free from all 'complexes' and obsessions, the worries and troubles that torment others. His mental health is perfect . . . he appreciates and

> enjoys things in the purest sense without self-projections. He is joyful, exultant, enjoying the pure life, his faculties pleased, free from anxiety, serene and peaceful. As he is free from selfish desire, hatred, ignorance, conceit, pride, and all such "defilements", he is pure and gentle, full of universal love.[107]

Again, this ultimate aim of the erasure of defilements, however true it may be for a form of Theravada, is to be contrasted with Augustine's own aim, namely, as described by TeSelle, of a soteriological ideal that approximates an angelic mode of obedience.[108] Engler's take on the Buddhist aim is that it is an "ideal fiction." Noting that discrete, hierarchically ordered stages of development may misleadingly indicate a linear trajectory ending in such an ideal fiction, Engler has modified his model, arguing that conventional and contemplative lines of development are interactive, complicated, and perhaps too thick to fully untangle. He presents evidence from Rorschach tests, case histories, detailed observations from within American Buddhist communities, and anecdotal evidence that some Buddhist masters have exhibited forms of defensiveness and pathology. This is particularly true within master-disciple relationships where the difficulties associated with transference—the "guru" problem—if not recognized and corrected can lead to subjugation and sexual abuse.[109]

Subsequent commentators agree. Jeff Rubin, for example, argues that in Engler's earlier model, "the complexity and multidimensionality of human experience and development is obscured by linear, hierarchical, developmental models."[110] Rather, Rubin argues that the relation between psychoanalysis and Buddhism "is more complex than the existing accounts suggest, forming not a singular pattern of influence but rather resembling a heterogeneous mosaic composed of elements that are—depending on the specific topic—antithetical, complementary and synergistic."[111] By "synergy" Rubin means that psychoanalysis can help Buddhism investigate unconscious determinants, idealizing transferences, life-cycle difficulties, and the like, while Buddhism can help psychoanalysis with non-self-centered subjective states and meditational techniques. For example, psychoanalysis has exposed how teachings like *anatta* can be used (especially for adolescents and those entering middle age) to forestall the creation of an adaptive identity and to rationalize the lack of self-esteem and feelings of emptiness. Additionally, it has posited that some drawn to meditation are experiencing a host of psychological problems, ranging from a fear of autonomy and refusal to assume adult responsibility to issues concerning incapacity for intimacy and passivity/dependency needs. Indeed, the notion of enlightenment can be cathected narcissistically to cater to the needs of archaic forms of grandiosity while student-teacher relationships, transported to Western cultural ground, can activate debilitating mirroring and idealizing forms of transference. With respect to deep, narcissistic deficiencies (such as Balint's "basic fault" or Kohut's archaic structures of narcissism), it is psychoanalytic therapy, and not Buddhist teaching and practice, that is the superior healing enterprise. In turn, Buddhist practices valorize and attempt to actualize and integrate non-self-centered subjective states. Such states are defined generally as being "open to the moment without a sense of time, unselfconscious but acutely aware, highly focused and engaged yet relaxed and without fear . . . non-self-centered subjectivity is characterized by heightened attentiveness, focus and clarity, attunement to the other as well as the self, non-self preoccupied exercise of agency, a sense of unity and timelessness, and non-self-annulling immersion in whatever one is doing."[112]

The above discussion reveals a true "dialogical" project within the broad confines of the psychology-and-religion movement, which, insofar as it has developed classic, adaptive, and transformational approaches to Buddhism, mirrors the historical sequence of models applied analytically to Augustine's writings. To summarize quickly, early psychoanalytic studies of Augustine looked for, and apparently found, evidence of oedipal and preoedipal conflicts that often interfered with his goals while resulting in theological formulations that served to obstruct rather than to open the path to a better Christian life. My engagement in this book affirms the need for psychoanalysis to adopt a dialogical, transformational, constructivist approach to mystical "experiences" and process—an approach that includes, though with qualifications, classic reductive and adaptive interpretations. The Buddhist theorists whose work I have looked at here follow this strategy both historically and conceptually.

However, in the dialogue between psychology and Buddhism, certain tendencies can impede our understanding of both mystical insight and mystical process. For example, in the effort to theorize about the More of Buddhism one finds, at times, a tendency toward perennialism that runs contrary to the dialogical, constructivist approach I have offered in this book. Engler, for example, indicates that the insight into *anatta* reveals "the" fundamental (no)reality, a stance that, as we have seen, is hard to square with the Shentong version of the "clear light" valorized by his fellow Buddhist (if Tibetan Buddhist) Judith Blackstone.[113] Blackstone, on the other hand, is willing to speak of a baseline as well—a "universality of nondual consciousness"—that she, at least, sees in traditions ranging from Vedanta to Kashmir Shaivism.[114] But a constructivist perspective begs to differ. Nondual states may well be beyond ordinary conceptual modes of knowing (which, as I have already indicated, is epistemologically problematic), but even so, they are never self-evident, being mediated with respect to certain linguistic conventions and a total religious matrix. Indeed, as Katz notes, perennialist appeals to the nondual falter for "different metaphysical entities can be 'described' by the same phrases if these phrases are indefinite enough."[115] In other words, it is not necessarily the case, to take one example Katz cites, that Eckhart's *nichts* is equivalent to the Buddhist *sunyata*.[116]

Additionally, I have stressed throughout this study that episodic insight cannot be wholly divorced from mystical process. Here again the differences between mystical systems are accentuated. For example, any intimation of the nondual in Eckhart is tied to a Christian Trinitarian metaphysic (with no reference to a doctrine of reincarnation), while in the case of Theravada Buddhism it is tied to reincarnation and the eventual goal of being an *arahant*. Indeed, no traditional form of Buddhism would describe the "developmental" path to enlightenment without recourse to the twin related concepts of karma and reincarnation. Such concepts are as central to Buddhism as, for example, God-given grace is to Christianity. As far as a lived life is concerned, then, the differences between the two mystical systems are vast. Psychoanalysis can only admit such diverse ideologies if they are understood to be transitional forms that are instrumental to the conduct of everyday life and the making sense of existential concerns. For example, while Buddhism might speak of not so much a single life cycle but the "lives cycle," there is no place for this as metaphysical statement or developmental fact in psychoanalytic theory. To integrate it baldly without qualification would be to turn psychoanalysis into a form of Buddhist psychology. On the other hand, as I have also argued with respect to Augustine's therapeia, any ideological notion understood as a transitional mode of experiencing is potentially useful—it can not only make sense of deep spiritual insights but can also help us weave a convincing narrative of the exigencies of life. Indeed, I have argued that it is here that the wider meaning of the term mysticism resides.

On Basements and Attics

The discussion in this concluding chapter offers more evidence to buttress the proposed transformational orientation I have urged throughout. Given the complexity of terms like "mysticism" and "spirituality" and the various definitional and hermeneutic strategies involved in studying them, a nonreductive constructivist and dialogical transformational approach is almost a requirement. Such an approach, which admits real differences among religious traditions, makes psychoanalysis into a bona fide partner in the interdisciplinary study of mysticism, and potentially provides insights that can inform the analyst-analysand relationship.

The approach I have advocated here replaces perennialism, generic oceanic feelings, and primary narcissism with an appreciation of the complexities and subtleties of those experiences, states, and dispositions that have been aggregated under the rubric of the mystical. A dialogical, transformational, constructivist approach allows for the possibility (even if it is deemed philosophically problematic) of the deep epistemological claims of the mystics in their comparative variety when qualified with respect to a constructivist Kantian framework. Their practical existential meaning is then relegated to process issues understood in terms of transitional modes of being. With respect to Augustine, my use of an expanded definition of Eros, of cognitive neuroscience and the formulations of the psychoanalytic mystics illustrates just such an approach. This argument indicates that psychoanalysis must learn to accept that certain mystical insights and experiences may well go beyond its existing theoretical frameworks, while depictions of the aims of mystical process may well end up relativizing psychoanalytic ones. It should also be evident that there are clear differences between types of religious insight, markers of development, and aims of process, and that these do not always conform to extant psychoanalytic theory. Indeed, many of the models discussed in this book relativize extant psychoanalytic notions of psychic development: Kakar's tragic/romantic understanding of *moksha;* Engler's distinction between conventional and contemplative lines of development, as well as his explication of Buddhist notions of the (Theravadin) *arahant,* or, with respect to Blackstone, the Tibetan rainbow body; Kripal's view of the tantric developmental scheme; and Augustine's intellectual visions and valorization of angelic obedience. While all are quite different from one another, they share the same general relation to conventional theories of psychoanalysis: they turn them on their head. This point is succinctly made by Kripal when he says, from the standpoint of the successful tantric, "Freud only got to the third Cakra."[117]

On the other hand, all the above also claim that psychoanalysis can play a pivotal role in addressing the inevitable developmental baggage one brings along on the mystical journey. One must ask about the relation between what we now know to be the developmental infrastructure of certain teachings and formulations and their less than helpful consequences for the modern sensibility.

Such an approach can, I believe, be imported into the clinical space. The modern period has given rise to a new social base of analysands inspired by inner-worldly mysticism and modern forms of spirituality. This in turn has occasioned the emergence of a mystical dimension and theorizing about the mystical in psychologies of multiple kinds, including psychoanalysis. The eminent training analyst psychoanalyst Steven Mitchell affirms that he has "worked with several patients who have had different kinds of mystical experiences," and notes that such experiences and insights "tend to become the basis for the patient's deep convictions concerning the nature of human beings and what life is all about."[118] Given this crucial existential observation, Mitchell thinks it time to revisit the standard Freudian recourse to pathology. He writes that while in the "old days," analysts could easily dismiss such convictions "by reducing them to psychodynamics," such a move "seems abhorrent to many of us now."[119] Yet this has left him in a conundrum of sorts. While agreeing with his patients that such experiences and insights may well provide glimpses into the deeper mysteries of existence, Mitchell confesses to struggling with just how to meet the challenge they pose to the analytic enterprise. Psychoanalytic engagements with the More can no longer be handled in terms of business as usual. A new way of configuring such deeper insights relative to psychoanalytic theorizing and practice needs to be articulated.

What I have proposed is that the variety of mystical phenomena communicated by patients immersed in a variety of traditions can be similarly accepted and worked through using a dialogical, transformational, constructivist approach. Along these lines, Freud taught that humanity evolves by way of cultural advance and generational change.[120] He saw psychoanalysis as a secular cure of souls, one designed to make social institutions more reality-based, to dissipate guilt and fear, and, as he once put it in his "Thoughts for the Times on War and Death," to turn egoistic impulses into altruistic ones.[121] Yet Freud had reservations about the possibilities of human progress, as evinced in his letter to Lou Andreas-Salomé in 1914 in which he proclaimed that humans were "organically unfitted" for living in groups (which is to say civilization), and further, that "We have to abdicate, and the *Great* Unknown, He or It, lurking behind Fate will someday repeat this *experiment* with another race."[122]

Let us hope that this dire assessment, written in the dark days of the Great War, is not the final judgment of psychoanalysis. Freud did not live to see the rise of a new psychoanalytic social base alert to the possibilities of spiritual transformation, and he knew little of the diversity of mysticism revealed by cross-cultural dialogue. As this new cultural movement comes to inform clinical practice, we may justifiably project that it will legitimate insights into human personality as enduring as those found in the mystics while transforming them through theories as imaginative as those bequeathed by psychoanalysis.

NOTES

INTRODUCTION

1. See, for example, William B. Parsons, *The Enigma of the Oceanic Feeling: Revisioning the Psychoanalytic Theory of Mysticism* (New York: Oxford University Press, 1999).

2. See Bernard McGinn, *The Foundations of Mysticism: Origins to the Fifth Century* (New York: Crossroad, 1991); John Peter Kenney, *The Mysticism of St. Augustine* (New York: Routledge, 2005).

3. Unless otherwise stated, all quotations from the *Confessions* are taken from *The Confessions of St Augustine*, trans. Rex Warner (New York: Mentor, 1963). All emphases in the texts from the *Confessions* are also from this edition.

4. See McGinn, *Foundations of Mysticism*, 232.

5. See Karl Weintraub, *The Value of the Individual: Self and Circumstance in Autobiography* (Chicago: University of Chicago Press, 1978); Henri Marrou, *Saint Augustin et la fin de la culture antique* (Paris: Éditions de Boccard, 1949); Robert O'Donnell, *St. Augustine's Confessions: The Odyssey of Soul* (Cambridge, MA: Harvard University Press, 1969).

6. See Weintraub, *Value of the Individual*, 39–40.

7. While the literature championing this perspective is vast, a recent paradigmatic example lies in the work of Kenney, *The Mysticism of St. Augustine.*

8. For an overview of the definitional problems and associated debates surrounding the term "mysticism," see William B. Parsons, ed., *Teaching Mysticism* (New York: Oxford University Press, 2011).

9. See Karl Weintraub, "St. Augustine's *Confessions:* The Search for a Christian Self," in *The Hunger of the Heart: Reflections on the Confessions of Augustine,* ed. Donald Capps and James E. Dittes, Monograph Series 8 (West Lafayette, IN: Society for the Scientific Study of Religion, 1990), 12.

10. See Peter Brown, *Augustine of Hippo* (Berkeley: University of California Press, 1967); Georges Gusdorf, "Conditions and Limits of Autobiography," in *Autobiography: Essays Theoretical and Critical,* ed. James Olney (Princeton, NJ: Princeton University Press, 1980); Krister Stendahl, "The Apostle Paul and the Introspective Conscience of the West," *Harvard Theological Review* 56, no. 3 (1963): 199–215.

11. I use Outler's language as cited by James E. Dittes in his essay "Continuities between the Life and Thought of Augustine," in *The Hunger of the Heart: Reflections on the Confessions of Augustine,* ed. Donald Capps and James E. Dittes, Monograph Series 8 (West Lafayette, IN: Society for the Scientific Study of Religion, 1990), 120.

12. See Donald Capps, "Augustine as Narcissist: Of Grandiosity and Shame," in *The Hunger of the Heart: Reflections on the Confessions of Augustine,* ed. Donald Capps and James E. Dittes, Monograph Series 8 (West Lafayette, IN: Society for the Scientific Study of Religion, 1990); Margaret Miles, "Infancy, Parenting and Nourishment in Augustine's *Confessions,*" in *The Hunger of the Heart: Reflections on the Confessions of Augustine,* ed. Donald Capps and James E. Dittes, Monograph Series 8 (West Lafayette, IN: Society for the Scientific Study of Religion, 1990).

13. Eugene TeSelle, "Augustine as Client and as Theorist," in *The Hunger of the Heart: Reflections on the Confessions of Augustine,* ed. Donald Capps and James E. Dittes, Monograph Series 8 (West Lafayette, IN: Society for the Scientific Study of Religion, 1990), 215.

14. See *The Confessions of St. Augustine,* trans. Warner, 10.14, 30, 32.

15. See William James, *The Varieties of Religious Experience* (New York: Modern Library, 1929); E. R. Dodds, "Augustine's Confessions: A Study of Spiritual Maladjustment," in *The Hunger of the Heart: Reflections on the Confessions of Augustine,* ed. Donald Capps and James E. Dittes, Monograph Series 8 (West Lafayette, IN: Society for the Scientific Study of Religion, 1990); Bernhard Legewie, *Augustinus: Eine Psychographie* (Bonn: A. Markus & E. Webers Verlag, 1925).

16. While this study does not utilize narrative theory, Mark Freeman's reading of Augustine, particularly with respect to the varying notions of development, comes close to that developed in this book. See his *Rewriting the Self* (New York: Routledge, 1993).

17. See Philip Rieff, *The Triumph of the Therapeutic* (New York: Harper, 1966).

18. As Freud put it, psychoanalysis is "a profession of lay curers of souls who need not be doctors and should not be priests." Sigmund Freud and Oskar Pfister, *Psychoanalysis and Faith: Dialogues with the Reverend Oskar Pfister,* ed. Heinrich Meng and Ernst L. Freud (New York: Basic Books, 1963), 125–26.

19. See Diane Jonte-Pace and William B. Parsons, eds., *Religion and Psychology: Mapping the Terrain* (New York: Routledge, 2001).

20. I take the term "modern spirituality" from Mary MacDonald (see her essay "Spirituality," in *The Encyclopedia of Religion,* ed. Lindsay Jones [New York:

Macmillan, 2005]). She distinguishes it from "classic spirituality," the latter being essentially churched.

21. See, for example, Robert Fuller, *Spiritual But Not Religious* (New York: Oxford University Press, 2001); G. William Barnard, "Diving into the Depths: Reflections on Psychology as a Religion," in *Religion and Psychology: Mapping the Terrain,* ed. Diane Jonte-Pace and William B. Parsons (New York: Routledge, 2001); William B. Parsons, "Psychologia Perennis and the Academic Study of Mysticism," in *Mourning Religion,* ed. William B. Parsons, Diane Jonte-Pace, and Susan E. Henking (New York: Oxford University Press, 2011).

22. For evidence that this is so, see Michael Eigen, "One Reality," in *The Couch and the Tree: Dialogues in Psychoanalysis,* ed. Anthony Molino (New York: North Point Press, 1998); Paul Cooper, "The Disavowal of the Spirit: Integration and Wholeness in Buddhism and Psychoanalysis," in the *Couch and the Tree: Dialogues in Psychoanalysis,* ed. Anthony Molino (New York: North Point Press, 1998); Anthony Molino, "Slouching towards Buddhism: A Conversation with Nina Coltart," in the *Couch and the Tree: Dialogues in Psychoanalysis,* ed. Anthony Molino (New York: North Point Press, 1998).

23. I use several terms to designate psychoanalytic theorizing about mysticism and mystical figures, including the "psychoanalytic mystics" (see Michael Eigen, *The Psychoanalytic Mystic* [London: Free Association Books, 1998]; Daniel Merkur, "Psychoanalytic Contributions on the Mystical," in *Changing the Scientific Study of Religion: Beyond Freud?,* ed. Jacob Belzen [New York: Springer-Verlag, 2009]), the "mystics of psychoanalysis" (see Sudhir Kakar, *The Analyst and the Mystic* [Chicago: University of Chicago Press, 1991]), and "mystical psychoanalysis" (a phrase used by Romain Rolland—see my *Enigma*). Allied with these terms is an approach termed "transformational," a term introduced and defined in *Enigma.* While that book was devoted in the main to Freud's interpretation of the oceanic feeling, it also mentioned the need to analyze other cases, of which Augustine was adduced as a primary candidate (121–22). The present work is an attempt to make good on that claim.

24. See Charles Kligerman, "A Psychoanalytic Study of the *Confessions* of St. Augustine," in *The Hunger of the Heart: Reflections on the Confessions of Augustine,* ed. Donald Capps and James E. Dittes, Monograph Series 8 (West Lafayette, IN: Society for the Scientific Study of Religion, 1990), 99.

25. In *The Hunger of the Heart: Reflections on the Scientific Study of Religion* (West Lafayette, IN: Society for the Scientific Study of Religion, Monograph Series 8, 1990), Donald Capps and James E. Dittes reveal that the term "basement theology" was coined as a result of a 1964 Yale University Divinity School seminar on continuities between the life and thought of various religious figures, which met in the basement, the idea being that classes in theology, which met upstairs, neglected such continuities. As Capps and Dittes put it, "the seminar . . . invited students to a kind of theological work that some, accustomed to the theology

'upstairs,' felt risky and alien . . . it was clear that they were engaging in a risky underground, even subversive activity" (ix).

26. For a good sampling of the early oedipal interpretations of Augustine, see the essays in Capps and Dittes, *Hunger of the Heart,* esp. chaps. 6–8.

27. See Philip Woollcott, "Some Considerations of Creativity and Religious Experience in St. Augustine of Hippo," *Journal for the Scientific Study of Religion* 5 (1966): 273–83, 283.

28. See David Bakan, "Augustine's *Confessions:* The Unentailed Self," in *The Hunger of the Heart: Reflections on the Confessions of Augustine,* ed. Donald Capps and James E. Dittes, Monograph Series 8 (West Lafayette, IN: Society for the Scientific Study of Religion, 1990), 111.

29. For a good sampling of preoedipal interpretations of Augustine, see the essays in Capps and Dittes, *Hunger of the Heart,* esp. chaps. 11–12; William Beers, "The Confessions of St. Augustine: Narcissistic Elements," *American Imago* 45 (1988): 107–25; Sandra Dixon, *Augustine: The Scattered and Gathered Self* (St. Louis: Chalice Press, 1999).

30. Beers, "Confessions of St. Augustine," 107.

31. See Capps, "Augustine as Narcissist"(it should be noted that Capps sees in Augustine's journey evidence of only *some* transformations of narcissism); William B. Parsons, "Augustine: Common-Man or Intuitive Psychologist?," *Journal of Psychohistory* 18 (1990): 155–79; idem, "Psychoanalysis and Mysticism: The Case of St. Augustine," in *Mysticism: A Variety of Psychological Perspectives,* ed. Jacob A. Belzen and Antoon Geels (Amsterdam: Rodopi, 2003); Dixon, *Augustine.*

32. See Kligerman, "A Psychoanalytic Study," 107.

33. Ibid., 108.

34. See Dittes, "Continuities."

35. See Capps, "Augustine as Narcissist," 172ff.

36. Beers, "Confessions of St. Augustine," 122.

37. See James E. Dittes, "Augustine: Search for a Fail-Safe God to Trust," in *The Hunger of the Heart: Reflections on the Confessions of Augustine,* ed. Donald Capps and James E. Dittes, Monograph Series 8 (West Lafayette, IN: Society for the Scientific Study of Religion, 1990), 259. Paul Elledge in his "Embracing Augustine: Reach, Restraint and Romantic Resolution in the Confessions" (in *The Hunger of the Heart: Reflections on the Confessions of Augustine,* ed. Donald Capps and James E. Dittes, Monograph Series 8 [West Lafayette, IN: Society for the Scientific Study of Religion, 1990]), similarly sees issues of basic trust in Augustine's mysticism.

38. See Volney Gay, "Augustine: The Reader as Self-Object," in *The Hunger of the Heart: Reflections on the Confessions of Augustine,* ed. Donald Capps and James E. Dittes, Monograph Series 8 (West Lafayette, IN: Society for the Scientific Study of Religion, 1990), 200–201.

39. Dixon, *Augustine,* 158.

40. Ibid., 159.

41. Ibid.

42. See Paula Fredriksen, "Augustine and His Analysts: The Possibility of a Psychohistory," *Soundings* 61 (1978): 206–27; and the essays by Richard Fenn, "Death Anxiety and the Power and Limits of Language," Margaret Miles, "Infancy, Parenting and Nourishment," and Eugene TeSelle, "Augustine as Client," all in *The Hunger of the Heart: Reflections on the Confessions of Augustine,* ed. Donald Capps and James E. Dittes, Monograph Series 8 (West Lafayette, IN: Society for the Scientific Study of Religion, 1990).

43. Fredriksen, "Augustine and His Analysts," 209.

44. See Bakan, "Augustine's *Confessions,*" 111–12.

45. See TeSelle, "Augustine as Client"; Fredriksen, "Augustine and His Analysts"; Dixon, *Augustine,* 184.

46. See Diane Jonte-Pace, "Augustine on the Couch: Psychohistorical (Mis) readings of the *Confessions,*" *Religion* 23 (1993): 71–83, 76.

47. Ibid.

48. See Fredriksen, "Augustine and His Analysts," 214.

49. See Pierre Courcelle, *Recherches sur les 'Confessions' de Saint Augustin* (Paris: Éditions de Boccard, 1968); Robert McMahon, *Augustine's Prayerful Ascent: An Essay on the Literary Form of the Confessions* (Athens: University of Georgia Press, 1990); Jonte-Pace, "Augustine on the Couch"; Leo Ferrari, "Paul at the Conversion of Augustine," *Augustinian Studies* 11 (1980): 5–20; Robert A. Johnson, "Comments on *Hunger of the Heart:* Reflections on the *Confessions* of Augustine" (manuscript); Elledge, "Embracing Augustine"; Fenn, "Augustine."

50. See Jonte-Pace, "Augustine on the Couch," 72.

51. For my use of the term "makes the truth," see John Cavadini's review of James O'Donnell's work on the *Confessions* ("Making Truth: A New Commentary on Augustine's *Confessions,*" *Religious Studies Review* 21 [1995]: 291–98).

52. See Jonte-Pace, "Augustine on the Couch," 77.

53. See Teselle, "Augustine as Client," 205.

54. Paul Rigby, "Augustine's Confessions: The Recognition of Fatherhood," in *The Hunger of the Heart: Reflections on the Confessions of Augustine,* ed. Donald Capps and James E. Dittes, Monograph Series 8 (West Lafayette, IN: Society for the Scientific Study of Religion, 1990), 146.

55. Ibid., 163.

56. See David Burrell, "Reading the *Confessions* of Augustine: An Exercise in Theological Understanding," *Journal of Religion* 50 (1970): 327–51.

57. Ibid. Also see Rigby, "Augustine's Confessions."

58. See Rigby, "Augustine's Confessions," 159; TeSelle, "Augustine as Client," 206.

59. See Teselle, "Augustine as Client," 206.

60. I take this term from Peter Homans in his essay "The Psychology and Religion Movement," in *The Encyclopedia of Religion,* ed. Mircea Eliade (New York: Macmillan, 1987), 66–74.

61. For an overview of the historical eras and also the various dialogical projects in the psychology-and-religion movement, see Jonte-Pace and Parsons, *Religion and Psychology;* William B. Parsons, "Psychology of Religion," in *The Encyclopedia of Religion,* ed. L. Jones (New York: Macmillan, 2005).

one RHETORIC

1. Jonte-Pace, "Augustine on the Couch," 72.

2. For paradigmatic instances of this, see Jonte-Pace, "Augustine on the Couch"; Dixon, *Augustine.*

3. Kligerman, "A Psychoanalytic Study," 105.

4. Weintraub, "St. Augustine's *Confessions,*" 30.

5. See Burrell, "Reading the *Confessions* of Augustine"; Jonte-Pace, "Augustine on the Couch"; Anne H. Hawkins, "St. Augustine: Archetypes of Family," in *The Hunger of the Heart: Reflections on the Confessions of Augustine,* ed. Donald Capps and James E. Dittes, Monograph Series 8 (West Lafayette, IN: Society for the Scientific Study of Religion, 1990).

6. McMahon, *Augustine's Prayerful Ascent;* Sabine MacCormack, *The Shadows of Poetry: Vergil in the Mind of Augustine* (Berkeley: University of California Press, 1998); John O'Meara, "Monica: The Mother of Augustine," *Furrow* 5 (1954): 555–62; Monica O'Ferrall, "Monica, the Mother of Augustine: A Reconsideration," *Recherches Augustiniennes* 10 (1975): 23–43.

7. Eric Ziolkowski, "St. Augustine: Aeneas' Antitype, Monica's Boy," *Literature and Theology* 9 (1995): 1–23.

8. Garry Wills, *St. Augustine* (New York: Vintage, 1999), xix.

9. Ibid.

10. Ibid., xviii.

11. See Capps, "Augustine as Narcissist"; Dodds, "Augustine's Confessions"; Leo Ferrari, "The Boyhood Beatings of Augustine," in *The Hunger of the Heart: Reflections on the Confessions of Augustine,* ed. Donald Capps and James E. Dittes, Monograph Series 8 (West Lafayette, IN: Society for the Scientific Study of Religion, 1990).

12. Jonte-Pace, "Augustine on the Couch," 73–4.

13. O'Ferrall, "Monica, the Mother of Augustine," 25. Courcelle posited the existence of the short life of Monica in his *Recherches sur les 'Confessions' de Saint Augustin.*

14. O'Ferrall, "Monica, the Mother of Augustine," 25.

15. Ibid., 30.

16. See Kim Power, *Veiled Desire: Augustine on Women* (New York: Continuum, 1996), 72–74.

17. See O'Ferrall, "Monica, the Mother of Augustine," 27. According to Pierre Courcelle's *Les Confessions de Saint Augustin dans le tradition littéraire* (Paris: Etudes Augustiniennes, 1963), Augustine's portrait of Monica as visionary may

have been influenced by the tradition of vision and dream narratives as developed in the African church.

18. Louis Bouyer, "Mysticism: An Essay on the History of the Word," in *Understanding Mysticism,* ed. Richard Woods (Garden City, NY: Image Books, 1980).

19. Ibid., 52–53.

20. Bernard McGinn is hardly alone in this regard. For example, the Buddologist Robert Gimello complains that "it is difficult to apply any of the widely accepted definitions or descriptions of mysticism to Buddhist praxis without the most serious reservations" (Gimello, "Mysticism and Meditation," in *Mysticism and Philosophical Analysis,* ed. Steven Katz [New York: Oxford University Press, 1979], 173), while the Islamicist Carl Ernst, warning that "not enough has been done to historicize and problematize the category of mysticism," notes that Sufi forms of "mysticism" cannot be properly understood absent some relation to Islam's focus on political, economic, and social issues (Ernst, "Between Orientalism and Fundamentalism: Problematizing the Teaching of Sufism," in *Teaching Islam,* ed. Brannon Wheeler [New York: Oxford University Press, 2003], 121). For a summary of the debates surrounding the term "mysticism" see the collection of essays in Parsons, *Teaching Mysticism.*

21. McGinn, *Foundations of Mysticism,* xvii.

22. Ibid., xv–xvi.

23. Ibid., xi–xx.

24. Kenney, *The Mysticism of St. Augustine.*

25. Andrew Louth, *The Origins of the Christian Mystical Tradition* (Oxford: Clarendon Press, 1981), 140. See also Paul Henry, *The Path to Transcendence: From Philosophy to Mysticism in Saint Augustine,* trans. Francis F. Burch (Pittsburgh: Pickwick, 1989); Eugene Teselle, "Augustine," in *An Introduction to the Medieval Mystics of Europe,* ed. Paul E. Szarmach (Albany: State University of New York Press, 1984).

26. There has been a staggering amount of attention, compiled by André Mandouze ("Ou en est la question de la mystique augustinienne?," in *Augustinus Magister* [Paris: L'Année théologique augustinienne, 1954]) and debated by many others, devoted to the issue of what Augustine "really" experienced—whether, for example, they were true Christian "infused" visions or mere intellectual ascents. This issue, while important, is not of concern in this chapter, which is devoted to more pressing literary arguments. However, I will return to address the question of Augustine's "experience" in the next chapter.

27. Henry, *The Path to Transcendence,* 28.

28. Louth, *Origins,* 129; Henry, *The Path to Transcendence,* 15–19; André Mandouze, "L'ecstase d'Ostie," in *Augustinus Magister* (Paris: L'Année théologique augustinienne, 1954).

29. See McGinn, *Foundations of Mysticism,* 251.

30. Ibid., 233.

31. For an analysis of the sense language employed by Augustine in the two visions, see McGinn, *Foundations of Mysticism,* 232ff.

32. TeSelle, "Augustine," 21–22.

33. Kenney, *The Mysticism of St. Augustine,* 110–28.

34. Ibid., see chap. 8.

35. Ibid., 113, 124.

36. For an exhaustive synopsis of the ecclesiastical and Christological dimensions of Augustine's mystical teaching, see McGinn, *Foundations of Mysticism,* 238–52.

37. Ibid., 234–35.

38. Ibid. See also Kenney, *The Mysticism of St. Augustine,* 111.

39. Henry, *The Path to Transcendence,* chap. 5.

40. See Power, *Veiled Desire,* 88–89.

41. See Jonte-Pace, "Augustine on the Couch," 72.

42. Ibid., 79.

43. Ibid.

44. See Grace Jantzen, *Power, Gender, and Christian Mysticism* (Cambridge: Cambridge University Press, 1995); Elliot Wolfson, *Through a Speculum That Shines* (Princeton, NJ: Princeton University Press, 1997); Amy Hollywood, *Sensible Ecstasy* (Chicago: University of Chicago Press, 2002).

two **VISION**

1. Michel de Certeau, "Mysticism," *Diacritics* 22 (1992): 11–25, 14.

2. Ibid., 24.

3. Lee Schmidt, "The Making of Modern Mysticism," *Journal of the American Academy of Religion* 71 (2003): 273–302, 288.

4. James, *Varieties of Religious Experience,* 370. For other perspectives on the use of the term "experience" in religious studies, see Robert Scharf, "Experience," in *Critical Terms for Religious Studies,* ed. Marc C. Taylor (Chicago: University of Chicago Press, 1987); Timothy Fitzgerald, "Experience," in *Guide to the Study of Religion,* ed. Willi Braun and Russell T. McCutcheon (London: Cassell, 2000).

5. James, *Varieties of Religious Experience,* 31–32.

6. The history of the term "spirituality" can be found in Walter Principe, "Toward Defining Spirituality," *Studies in Religion* 12 (1983): 127–41. For a history of the churched use of the term, see Bernard McGinn, "The Letter and the Spirit: Spirituality as an Academic Discipline," in *Minding the Spirit: The Study of Christian Spirituality,* ed. Elizabeth A. Dryer and Marc S. Burrows (Baltimore, MD: Johns Hopkins University Press, 2005).

7. See David Wulff, *Psychology of Religion: Classic and Contemporary,* 2nd ed. (New York: John Wiley and Sons, 1997).

8. Principe, "Toward Defining Spirituality."

9. MacDonald, "Spirituality."

10. See Fuller, *Spiritual But Not Religious;* John Blake, "Are There Dangers in Being 'Spiritual But Not Religious?'" (http://articles.cnn.com/2010-06-03/living/spiritual.but.not.religious_1_spiritual-community-religious-god?_s=PM:LIVING).

11. See Fuller, *Spiritual But Not Religious.*

12. James, *Varieties of Religious Experience,* 410.

13. In this section I draw from a previous study, *Enigma,* the appendix of which has the entirety of the correspondence between Freud and Rolland.

14. Sigmund Freud, *The Future of an Illusion,* vol. 20 of *The Standard Edition of the Complete Psychological Works of Sigmund Freud,* trans. and ed. James Strachey (London: Hogarth Press, 1966–74, first published 1927), 39.

15. Sigmund Freud to Oskar Pfister, November 25, 1928, in Freud and Pfister, *Psychoanalysis and Faith,* 125–26.

16. See Parsons, *Enigma,* chaps. 1 and 2.

17. This pivotal letter can be found in Parsons, *Enigma,* 173–74.

18. Ibid., 170.

19. See Rolland's letter to Freud of December 5, 1927, in Parsons, *Enigma,* 173–74.

20. Parsons, *Enigma,* 90, 92, 95–96.

21. Ibid., chap. 5.

22. Ibid.

23. Ibid.

24. Ibid., 173–74.

25. See Teresa of Avila, *The Interior Castle* (New York: Paulist Press, 1979), mansion seven.

26. See Arthur Osborne, *Ramana Maharshi and the Path of Self-Knowledge* (New York: Samuel Weiser, 1973).

27. Sigmund Freud, *Civilization and Its Discontents,* vol. 21 of *The Standard Edition of the Complete Psychological Works of Sigmund Freud,* trans. and ed. James Strachey (London: Hogarth Press, 1966–74, first published 1930), 65.

28. Ibid., 68.

29. For these letters, see Parsons, *Enigma,* 174–75.

30. For an articulation of this perspective, see Kenney, *The Mysticism of St. Augustine.*

31. Ibid., 67.

32. Steven Katz, *Mysticism and Philosophical Analysis* (New York: Oxford University Press, 1979), 26.

33. Rufus Jones, *Studies in Mystical Religion* (New York: Russell and Russell, 1909), xxxiv.

34. Katz, *Mysticism and Philosophical Analysis,* 27.

35. Kenney, *The Mysticism of St. Augustine,* 85.

36. Louth, *Origins,* 137.

37. Kenney, *The Mysticism of St. Augustine,* 118.

38. McGinn, *Foundations of Mysticism,* 242.

39. Ibid., xvi.

40. Ibid., xvi–xvii.

41. Ibid., 242.

42. Ibid., chap. 7.

43. Ibid., 253.

44. Ibid.; see 237, 253, 255.

45. Kenney, *The Mysticism of St. Augustine,* 128.

46. Augustine, *The Literal Meaning of Genesis,* trans. and annotated by John H. Taylor (New York: Newman Press, 1982), 12.24.50.

47. Ibid., 12.14.29.

48. Ibid., 12.7.16.

49. Ibid.

50. Ibid., 12.24.50.

51. Ibid., 12.26.54.

52. Ibid., 12.31.59.

53. See Augustine, *Literal Meaning of Genesis* 12; Kenney, *The Mysticism of St. Augustine,* 131ff.

54. Ibid., 12.28.56.

55. See the discussion by McGinn in *Foundations of Mysticism,* 240–41.

56. Ibid., 258.

57. See ibid., 230ff. I have been unable to find a single acknowledgment, much less a sustained engagement, of this ongoing debate in the psychoanalytic literature on Augustine. Abbot Butler was perhaps the most strident in his view that Augustine had experienced the highest form of intellectual vision. See his *Western Mysticism* (New York: E. P. Dutton, 1923) and also the essays in Frederick Van Fleteren, Joseph C. Schnaubelt, and Joseph Reino, eds., *Augustine: Mystic and Mystagogue,* vol. 3 of Collectanea Augustiniana (New York: Peter Lang, 1994).

58. John Smith, "William James's Account of Mysticism," in *Mysticism and Religious Traditions,* ed. Steven Katz (New York: Oxford University Press, 1983), 253.

59. James, *Varieties of Religious Experience,* 390.

60. Ibid., 389.

61. Ibid., 389.

62. Ibid., 391.

63. Ibid., 396.

64. See Kenney, *The Mysticism of St. Augustine,* 143.

65. Katz, *Mysticism and Philosophical Analysis,* 22–23.

66. Steven Katz, "On Mysticism," *Journal for the American Academy of Religion* 56 (1988): 751–61.

67. See Anthony Perovich, "Does the Philosophy of Mysticism Rest on a Mistake?," in *The Problem of Pure Consciousness,* ed. Robert K. C. Forman (New York: Oxford, 1990).

68. Katz, *Mysticism and Philosophical Analysis,* 59.

69. Ibid., 27.

70. See, for example, Perovitch, "Does the Philosophy of Mysticism Rest on a Mistake?," and also Jorge Ferrer (with Jacob H. Sherman), *The Participatory Turn: Spirituality, Mysticism, Religious Studies* (Albany: State University of New York Press, 2010).

three **VISION INTERPRETED**

1. For example, see Frank Sulloway, *Freud: Biologist of the Mind: Beyond the Psychoanalytic Legend* (New York: Basic Books, 1983); Paul Ricoeur, *Freud and Philosophy* (New Haven, CT: Yale University Press, 1970); Peter Homans, *Theology after Freud* (Indianapolis: Bobbs-Merrill, 1970); Bruno Bettelheim, *Freud and Man's Soul* (New York: Vintage, 1984).

2. See Ernst L. Freud, ed., *The Letters of Sigmund Freud* (New York: Basic Books, 1960), 339–40.

3. Giovanni Papini, "A Visit to Freud," *Review of Existential Psychology and Psychiatry* 9 (1969): 130–34; Henry Ellenberger, *The Discovery of the Unconscious* (New York: Basic Books, 1970), 460, 467.

4. Sigmund Freud, *Group Psychology and the Analysis of the Ego,* vol. 18 of *The Standard Edition of the Complete Psychological Works of Sigmund Freud,* trans. and ed. James Strachey (London: Hogarth Press, 1966–74, first published 1921), 90–91.

5. See Sigmund Freud, *The Ego and the Id,* vol. 19 of *The Standard Edition of the Complete Psychological Works of Sigmund Freud,* trans. and ed. James Strachey (London: Hogarth Press, 1966–74, first published 1923), 25.

6. See Parsons, *Enigma,* 50ff.

7. See James Tabor, *Things Unutterable* (New York: University Press of America, 1986). In saying this, surely Augustine had Paul right when, in rejecting the Plotinian *henosis,* he spoke of a spiritual architecture in which creator and created were distinct and union with the ontological substance was impossible. The point, rather, is that there is no evidence to suggest that Augustine had knowledge of the Jewish merkavah world in which Paul operated—that indeed his exegesis of Paul's ascent was invariably a creative misreading based on personal experience in tandem with extant Christian and Platonic cultural material. Moreover, this was not the only instance in which he creatively misread Paul, as is noted by Krister Stendahl's gloss on Augustine's (mis)reading of the "two wills" of Romans. I say more about the latter shortly.

8. Jacques Lacan, "God and the Jouissance of Women," in *Feminine Sexuality: Jacques Lacan and the École Freudian,* ed. Juliet Mitchell and Jacqueline Rose (New York: W. W. Norton, 1982), 147.

9. Ibid.

10. See Richard E. Webb and Michael Sells, "Lacan and Bion: Psychoanalysis and the Mystical Language of Unsaying," *Theory and Psychology* 5 no. 2 (1995): 195–215.

11. Sudhir Kakar, "Clinical Work and Cultural Imagination," *Psychoanalytic Quarterly* 64 (no. 2 (1995): 265–81, 281.

12. Ibid., 289, 292.

13. See, for example, Sudhir Kakar, *The Inner World: A Psycho-Analytic Study of Childhood and Society in India* (Delhi: Oxford University Press, 1981), chap. 2; idem, *The Analyst and the Mystic,* chap. 1.

14. Kakar, *Inner World,* 27.

15. Jeffrey Kripal, *Kali's Child: The Mystical and the Erotic in the Life and Teachings of Ramakrishna* (Chicago: University of Chicago Press, 1995), 24.

16. Ibid., 23.

17. Ibid.

18. Ibid., 326.

19. Ibid., 323–24.

20. Ibid., 43.

21. Freud, *Civilization and Its Discontents,* 72.

22. See Parsons, *Enigma,* 175.

23. See, for example, Jeffrey Moussaieff Masson, *The Assault on Truth* (New York: Farrar, Straus and Giroux, 1984), appendix A; Daniel Merkur, *The Explorations of the Psychoanalytic Mystics* (Amsterdam: Rodopi, 2010); Henri Vermorel and Madeleine Vermorel, *Sigmund Freud et Romain Rolland Correspondance 1923–1936* (Paris: Presses Universitaires de France, 1993).

24. See Parsons, *Enigma,* chap. 2.

25. Ibid., 48.

26. Ibid.

27. Ibid.

28. Ibid., 48ff.

29. Ibid., 70–71.

30. Ibid., 176–77.

31. Freud, *Future of an Illusion,* 28. I have unpacked in greater detail this passage and its relation to Rolland in my *Enigma,* chap. 4.

32. Ibid., 31–32.

33. Sigmund Freud, *New Introductory Lectures on Psychoanalysis,* vol. 22 of *The Standard Edition of the Complete Psychological Works of Sigmund Freud,* trans. and ed. James Strachey (London: Hogarth Press, 1966–74, first published 1933), 71.

34. See Sigmund Freud, *Moses and Monotheism,* vol. 23 of *The Standard Edition of the Complete Psychological Works of Sigmund Freud,* trans. and ed. James Strachey (London: Hogarth Press, 1966–74, first published 1939), 300.

35. See E. L. Freud, *Letters,* 427.

36. See Freud, *Moses and Monotheism,* 299.

37. Ibid., 99.

38. Ernest Jones, *The Life and Work of Sigmund Freud,* 3 vols. (New York: Basic Books, 1953–57), 3:313.

39. See Masson, *Assault on Truth.*

40. Freud, *Introductory Lectures,* 461.

41. See Jones, *Life and Work of Sigmund Freud,* vol. 3, chap. 13.

42. Freud, *Moses and Monotheism,* 98.

43. Ibid., 100.

44. Ibid., 85.

45. Ibid., 133–34.

46. Ibid.

47. See Parsons, "Psychology of Religion."

48. See James, *Varieties of Religious Experience.*

49. Carl Jung, *Memories, Dreams, Reflections* (New York: Vintage, 1961), 199.

50. See Frederic Myers, *Human Personality and Its Survival of Bodily Death* (Charlottesville, VA: Hampton Roads, 2001).

51. See Jonathan Garb, *Shamanic Trance in Modern Kabbalah* (Chicago: University of Chicago Press, 2011).

52. See Merkur, *Explorations of the Psychoanalytic Mystics.*

53. Philip Woollcott and Prakash Desai, "Religious and Creative States of Illumination: A Perspective from Psychiatry," in *Religious and Ethical Factors in Psychiatric Practice,* ed. Donald S. Browning, Thomas Jobe, and Ian S. Evison (Chicago: Nelson Hall, 1990).

54. See James Jones, "Hans Loewald: The Psychoanalyst as Mystic," *Psychoanalytic Review* 88 (2001): 793–804; idem, *Terror and Transformation* (New York: Routledge, 2002).

55. See Erik Erikson, *Young Man Luther* (New York: W. W. Norton, 1962).

56. Ibid., 109.

57. Ibid.

58. Wilfred Bion, *Attention and Interpretation* (New York: Jason Aronson, 1983), 26.

59. Heinz Kohut, "Forms and Transformations of Narcissism," in *The Search for the Self,* ed. Paul Ornstein (New York: International Universities Press, 1978), 456.

60. Ibid., 455–56.

61. I make this point in detail in my *Enigma,* chaps. 5–7.

62. Heinz Kohut, "On Leadership." In *Self Psychology and the Humanities*, ed. Charles B. Strozier (New York: W. W. Norton, 1985), 70.

63. Ibid.

64. Ibid., 70–71.

65. See Merkur, *Explorations of the Psychoanalytic Mystics;* Kelly Raab, "Creativity and Transcendence in the Work of Marion Milner," *American Imago* 57 (2000): 185–214.

66. See Jones, *Life and Work of Sigmund Freud,* vol. 3, chap. 14.

67. Ibid.

68. Sigmud Freud, "Dreams and Occultism," in vol. 22 of *The Standard Edition of the Complete Psychological Works of Sigmund Freud,* trans. and ed. James Strachey (London: Hogarth Press, 1966–74, first published 1933), 54–55.

69. Kohut, "Forms and Transformations of Narcissism," 453.

70. Kakar, *Inner World,* 19.

71. Ibid., 20.

72. Aurthur Deikman, "Deautomatization and the Mystic Experience," in *Understanding Mysticism,* ed. Richard Woods (Garden City, NY: Image Books, 1980).

73. Ibid., 256.

74. Ibid., 258.

75. Kelly Bulkeley, "Freud and Neuroscience: A Return to Origins," in *Disciplining Freud on Religion,* ed. Gregory Kaplan and William B. Parsons (Lanham, MD: Lexington Books, 2010).

76. See Kelly Bulkeley, *The Wondering Brain* (New York: Routledge, 2003), 172.

77. Ibid., 155, 157.

78. Ibid., 155.

79. Ibid.

80. Ibid., 160.

81. Ibid., 163–65.

82. See Mark Fox, *Religion, Spirituality, and the Near-Death Experience* (London: Routledge, 2003).

83. See, for example, Lee Bailey and Jenny Yates, eds., *The Near-Death Experience: A Reader* (New York: Routledge, 1996).

84. See Paul Badham, "Religious and Near-Death Experience in Relation to Belief in a Future Life." Second Series Occasional Paper 13 (Oxford: Religious Experience Centre, 1997).

85. See the contributions in Bailey and Yates, *Near-Death Experience;* Mark Fox, *Religion, Spirituality, and the Near-Death Experience;* Carol Zaleski, *Otherworld Journeys* (New York: Oxford University Press, 1987).

86. Zaleski, *Otherworld Journeys,* 180.

87. Ibid., 86.

four **THERAPEIA**

1. McGinn, *Foundations of Mysticism,* xv.

2. Ibid., xvi.

3. I use the notion of modern psychologies having a religio-ethical dimension in the sense articulated by Donald S. Browning in his *Religious Thought and the Modern Psychologies* (Philadelphia: Fortress Press, 1987).

4. In Louis Beirnaert, "Romain Rolland: Les derniéres etapes du voyage intérieur," *Etudes* 44 (1945): 250–56.

5. Romain Rolland, *Mémoires et fragments du Journal* (Paris: Éditions Albin Michel, 1956), 23.

6. Ibid., 23–25.

7. Romain Rolland, *Journey Within* (New York: Philosophical Library, 1947), 24–25.

8. Romain Rolland, *Life of Vivekananda* (Calcutta: Advaitta Ashrama, 1988), 183–84, 231–32.

9. Miles, "Infancy, Parenting and Nourishment," 224.

10. Kenney, *The Mysticism of St. Augustine,* 122.

11. Ibid., 106–7.

12. Ibid., 108–9.

13. Louth, *Origins,* 142.

14. Ibid., 143.

15. Kenney, *The Mysticism of St. Augustine,* 107.

16. McGinn, *Foundations of Mysticism,* 244–45.

17. TeSelle, "Augustine," 27–8.

18. Teselle, "Augustine as Client," 213–14.

19. See D. W. Winnicott, *Playing and Reality* (New York: Penguin, 1971).

20. Ibid., chaps. 1, 7.

21. Michael Eigen, "The Area of Faith in Winnicott, Lacan, and Bion," *International Journal of the American Psychoanalytic Association* 27 (1969): 413–33, 431.

22. Ibid.

23. Ana-Maria Rizzuto, *The Birth of the Living God* (Chicago: University of Chicago Press, 1979).

24. Ibid., 47.

25. Ibid., 51.

26. Ibid., 177.

27. Ibid., 44.

28. Ibid., 48–49.

29. Ibid., 51.

30. Ibid., 182.

31. Kakar, *Inner World,* 15.

32. Ibid., 50–51.

33. Ibid., 28–29.

34. Here I follow, with some qualifications and additions, a previous line of argument undertaken in two of my essays on Augustine: "St. Augustine: Common-Man or Intuitive Psychologist?" and "Psychoanalysis and Mysticism: The Case of St. Augustine."

35. Brown, *Augustine of Hippo,* 46.

36. Ibid., 51.

37. See Rizzuto, *Birth of the Living God,* 20ff.

38. See Donald Capps, "Parabolic Events in Augustine's Autobiography," *Theology Today* 40 (1983): 260–72.

39. Peter Brown makes similar observations in his *Augustine of Hippo.*

40. Kenney, *The Mysticism of St. Augustine,* 95.

41. Brown, *Augustine of Hippo,* 94–5, 80–105.

42. Ibid., 95.

43. Ibid.

44. See Capps and Dittes, *The Hunger of the Heart,* xx. It should be noted that Capps, at least, would probably agree that all we have here is "portraits"—that a "photograph" of Augustine is beyond our purview. Nevertheless, many other studies are far less nuanced and give the impression of offering something more definitive.

45. See Capps, "Parabolic Events in Augustine's Autobiography"; John Updike, "Augustine's Concubine," in *Problems and Other Stories* (New York: Alfred A. Knopf, 1979).

CONCLUSION

1. My use of the term "psychology-and-religion movement" and its relation to the dialogical entities has been elaborated in a previous publication (see Jonte-Pace and Parsons, *Psychology and Religion*).

2. The term was coined by Peter Homans in his *Jung in Context* (Chicago: University of Chicago Press, 1995).

3. For example, the paradigmatic textbook in the psychology of religion is David Wulff's *Psychology of Religion.* For a textbook on empirical approaches see Bernard Spilka, Ralph W. Hood, Jr., and Richard L. Gorsuch, *The Psychology of Religion: An Empirical Approach* (New York: Guilford Press, 2003).

4. See David Wulff, "Psychology of Religion: An Overview," in *Religion and Psychology: Mapping the Terrain,* ed. Diane Jonte-Price and William B. Parsons (New York: Routledge, 2001).

5. For more detail, see my essay "Psychology of Religion."

6. See Joseph Maréchal, *Studies in the Psychology of the Mystics* (Albany, NY: Magi Books, 1964).

7. See Homans, *Jung in Context.*

8. See the introduction to Jonte-Pace and Parsons, *Religion and Psychology.*

9. Max Weber, *The Protestant Ethic and the Spirit of Capitalism* (New York: Charles Scribner's Sons, 1958).

10. See Philip Rieff, *The Feeling Intellect* (Chicago: University of Chicago Press, 1990). In particular, see chap. 2, "The American Transference: From Calvin to Freud."

11. For example, I would cite as exceptions the early essay by Philip Woollcott and Sandra Dixon's more recent *Augustine.* Even here, however, such exceptions must be viewed in context. Dixon's book was based on a dissertation directed by

Bernard McGinn, perhaps the leading contemporary scholar of Christian mysticism, while Woollcott experimented with mystical techniques, a fact that eventuated in a later essay (with Prekash Desai) on a mystical line of development. In other words, I would consider Woollcott to have been influenced by the culture of modern spirituality and inner-worldly mysticism.

12. H. S. Hughes, *The Sea Change* (New York: McGraw-Hill, 1977); Peter Lasch, *The Culture of Narcissism* (New York: W. W. Norton, 1991); Peter Homans, *The Ability to Mourn* (Chicago: University of Chicago Press, 1989).

13. See Roland Robertson, *Meaning and Change* (New York: New York University Press, 1978); Philip Wexler, *The Mystical Society* (Boulder CO: Westview Press, 2000); Alton Pollard, *Mysticism and Social Change* (New York: Peter Lang, 1992); Harry Hunt, *Lives in Spirit: Precursors and Dilemmas of a Secular Western Mysticism* (Albany: State University of New York Press, 1995).

14. See Robertson, *Meaning and Change.*

15. As stated by John Blake in his "Are There Dangers in Being 'Spiritual But Not Religious?' " The latter can be found at http://articles.cnn.com/2010-06-03/living/spiritual.but.not.religious_1_spiritual-community-religious-god?_s=PM:LIVING.

16. See Jeffrey Kripal, *Esalen* (Chicago: University of Chicago Press, 2008); Wexler, *Mystical Society;* Elaine Eklund, *Science vs. Religion: What Scientists Really Think* (New York: Oxford University Press, 2010).

17. Weber, *Protestant Ethic,* 55.

18. See Homans, *Ability to Mourn,* 122ff.; idem, *Jung in Context.*

19. See Marthe Robert, *From Oedipus to Moses* (Garden City, NY: Anchor Books, 1976).

20. See Certeau, "Mysticism."

21. Rolland, *Mémoires,* 23.

22. Rolland, *Journey Within,* 17.

23. See Rolland, *Life of Vivekananda,* 346ff.

24. See Rolland's letter to Freud of December 5, 1927, in Parsons, *Enigma,* 173–74.

25. Ibid., 259.

26. Rolland, *Life of Vivekananda,* pt. 1, chap. 4; 348n1.

27. See D. K. Roy, *Among the Great* (Bombay: N. M. Tripathi, Nalanda Publications, 1945), 71–72.

28. Rolland, *Life of Vivekananda,* 176–77.

29. Carl Jung, *Psychology and Religion* (New Haven, CT: Yale University Press, 1938), 4–6.

30. R. C. Bucke, *Cosmic Consciousness: A Study in the Evolution of the Human Mind* (New York: Citadel Press, 1993), 8.

31. Ibid., 316–17.

32. Ibid., 9ff.

33. Ibid., 3.

34. Ibid., 2.

35. Ibid., 318.

36. Abraham Maslow, *Religion, Values and Peak-Experiences* (New York: Penguin, 1954), 19–20.

37. Ibid., 28.

38. From Anthony Sutich, "Transpersonal Psychology: An Emerging Force," *Journal of Humanistic Psychology* 8 (1968): 77–78, 78.

39. See Jorge Ferrer, *Revisioning Transpersonal Psychology* (Albany: State University of New York Press, 2002).

40. Kenneth Ring, "Near-Death Experiences: Implications for Human Evolution and Planetary Transformation," in *The Near-Death Experience: A Reader,* ed. Lee Bailey and Jenny Yates (New York: Routledge, 1996), 194.

41. Jill Taylor, *My Stroke of Insight* (New York: Penguin, 2009), 187.

42. Robert Ornstein, *The Psychology of Consciousness* (New York: Harcourt Brace, 1972); Richard Woods, ed., *Understanding Mysticism* (Garden City, NJ: Image, 1980).

43. See Bion, *Attention and Interpretation,* 16; idem, *A Memoir of the Future* (London: Karnac Books, 1975), 112.

44. See Kohut, "On Leadership," 70.

45. Ibid., 71.

46. See Freud, *Future of an Illusion,* 32.

47. Sigmund Freud, *The Psychopathology of Everyday Life,* vol. 6 of *The Standard Edition of the Complete Psychological Works of Sigmund Freud,* trans. and ed. James Strachey (London: Hogarth Press, 1966–74, first published 1901), 258–59.

48. See Rieff, *Triumph of the Therapeutic.*

49. Ibid.; see esp. chap. 3.

50. Ibid.

51. I use this term and define it in my essay "Psychoanalytic Spirituality," in *Spirituality and Religion: Psychoanalytic Perspectives,* ed. Jerome A. Winer and James William Anderson (Catskill, NY: Mental Health Resources, 2007), 83–97. My analysis here follows and elaborates lines of argument laid down in that essay.

52. For a full treatment of Jung's conversation with Hisamatsu, see pt. 2 (pp. 101–42) of Daniel Meckel and Robert Moore, eds., *Self and Liberation: The Jung/Buddhism Dialogue* (New York: Paulist Press, 1992); Hawkins, "St. Augustine," 237–54.

53. Raymond Schwab, *The Oriental Renaissance* (New York: Columbia University Press, 1987), 7.

54. See my "Psychoanalysis Meets Buddhism: Development of a Dialogue," in *Changing the Scientific Study of Religion: Beyond Freud?,* ed. Jacob Belzen (New York: Springer-Verlag, 2009), 179–210.

55. I have spoken more at length about this in two of my essays, "Themes and Debates in the Psychology-Comparativist Dialogue," in *Religion and Psychology: Mapping the Terrain,* ed. Diane Jonte-Price and William B. Parsons (London: Routledge, 2001), and "Psychoanalysis Meets Buddhism."

56. See T. G. Vaidyanathan and Jeffrey J. Kripal, eds., *Vishu on Freud's Desk* (Delhi: Oxford University Press, 2002); Gananath Obeyesekere, *The Awakened Ones* (New York: Columbia University Press, 2012).

57. See, for example, Narasingha Sil, *Ramakrishna Paramahamsa* (New York: Brill, 1991); William B. Parsons, "Mourning and Method in Psychoanalytic Studies of Indian Thought," in *Mourning Religion*, ed. William B. Parsons, Diane Jonte-Pace, and Susan E. Henking (Charlottesville: University of Virginia Press, 2008).

58. Jeffrey Kripal, *Roads of Excess, Palaces of Wisdom: Eroticism and Reflexivity in the Study of Mysticism* (Chicago: University of Chicago Press, 2001), 92.

59. Ibid., 90.

60. Ibid., 90–91.

61. Ibid., 91.

62. Ibid., 92–93.

63. Ibid., 93.

64. Ibid., 93.

65. Ibid., 94–95.

66. Ibid., 97.

67. Ibid., 96.

68. Ibid., 202.

69. Ibid., 201.

70. Ibid., 202.

71. Kripal, *Esalen.*

72. In this section I draw from a previous essay, "Mourning and Method in Psychoanalytic Studies of Indian Thought."

73. Kakar, *Inner World,* 13.

74. Idem, *Shamans, Mystics, Doctors* (New York: Alfred A. Knopf, 1982), 220.

75. Ibid., 12–13.

76. Ibid., 12.

77. Ibid., 13.

78. Ibid.

79. Ibid.

80. Sudhir Kakar, "Reflections on Psychoanalysis, Indian Culture and Mysticism," *Journal of Indian Philosophy* 10 (1982): 292.

81. Ibid., 296.

82. Ibid., 289, 292.

83. See, for example, Kakar, *Inner World,* chap. 2, and *The Analyst and the Mystic,* chap. 1.

84. Kakar, *The Analyst and the Mystic,* 30.

85. Kakar, "Reflections on Psychoanalysis," 292.

86. In the following section on Buddhism I take liberally from a previous essay, "Psychoanalysis Meets Buddhism."

87. Franz Alexander, "Buddhist Training as Artificial Catatonia," *Psychoanalytic Review* 18, no. 2 (1931): 129–41, 136.

88. See Joe Tom Sun, "Psychology in Primitive Buddhism," in *The Couch and the Tree: Dialogues in Psychoanalysis,* ed. Anthony Molino (New York: North Point Press, 1998). As an interesting aside, in 1924 Thompson was on board a U.S. Navy transport passing through the Panama Canal when he met a woman and her twelve-year-old son. Thompson took a shine to the boy and taught him how to train cats and introduced him to psychoanalysis. The boy took it all in, and it had an important influence on his later work. The boy's name was Lafayette Ronald Hubbard—better known as L. Ron Hubbard, the founder of Scientology. Apparently L. Ron memorized many of Thompson's tales and later claimed them as his own. In any event, it was through Thompson that Hubbard was first exposed to psychoanalysis. My thanks to Daniel Benveniste for making this clear to me. See his "The Early History of Psychoanalysis in San Francisco," *Psychoanalysis and History* 8, no. (2006): 195–233.

89. Sun, "Psychology in Primitive Buddhism," 6.

90. Masson's work is particularly notable in that he was trained first as an Indologist (at Harvard) and then as a psychoanalyst. Indeed, his many publications on Eastern religions engage not only the original texts, crucial commentaries, and secondary sources but also pivotal studies in the social scientific and comparative study of mysticism in ways absent in his forebears. For example, he is able to analyze, critique, and ultimately dismiss the noetic claims of the mystics sympathetically rendered by W. T. Stace in his classic work, *Mysticism and Philosophy,* move quickly to dismiss those arguments of cultural relativism that mitigate the cross-cultural hermeneutic power of applied psychoanalysis, and then, drawing on predecessors such as Lewin, Morel, and Freud (especially his case history of the psychotic Schreber), easily render Eastern religion and its accoutrements as indicative of pathology. Masson can confidently state, for example, that Vedanta philosophy, with its emphasis on the world as illusion, can only signify derealization, depersonalization, and aggressive annihilation fantasies. The tantric emphasis on celibacy, watching one's breath, and quieting the mind betrays an inability to work through the dangerous possibilities inherent in sexual excitement. The ascetic diet can be explained with recourse to anorexia nervosa. The narrative of Krishna's encounter with the hunchback indicates oedipal issues and castration anxiety. Ramakrishna is a "happy" pervert only because the pathology inherent in his religio-cultural surround countenanced, if not encouraged, his bizarre behavior.

Most important for our purposes, Masson thinks he has ascertained the true meaning of Buddhism. For Masson, the first noble truth is symptomatic: Gotama Buddha suffered from depression. Early in life, speculates Masson, the Buddha must have been abandoned by loved ones, a deep wound that led to a recurrent depressive state and the need for a cure. He found that cure in meditation, which facilitated regression and the dim awareness of trauma. Unable to fully derepress the trauma in an ego-syntonic manner, the Buddha resorted to a defensive maneuver: a manic denial, set forth as the state of nirvana. Detachment, eradication of passion, and quiescence in the bliss of nirvana were hailed as the cure. Derealization and depersonalization were inevitable concomitants of this process and signify aggressive annihilation fantasies. The repressed need for love found expression in the creation of mythological worlds filled with imaginary beings. The doctrine of reincarnation is but the return of split-off remnants of repressed experiences and periods of childhood. With respect to Augustine, Masson would undoubtedly see his mysticism (and particularly the "echo" of his ascents in *Confessions* 10.40) as indicative of mania. Along these lines, it is interesting that Kripal was set to follow Masson's dogmatic pathologizing of Ramakrishna until "that night" (while Kakar, in contrast, has not been shy about his animosity toward Masson's work)—a fact that lends credence to the view that psychoanalysis is itself a body of diverse theories vis-à-vis religion. I have addressed the relation between the views of Masson, Kakar, and Kripal and put them in psychobiographical context in my "Mourning and Method in Psychoanalytic Studies of Indian Religion." For a detailed history of the psychoanalytic encounter with Hinduism, see Vaidyanathan and Kripal, *Vishnu on Freud's Desk,* and Roland, *In Search of Self in India and Japan.*

91. See my "Psychoanalysis Meets Buddhism," 190ff.

92. See David McMahan, *The Making of Buddhist Modernism* (New York: Oxford University Press, 2008); Charles Prebish and Martin Baumann, eds., *Westward Dharma: Buddhism beyond Asia* (Berkeley: University of California Press, 2002).

93. See Robert H. Scharf, "The Zen of Japanese Nationalism." In *Curators of the Buddha: The Study of Buddhism under Colonialism,* ed. Donald S. Lopez (Chicago: University of Chicago Press, 1995).

94. See my "Psychoanalysis Meets Buddhism," 190ff.

95. Karen Horney, "Free Associations and the use of the Couch," in *The Couch and the Tree: Dialogues in Psychoanalysis,* ed. Anthony Molino (New York: North Point Press, 1998), 35–36.

96. Erik Fromm, D. T. Suzuki, and R. de Martino, eds., *Psychoanalysis and Zen Buddhism* (New York: Harper, 1960), 135.

97. See Herbert Fingarette, *The Self in Transformation* (New York: Harper and Row, 1965).

98. See Cooper, "The Disavowal of the Spirit"; Eigen, "One Reality," 225.

99. See, for example, Merkur, "Psychoanalytic Contributions on the Mystical"; Barry Magid, *Ordinary Mind: Exploring the Common Ground of Zen and Psychoanalysis* (New York: Wisdom Publications, 2002); Parsons, "Psychoanalysis Meets Buddhism"; Jeffrey Rubin, "Spirituality and the Self," *Journal of Religion and Health* 43 (2004): 217–20.

100. Mark Epstein, *Thoughts without a Thinker* (New York: Basic Books, 1995), 130.

101. Jack Engler, "Reply: Can We Say What the Self 'Really' Is?," in *Psychoanalysis and Buddhism*, ed. Jeremy Safran (Boston: Wisdom Publications, 2003), 92–93.

102. Ibid., 87.

103. Epstein, *Thoughts without a Thinker*, 47.

104. See Judith Blackstone, *The Empathic Ground* (Albany: State University of New York Press, 2007), chap. 1.

105. Ibid., 25, 48ff.

106. Jack Engler, "Therapeutic Aims in Psychotherapy and Buddhism," in *Transformations of Consciousness*, ed. Ken Wilber, Jack Engler, and Daniel Brown (Boston: Shambala, 1986).

107. Wapola Rahula, *What the Buddha Taught* (New York: Grove, 1974), 43.

108. The notion of Buddhism leading to an end to all suffering was, of course, one of the sticking points in the famous "conversation" between Jung and the Zen master Shin'ichi Hisamatsu. For the latter, see Meckel and Moore, *Self and Liberation*.

109. Jack Engler, "Being Somebody and Being Nobody: A Reexamination of the Understanding of Self in Psychoanalysis and Buddhism," in *Psychoanalysis and Buddhism*, ed. Jeremy Safran (Boston: Wisdom Publications, 2003).

110. Jeffrey Rubin, *Psychotherapy and Buddhism* (New York: Plenum Press, 1996), 41.

111. Ibid., 51.

112. Ibid., 69. Rubin himself engaged in an instructive analysis with a bona fide Zen master, which can be found in the essay by Chip Brown at http://www.nytimes.com/2009/04/26/magazine/26zen-t.html.

113. See Jeremy Safran, ed., *Psychoanalysis and Buddhism* (Boston: Wisdom Publications, 2003), chap. 1.

114. See Blackstone, *Empathic Ground*, 8.

115. See Katz, *Mysticism and Philosophical Analysis*, 51.

116. Ibid., 53.

117. Kripal, *Kali's Child*, 43.

118. See Safran, *Psychoanalysis and Buddhism*, 85–86.

119. Ibid.

120. This is certainly the implication of his view that the *Über-Ich* had its origin in the past—in the repeated primal deed—and that moral advance, while slow, was taking place generationally, best evinced in the surpassing of cannibalism.

121. See Sigmund Freud, "Thoughts for the Times on War and Death," in vol. 14 of *The Standard Edition of the Complete Psychological Works of Sigmund Freud*, trans. and ed. James Strachey (London: Hogarth Press, 1966–74, first published 1915).

122. See Jones, *Life and Work of Sigmund Freud*, 2:177.

BIBLIOGRAPHY

Alexander, Franz. "Buddhistic Training as an Artificial Catatonia." *Psychoanalytic Review* 18, no. 2 (1931): 129–41.

Augustine. *The Confessions of St. Augustine.* Translated by Rex Warner. New York: Mentor, 1963.

Augustine. *The Literal Meaning of Genesis.* Vol. 2. Translated and annotated by John H. Taylor. New York: Newman Press, 1982.

Badham, Paul. "Religious and Near-Death Experience in Relation to Belief in a Future Life." Second Series Occasional Paper 13. Oxford: Religious Experience Centre, 1997.

Bailey, Lee, and Jenny Yates, eds. *The Near-Death Experience: A Reader.* New York: Routledge, 1996.

Bakan, David. "Augustine's *Confessions:* The Unentailed Self." In Capps and Dittes, *Hunger of the Heart,* 109–16.

Barnard, G. William. "Diving into the Depths: Reflections on Psychology as a Religion." In Jonte-Pace and Parsons, *Religion and Psychology,* 297–318.

Beers, William. "The Confessions of St. Augustine: Narcissistic Elements." *American Imago* 45 (1988): 107–25.

Beirnaert, Louis. "Romain Rolland: Les derniéres etapes du voyage intérieur." *Etudes* 44 (1945): 250–56.

Benveniste, Daniel. "The Early History of Psychoanalysis in San Francisco." *Psychoanalysis and History* 8, no. 2 (2006): 195–233.

Bettelheim, Bruno. *Freud and Man's Soul.* New York: Vintage, 1984.

Bion, Wilfred. *Attention and Interpretation.* New York: Jason Aronson, 1983.

———. *A Memoir of the Future.* London: Karnac Books, 1975.

Blackstone, Judith. *The Empathic Ground: Intersubjectivity and Nonduality in the Psychotherapeutic Process.* Albany: State University of New York Press, 2007.

Bouyer, Louis. "Mysticism: An Essay on the History of the Word." In Woods, *Understanding Mysticism*, 42–56.

Brown, Peter. *Augustine of Hippo*. Berkeley: University of California Press, 1967.

Browning, Donald S. *Religious Thought and the Modern Psychologies*. Philadelphia: Fortress Press, 1987.

Bucke, R. C. *Cosmic Consciousness: A Study in the Evolution of the Human Mind*. New York: Citadel Press, 1993.

Bulkeley, Kelly. "Freud and Neuroscience: A Return to Origins." In *Disciplining Freud on Religion*, ed. Gregory Kaplan and William B. Parsons, 147–67. Lanham, MD: Lexington Books, 2010.

———. *The Wondering Brain: Thinking about Religion with and beyond Cognitive Neuroscience*. New York: Routledge, 2003.

Burrell, David. "Reading the *Confessions* of Augustine: An Exercise in Theological Understanding." *Journal of Religion* 50 (1970): 327–51.

Butler, Cuthbert. *Western Mysticism*. New York: E. P. Dutton, 1923.

Capps, Donald. "Augustine as Narcissist: Of Grandiosity and Shame." In Capps and Dittes, *Hunger of the Heart*, 109–16.

———. "Parabolic Events in Augustine's Autobiography." *Theology Today* 40 (1983): 260–72.

Capps, Donald, and James E. Dittes, eds. *The Hunger of the Heart: Reflections on the Confessions of Augustine*. Monograph Series 8. West Lafayette, IN: Society for the Scientific Study of Religion, 1990.

Cavadini, John. "Making Truth: A New Commentary on Augustine's *Confessions*." *Religious Studies Review* 21 (1995): 291–98.

Certeau, Michel de. "Mysticism." *Diacritics* 22 (1992): 11–25.

Cooper, Paul. "The Disavowal of the Spirit: Integration and Wholeness in Buddhism and Psychoanalysis." In Anthony Molino, *The Couch and the Tree*, 231–46.

———. "Unconscious Processes: Zen and Psychoanalytic Versions." *Journal of Religion and Health* 39, no. 1 (2000): 57–69.

Courcelle, Pierre. *Les Confessions de Saint Augustin dans le tradition littéraire*. Paris: Etudes Augustiniennes, 1963.

———. *Recherches sur les 'Confessions' de Saint Augustin*. Paris: Éditions de Boccard, 1968.

Deikman, Arthur. "Deautomatization and the Mystic Experience." In Woods, *Understanding Mysticism*, 240–60.

Dittes, James E. "Augustine: Search for a Fail-Safe God to Trust." In Capps and Dittes, *Hunger of the Heart*, 255–65.

———. "Continuities between the Life and Thought of Augustine." In Capps and Dittes, *Hunger of the Heart*, 117–33.

Dixon, Sandra. *Augustine: The Scattered and Gathered Self*. St. Louis: Chalice Press, 1999.

Dodds, E. R. "Augustine's Confessions: A Study of Spiritual Maladjustment." In Capps and Dittes, *Hunger of the Heart,* 41–55.

Eklund, Elaine. *Science vs. Religion: What Scientists Really Think.* New York: Oxford University Press, 2010.

Eigen, Michael. "The Area of Faith in Winnicott, Lacan, and Bion." *International Journal of the American Psychoanalytic Association* 27 (1969): 413–33.

———. *The Psychoanalytic Mystic.* London: Free Association Books, 1998.

———. "One Reality." In Molino, *The Couch and the Tree,* 217–30.

Elledge, Paul. "Embracing Augustine: Reach, Restraint and Romantic Resolution in the Confessions." In Capps and Dittes, *Hunger of the Heart,* 265–86.

Ellenberger, Henry. *The Discovery of the Unconscious.* New York: Basic Books, 1970.

Engler, Jack. "Being Somebody and Being Nobody: A Reexamination of the Understanding of Self in Psychoanalysis and Buddhism." In Safran, *Psychoanalysis and Buddhism,* 35–80.

———. "Reply: Can We Say What the Self 'Really' Is?" In Safran, *Psychoanalysis and Buddhism,* 86–100.

———. "Therapeutic Aims in Psychotherapy and Buddhism." In *Transformations of Consciousness,* ed. K. Wilber, J. Engler, and D. Brown, 17–52. Boston: Shambhala, 1986.

Epstein, Mark. *Thoughts without a Thinker.* New York: Basic Books, 1995.

Erikson, Erik H. *Young Man Luther.* New York: W. W. Norton, 1962.

Ernst, Carl. "Between Orientalism and Fundamentalism: Problematizing the Teaching of Sufism." In *Teaching Islam,* ed. Brannon Wheeler, 108–23. New York: Oxford University Press, 2003.

Fenn, Richard. "Augustine: Death Anxiety and the Power and Limits of Language." In Capps and Dittes, *Hunger of the Heart,* 314–34.

Ferrari, Leo. "The Boyhood Beatings of Augustine." In Capps and Dittes, *Hunger of the Heart,* 55–67.

———. "Paul at the Conversion of Augustine." *Augustinian Studies* 11 (1980): 5–20.

Ferrer, Jorge. *Revisioning Transpersonal Theory.* Albany: State University of New York Press, 2002.

Ferrer, Jorge, with Jacob H. Sherman. *The Participatory Turn: Spirituality, Mysticism, Religious Studies.* Albany: State University of New York Press, 2010.

Fingarette, Herbert. *The Self in Transformation.* New York: Harper and Row, 1965.

Fitzgerald, Timothy. "Experience." In *Guide to the Study of Religion,* ed. Willi Braun and Russell T. McCutcheon, 125–39. London: Cassell, 2000.

Fox, Mark. *Religion, Spirituality, and the Near-Death Experience.* London: Routledge, 2003.

Fredriksen, Paula. "Augustine and His Analysts: The Possibility of a Psychohistory." *Soundings* 61 (1978): 206–27.

Freeman, Mark. *Rewriting the Self.* New York: Routledge, 1993.

Freud, Ernst L., ed. *The Letters of Sigmund Freud.* New York: Basic Books, 1960.

Freud, Sigmund. *The Standard Edition of the Complete Psychological Works of Sigmund Freud.* Trans. and ed. James Strachey. 24 vols. London: Hogarth Press, 1966–1974.

———. *The Psychopathology of Everyday Life.* Vol. 6 of *The Standard Edition* (first published 1901).

———. "Thoughts for the Times on War and Death." In vol. 14 of *The Standard Edition* (first published 1915).

———. *Group Psychology and the Analysis of the Ego.* Vol. 18 of *The Standard Edition* (first published 1921).

———. *The Ego and the Id.* Vol. 19 of *The Standard Edition* (first published 1923).

———. *The Future of an Illusion.* Vol. 20 of *The Standard Edition* (first published 1927).

———. *Civilization and Its Discontents.* Vol. 21 of *The Standard Edition* (first published 1930).

———. "Dreams and Occultism." In vol. 22 of *The Standard Edition* (first published 1933).

———. *New Introductory Lectures on Psychoanalysis.* Vol. 22 of *The Standard Edition* (first published 1933).

———. *Moses and Monotheism.* Vol. 23 of *The Standard Edition* (first published 1939).

Freud, Sigmund, and Oskar Pfister. *Psychoanalysis and Faith: Dialogues with the Reverend Oskar Pfister.* Ed. Heinrich Meng and Ernst L. Freud. New York: Basic Books, 1963.

Fromm, Erik, D. T. Suzuki, and R. de Martino, eds. *Zen Buddhism and Psychoanalysis.* New York: Harper, 1960.

Fuller, Robert. *Spiritual But Not Religious.* New York: Oxford University Press, 2001.

Garb, Jonathan. *Shamanic Trance in Modern Kabbalah.* Chicago: University of Chicago Press, 2011.

Gay, Volney. "Augustine: The Reader as Self-Object." In Capps and Dittes, *Hunger of the Heart,* 185–202.

Gimello, Robert. "Mysticism and Meditation." In Katz, *Mysticism and Philosophical Analysis,* 170–99.

Gusdorf, Georges. "Conditions and Limits of Autobiography." In *Autobiography: Essays Theoretical and Critical,* ed. James Olney, 28–48. Princeton, NJ: Princeton University Press, 1980.

Hawkins, Anne H. "St. Augustine: Archetypes of Family." In Capps and Dittes, *Hunger of the Heart,* 237–54.

Henry, Paul. *The Path to Transcendence: From Philosophy to Mysticism in Saint Augustine.* Translated by Francis F. Burch. Pittsburgh: Pickwick, 1981.

Hollywood, Amy. *Sensible Ecstasy.* Chicago: University of Chicago Press, 2002.

Homans, Peter. *The Ability to Mourn.* Chicago: University of Chicago Press, 1989.

———. *Jung in Context.* Chicago: University of Chicago Press, 1995.

———. “The Psychology and Religion Movement.” In *The Encyclopedia of Religion,* ed. Mircea Eliade. Vol. 12, 66–74. New York: Macmillan, 1987.

———. *Theology after Freud.* Indianapolis, IN: Bobbs-Merrill, 1970.

Horney, Karen. “Free Associations and the Use of the Couch.” In Molino, *The Couch and the Tree,* 35–36.

Hughes, H. S. *The Sea Change.* New York: McGraw-Hill, 1977.

Hunt, Harry. *Lives in Spirit: Precursors and Dilemmas of a Secular Western Mysticism.* Albany: State University of New York Press, 2003.

James, William. *The Varieties of Religious Experience.* New York: Modern Library, 1929.

Jantzen, Grace. *Power, Gender, and Christian Myticism.* Cambridge: Cambridge University Press, 1995.

Johnson, Robert A. “Comments on *The Hunger of the Heart:* Reflections on the *Confessions* of Augustine.” Manuscript.

Jones, Ernest. *The Life and Work of Sigmund Freud.* 3 vols. New York: Basic Books, 1953–57.

Jones, James. “Hans Loewald: The Psychoanalyst as Mystic.” *Psychoanalytic Review* 88 (2001): 793–804.

———. *Terror and Transformation.* New York: Routledge, 2002.

Jones, Rufus. *Studies in Mystical Religion.* New York: Russell and Russell, 1909.

Jonte-Pace, Diane. “Augustine on the Couch: Psychohistorical (Mis)readings of the *Confessions.*” *Religion* 23 (1993): 71–83.

Jonte-Pace, Diane, and William B. Parsons, eds. *Religion and Psychology: Mapping the Terrain.* New York: Routledge, 2001.

Jung, Carl. *Memories, Dreams, Reflections.* New York: Vintage, 1961.

———. *Psychology and Religion.* New Haven, CT: Yale University Press, 1938.

Kakar, Sudhir. *The Analyst and the Mystic.* Chicago: University of Chicago Press, 1991.

———. “Clinical Work and Cultural Imagination.” *Psychoanalytic Quarterly* 64, no. 2 (1995): 265–81.

———. *The Inner World: A Psycho-Analytic Study of Childhood and Society in India.* Delhi: Oxford University Press, 1981.

———. *Shamans, Mystics, Doctors.* New York: Alfred A. Knopf, 1982.

———. “Reflections on Psychoanalysis, Indian Culture and Mysticism,” *Journal of Indian Philosophy* 10 (1982): 289–98.

Katz, Steven. *Mysticism and Philosophical Analysis.* New York: Oxford University Press, 1979.

———. “On Mysticism.” *Journal for the American Academy of Religion* 56 (1988): 751–61.

Kenney, John Peter. *The Mysticism of St. Augustine.* New York: Routledge, 2005.

Kligerman, Charles. “A Psychoanalytic Study of *The Confessions* of St. Augustine.” In Capps and Dittes, *Hunger of the Heart,* 95–109.

Kohut, Heinz. “Forms and Transformations of Consciousness.” In *The Search for the Self*, ed. Paul Ornstein, 427–60. New York: International Universities Press, 1978.

———. “On Leadership.” In *Self Psychology and the Humanities*, ed. Charles B. Strozier, 51–72. New York: W. W. Norton, 1985.

Kripal, Jeffrey. *Esalen*. Chicago: University of Chicago Press, 2008.

———. *Kali's Child: The Mystical and the Erotic in the Life and Teachings of Ramakrishna*. Chicago: University of Chicago Press, 1995.

———. *Roads of Excess, Palaces of Wisdom: Eroticism and Reflexivity in the Study of Mysticism*. Chicago: University of Chicago Press, 2001.

Lacan, Jacques. “God and the Jouissance of Women.” In *Feminine Sexuality: Jacques Lacan and the École Freudian*, ed. Juliet Mitchell and Jacqueline Rose, 137–49. New York: W. W. Norton, 1982.

Lasch, Chistopher. *The Culture of Narcissism*. New York: W. W. Norton, 1991.

Legewie, Bernhard. *Augustinus: Eine Psychographie*. Bonn: A. Markus & E. Webers Verlag, 1925.

Louth, Andrew. *The Origins of the Christian Mystical Tradition*. Oxford: Clarendon Press, 1981.

MacCormack, Sabine. *The Shadows of Poetry: Vergil in the Mind of Augustine*. Berkeley: University of California Press, 1998.

MacDonald, Mary. “Spirituality.” In *The Encyclopedia of Religion*, ed. Lindsay Jones, 8718–21. New York: Macmillan, 2005.

Magid, Barry. *Ordinary Mind: Exploring the Common Ground of Zen and Psychoanalysis*. New York: Wisdom Publications, 2002.

Mandouze, André. “L'ecstase d'Ostie.” In *Augustinus Magister*, 67–84. Paris: L'Année théologique augustinienne, 1954.

———. “Ou en est la question de la mystique augustinienne?” In *Augustinus Magister*, 3:103–68. Paris: L'Année théologique augustinienne, 1954.

Maréchal, Joseph. *Studies in the Psychology of the Mystics*. Albany, NY: Magi Books, 1964.

Marrou, Henri. *Saint Augustin et la fin de la culture antique*. Paris: Éditions de Boccard, 1949.

Maslow, Abraham. *Religion, Values and Peak-Experiences*. New York: Penguin, 1954.

Masson, Jeffrey Moussaieff. *The Assault on Truth: Freud's Suppression of the Seduction Theory*. New York: Farrar, Straus and Giroux, 1984.

———. *The Oceanic Feeling: The Origin of Religious Sentiment in Ancient India*. Dordrecht: D. Riedel, 1980.

McGinn, Bernard. *The Foundations of Mysticism: Origins to the Fifth Century*. New York: Crossroad, 1991.

———. “The Letter and the Spirit: Spirituality as a Academic Discipline.” In *Minding the Spirit: The Study of Christian Spirituality*, ed. Elizabeth A. Dreyer and Marc S. Burrows, 25–41. Baltimore, MD: Johns Hopkins University Press, 2005.

McMahan, David. *The Making of Buddhist Modernism.* New York: Oxford University Press, 2008.

McMahon, Robert. *Augustine's Prayerful Ascent: An Essay on the Literary Form of the Confessions.* Athens: University of Georgia Press, 1990.

Meckel, Daniel, and Robert Moore, eds. *Self and Liberation: The Jung-Buddhism Dialogue.* New York: Paulist Press, 1992.

Merkur, Daniel. "Psychoanalytic Contributions on the Mystical." In *Changing the Scientific Study of Religion: Beyond Freud?,* ed. Jacob A. Belzen, 111–40. New York: Springer, 2009.

———. *The Explorations of the Psychoanalytic Mystics.* Amsterdam: Rodopi, 2010.

Miles, Margaret. "Infancy, Parenting and Nourishment in Augustine's *Confessions.*" In Capps and Dittes, *Hunger of the Heart,* 219–37.

Molino, Anthony, ed. *The Couch and the Tree: Dialogues in Psychoanalysis.* New York: North Point Press, 1998.

———. "Slouching towards Buddhism: A Conversation with Nina Coltart." In Molino, *The Couch and the Tree,* 170–82.

Myers, Frederic. *Human Personality and Its Survival of Bodily Death.* Charlottesville, VA: Hampton Roads, 2001.

Obeyesekere, Gananath. *The Awakened Ones: Phenomenology of Visionary Experience.* New York: Columbia University Press, 2012.

O'Connell, Robert. *St. Augustine's Confessions: The Odyssey of Soul.* Cambridge, MA: Harvard University Press, 1969.

———. *St. Augustine's Early Theory of Man,* a.d. *386–391.* Cambridge, MA: Harvard University Press, 1968.

O'Donnell, James. *Augustine: Confessions II: Commentary on Books 1–7. Confession III: Commentary on Books 8–13.* New York: Oxford University Press, 1992.

O'Donnell, Robert. *St. Augustine's Confessions: The Odyssey of Soul.* Cambridge, MA: Harvard University Press, 1969.

O'Ferrall, Margaret. "Monica, the Mother of Augustine: A Reconsideration." *Recherches Augustiniennes* 10 (1975): 23–43.

O'Meara, John. "Monica: The Mother of Augustine." *Furrow* 5 (1954): 555–62.

Ornstein, Robert. *The Psychology of Consciousness.* New York: Harcourt Brace, 1972.

Osborne, Arthur. *Ramana Maharshi and the Path of Self-Knowledge.* New York: Samuel Weiser, 1973.

Papini, Giovanni. "A Visit to Freud." *Review of Existential Psychology and Psychiatry* 9 (1969): 130–34.

Parsons, William B. "Augustine: Common-Man or Intuitive Psychologist?" *Journal of Psychohistory* 18 (1990): 155–79.

———. *The Enigma of the Oceanic Feeling: Revisioning the Psychoanalytic Theory of Mysticism.* New York: Oxford University Press, 1999.

———. "Mourning and Method in Psychoanalytic Studies of Indian Thought." In *Mourning Religion*, ed. William B. Parsons, Diane Jonte-Pace, and Susan E. Henking, 63–80. Charlottesville: University of Virginia Press, 2008.

———. "Psychoanalysis and Mysticism: The Case of St. Augustine." In *Mysticism: A Variety of Psychological Perspectives*, ed. Jacob A. Belzen and Antoon Geels, 151–78. Amsterdam: Rodopi, 2003.

———. "Psychoanalysis Meets Buddhism: Development of a Dialogue." In *Changing the Scientific Study of Religion: Beyond Freud?*, ed. Jacob A. Belzen, 179–210. New York: Springer, 2009.

———. "Psychoanalytic Spirituality." In *Spirituality and Religion: Psychoanalytic Perspectives*, ed. Jerome A. Winer and James William Anderson, 83–97. Catskill, NY: Mental Health Resources, 2007.

———. "Psychologia Perennis and the Academic Study of Mysticism." In *Mourning Religion*, ed. William B. Parsons, Diane Jonte-Pace and Susan E. Henking, 97–123. Charlottesville: University of Virginia Press, 2008.

———. "Psychology of Religion." In *The Encyclopedia of Religion*, ed. Lindsay Jones, 7473–81. New York: Macmillan, 2005.

———, ed. *Teaching Mysticism*. New York: Oxford University Press, 2011.

———. "Themes and Debates in the Psychology-Comparativist Dialogue." In Jonte-Pace and Parsons, *Religion and Psychology*, 229–53.

Perovich, Anthony. "Does the Philosophy of Mysticism Rest on a Mistake?" In *The Problem of Pure Consciousness*, ed. Robert K. C. Forman, 237–53. New York: Oxford, 1990.

Pollard, Alton. *Mysticism and Social Change*. New York: Peter Lang, 1992.

Power, Kim. *Veiled Desire: Augustine on Women*. New York: Continuum, 1996.

Prebish, Charles, and Martin Baumann, eds. *Westward Dharma: Buddhism beyond Asia*. Berkeley: University of California Press, 2002.

Principe, Walter. "Toward Defining Spirituality." *Studies in Religion* 12 (1983): 127–41.

Raab, Kelly. "Creativity and Transcendence in the Work of Marion Milner." *American Imago* 57 (2000): 185–214.

Rahula, Wapola. *What the Buddha Taught*. New York: Grove, 1974.

Ricoeur, Paul. *Freud and Philosophy*. New Haven, CT: Yale University Press, 1970.

Rieff, Philip. *The Feeling Intellect*. Chicago: University of Chicago Press, 1990.

———. *The Triumph of the Therapeutic*. New York: Harper, 1966.

Rigby, Paul. "Augustine's Confessions: The Recognition of Fatherhood." In Capps and Dittes, *Hunger of the Heart*, 143–68.

Ring, Kenneth. "Near-Death Experiences: Implications for Human Evolution and Planetary Transformation." In Bailey and Yates, *The Near-Death Experience*, 179–98.

Rizzuto, Ana-Maria. *The Birth of the Living God*. Chicago: University of Chicago Press, 1979.

Robert, Marthe. *From Oedipus to Moses*. Garden City, NY: Anchor Books, 1976.

Robertson, Roland. *Meaning and Change*. New York: New York University Press, 1978.

Roland, Alan. *In Search of Self in India and Japan*. Princeton, NJ: Princeton University Press, 1989.

Rolland, Romain. *Journey Within*. New York: Philosophical Library, 1947.

———. *The Life of Vivekananda*. Calcutta: Advaita Ashrama, 1988.

———. *Mémoires et fragments du Journal*. Paris: Éditions Albin Michel, 1956.

Roy, D. K. *Among the Great*. Bombay; N. M. Tripathi, Nalanda Publications, 1945.

Rubin, Jeffrey. *Psychotherapy and Buddhism*. New York: Plenum Press, 1996.

———. "Spirituality and the Self." *Journal of Religion and Health* 43 (2004): 217–20.

Safran, Jeremy D., ed. *Psychoanalysis and Buddhism: An Unfolding Dialogue*. Boston: Wisdom Publications, 2003.

Scharf, Robert H. "Experience." In *Critical Terms for Religious Studies*, ed. Marc C. Taylor, 94–116. Chicago: University of Chicago Press, 1998.

———. "The Zen of Japanese Nationalism." In *Curators of the Buddha: The Study of Buddhism under Colonialism*, ed. Donald S. Lopez, 107–161. Chicago: University of Chicago Press, 1995.

Schmidt, Lee. "The Making of Modern Mysticism." *Journal of the American Academy of Religion* 71 (2003): 273–302.

Schwab, Raymond. *The Oriental Renaissance*. New York: Columbia University Press, 1987.

Sil, Narasingha. *Ramakrishna Paramahamsa*. New York: Brill, 1991.

Smith, John. "William James's Account of Mysticism." In *Mysticism and Religious Traditions*, ed. Steven T. Katz, 247–279. New York: Oxford University Press, 1983.

Spilka, Bernard, Ralph W. Hood, Jr., and Richard L. Gorsuch. *The Psychology of Religion: An Empirical Approach*. New York: Guilford Press, 2003.

Stendahl, Krister. "The Apostle Paul and the Introspective Conscience of the West." *Harvard Theological Review* 56, no. 3 (1963): 199–215.

Sulloway, Frank. *Freud: Biologist of the Mind: Beyond the Psychoanalytic Legend*. New York: Basic Books, 1983.

Sun, Joe Tom. "Psychology in Primitive Buddhism." In Molino, *The Couch and the Tree*, 3–11.

Sutich, Anthony. "Transpersonal Psychology: An Emerging Force." *Journal of Humanistic Psychology* 8 (1968):77–78.

Tabor, James. *Things Unutterable*. New York: University Press of America, 1986.

Taylor, Jill. *My Stroke of Insight*. New York: Penguin, 2009.

Teresa of Avila. *The Interior Castle*. The Classics of Western Spirituality. Mahwah, NJ: Paulist Press, 1979.

TeSelle, Eugene. "Augustine." In *An Introduction to the Medieval Mystics of Europe*, ed. Paul E. Szarmach, 19–37. Albany: State University of New York Press, 1984.

———. "Augustine as Client and as Theorist." In Capps and Dittes, *Hunger of the Heart*, 185–216.

Updike, John. "Augustine's Concubine." In *Problems and Other Stories*, 132–40. New York: Alfred A. Knopf, 1979.

Vaidyanathan, T. G., and Jeffrey J. Kripal, eds. *Vishnu on Freud's Desk: A Reader in Psychoanalysis and Hinduism*. Delhi: Oxford University Press, 2002.

Van Fleteren, Frederick, Joseph C. Schnaubelt, and Joseph Reino, eds. *Augustine: Mystic and Mystagogue*. Vol. 3 of Collectanea Augustiniana. New York: Peter Lang, 1994.

Vermorel, Henri, and Madeleine Vermorel, *Sigmund Freud et Romain Rolland Correspondance 1923–1936*. Paris: Presses Universitaires de France, 1993.

Webb, Richard E., and Michael Sells. "Lacan and Bion: Psychoanalysis and the Mystical Language of Unsaying." *Theory and Psychology* 5, no. 2 (1995): 195–215.

Weber, Max. *The Protestant Ethic and the Spirit of Capitalism*. New York: Charles Scribner's Sons, 1958.

Weintraub, Karl. "St. Augustine's *Confessions:* The Search for a Christian Self." In Capps and Dittes, *Hunger of the Heart*, 3–31.

———. *The Value of the Individual: Self and Circumstance in Autobiography*. Chicago: University of Chicago Press, 1978.

Wexler, Philip. *The Mystical Society*. Boulder, CO: Westview Press, 2000.

Wills, Garry. *St. Augustine*. New York: Vintage, 1999.

Winnicott, D. W. *Playing and Reality*. New York: Penguin, 1971.

Wolfson, Elliot. *Through a Speculum That Shines*. Princeton, NJ: Princeton University Press, 1997.

Woods, Richard, ed. *Understanding Mysticism*. Garden City, NY: Image, 1980.

Woollcott, Philip. "Some Considerations of Creativity and Religious Experience in St. Augustine of Hippo." *Journal for the Scientific Study of Religion* 5 (1966): 273–83.

Woollcott, Philip, and Prakash Desai. "Religious and Creative States of Illumination: A Perspective from Psychiatry." In *Religious and Ethical Factors in Psychiatric Practice*, ed. Donald S. Browning, Thomas Jobe, and Ian S. Evison, 230–63. Chicago: Nelson Hall, 1990.

Wulff, David. *Psychology of Religion: Classic and Contemporary*. 2nd ed. New York: John Wiley and Sons, 1997.

———. "Psychology of Religion: An Overview." In Jonte-Pace and Parsons, *Religion and Psychology*, 15–29.

Zaleski, Carol. *Otherworld Journeys*. New York: Oxford University Press, 1987.

Ziolkowski, Eric. "St. Augustine: Aeneas' Antitype, Monica's Boy." *Literature and Theology* 9 (1995): 1–23.

INDEX

RECENT BOOKS IN THE STUDIES IN RELIGION AND CULTURE SERIES

Lynda Sexson / *Ordinarily Sacred*

John D. Barbour / *Versions of Deconversion: Autobiography and the Loss of Faith*

Gary L. Ebersole / *Captured by Texts: Puritan to Postmodern Images of Indian Captivity*

Laurie L. Patton and Wendy Doniger, editors / *Myth and Method*

Michael L. Raposa / *Boredom and the Religious Imagination*

Peter Homans, editor / *Symbolic Loss: The Ambiguity of Mourning and Memory at Century's End*

Winston Davis, editor / *Taking Responsibility: Comparative Perspectives*

John P. Burris / *Exhibiting Religion: Colonialism and Spectacle at International Expositions, 1851–1893*

Jeffrey W. Robbins / *Between Faith and Thought: An Essay on the Ontotheological Condition*

Michael L. Raposa / *Meditation and the Martial Arts*

John D. Barbour / *The Value of Solitude: The Ethics and Spirituality of Aloneness in Autobiography*

Roger Caillois / *Pontius Pilate*

David M. Craig / *John Ruskin and the Ethics of Consumption*

Clayton Crockett, editor / *Religion and Violence in a Secular World: Toward a New Political Theology*

Greg Johnson / *Sacred Claims: Repatriation and Living Tradition*

Frederick J. Ruf / *Bewildered Travel: The Sacred Quest for Confusion*

Jonathan Rothchild, Matthew Myer Boulton, and Kevin Jung, editors / *Doing Justice to Mercy: Religion, Law, and Criminal Justice*

Gabriel Vahanian / *Praise of the Secular*

William B. Parsons, Diane Jonte-Pace, and Susan E. Henking, editors / *Mourning Religion*

Victor E. Taylor / *Religion after Postmodernism: Retheorizing Myth and Literature*

J. Heath Atchley / *Encountering the Secular: Philosophical Endeavors in Religion and Culture*

Jeffrey S. Bennett / *When the Sun Danced: Myth, Miracles, and Modernity in Early Twentieth-Century Portugal*

Wesley A. Kort / *Textual Intimacy: Autobiography and Religious Identities*

Carl Raschke / *Postmodernism and the Revolution in Religious Theory: Toward a Semiotics of the Event*

Daniel Boscaljon / *Vigilant Faith: Passionate Agnosticism in a Secular World*

William B. Parsons / *Freud and Augustine in Dialogue: Psychoanalysis, Mysticism, and the Culture of Modern Spirituality*